C 25

R3. 6

Imperial Germany

**Modern
Scholarship on
European History**

Henry A.
Turner, Jr.

General Editor

Imperial Germany

EDITED WITH AN INTRODUCTION
BY JAMES J. SHEEHAN

New Viewpoints
A Division of Franklin Watts
New York/London/1976

New Viewpoints
A Division of Franklin Watts
730 Fifth Avenue
New York, New York 10019

Library of Congress Cataloging in Publication Data
Imperial Germany.

(Modern scholarship on European history)
CONTENTS: Social and economic development: Born,
K. E. Structural changes in German social and economic
development at the end of the nineteenth century. Rosenberg, H. Political and social consequences of the Great
Depression of 1873–1896 in central Europe. —Elites and
institutions: Sheehan, J. J. Conflict and cohesion among
German elites in the nineteenth century. Angress, W. T.
Prussia's army and the Jewish reserve officer controversy
before World War I. Röhl, J. C. G. Higher civil servants
in Germany, 1890–1900. —Foreign policy: domestic origins and consequences: Pflanze, O. Bismarck's Realpolitik. Wehler, H.-U. Bismarck's imperialism, 1862–1890.
Mommsen, W. J. Domestic factors in German foreign
policy before 1914.
    1. Germany—History—1871–1918—Addresses, essays,
lectures. I. Sheehan, James J.
DD220.I63   943.08   75–28083
ISBN 0–531–05374–1
ISBN 0–531–05581–7 pbk.

Manufactured in the United States of America
5 4 3 2 1

Contents

Introduction

Main Themes in Nineteenth-Century German History

The sharp conflict between a natural, deeply-rooted spirit of dissension and an equally intense impulse toward unity has made our social life extremely interesting and instructive, but also extremely troubled.

W. H. Riehl (1851)

In the German-speaking lands of central Europe, as in many other parts of the world, the seventh decade of the nineteenth century was a time of reorganization and reform. As in the United States and Italy, long-standing regional conflicts entered a new stage when the economically advanced north fought a war to impose its will on a more "backward" south. As in France and England, political changes were introduced in order to absorb pressures for greater popular participation in public life. And finally, as in Japan and Russia, social and economic institutions were altered in an attempt to provide a new basis for material growth and national power. Historians have often pointed out that one of the distinctive features of the German situation was the way in which Germany was forced to confront two or more general problems of development at the same time. Equally important was the fact that in

Germany the instruments of change existing in other nations interacted: as in western Europe and the United States, popular movements played an important role in the great events of 1866–1871, but as in Japan and Russia, people from traditional elites were the chief agents and beneficiaries of change. The future of the German Empire created in 1871 was in large part determined by the continued interplay of national, political, and social conflicts and by the persistent tension between popular political movements and the interests and values of traditional elites.

I

To most contemporaries, the creation of the German nation was itself the most significant product of the years 1866 and 1871. It was this apparent fulfillment of deeply rooted longings for unity that evoked from men like Heinrich von Sybel such expressions of delight and historic enthusiasm:

> *How have we deserved God's blessing to be able to experience such great and mighty events? And how will we now live? What has been the subject of our wishes and efforts for twenty years is now achieved in an endlessly glorious way.*

A hundred years earlier, in the last decades of the eighteenth century, the idea of German nationhood had few adherents. At that time, the basic loyalties of most Germans were locally rooted in a particular town or region, or perhaps directed toward a dynasty or state. Those who thought of themselves as "Germans" usually regarded this as a source of cultural rather than political or national identification. The impact of the French Revolution and the Napoleonic invasions affected the evolution of German nationalism in two important ways. First, after having defeated the major German states, Napoleon introduced a massive reorganization of central Europe: the old Holy Roman Empire was destroyed and many of its smallest components—tiny splinter

states, free cities, bishoprics, and principalities—were absorbed
into a few middle-sized states created by the conqueror. By radi-
cally simplifying the map, Napoleon undermined the institutional
basis of localism, severed ties of local allegiance, and thereby
prepared the way for the development of larger-scale organizations and commitments. Second, the Napoleonic conquest
evoked a patriotic response from many Germans that found its
victorious fulfillment in the so-called wars of liberation against
the French. In many ways, this patriotism was an old-fashioned
kind of hostility toward foreign invaders, but, as myth and ritual,
the story and celebration of Germany's liberation from Napoleon
became an important feature of national ideologies after 1815.

The growth of nationalism during the first half of the nineteenth
century was not merely the result of collective enthusiasms. Between 1815 and 1848, hard-surfaced roads, improved mail service, and eventually railroads helped to establish the connective
tissues of a collective existence. A Customs Union—the *Zollverein*—established by Prussia, served to unite most German states
into a single economic system and, by excluding Austria, foreshadowed the eventual triumph of a Prussian-led nation state.
These material changes in German life encouraged some people
to advocate national unity because they saw its economic advantages: a larger market for their goods, easier access to raw materials, a more powerful economic unit to promote their interests. At
the same time, political dissatisfaction with the repressive measures of Metternich's German Confederation helped to feed the
longings for a nation among those who wanted a way out of the
restrictive social and political world of the "restoration." To
these people, the nation would at once integrate and emancipate
the free energies of the German Volk. Within a short time after
1815, therefore, the goal of national unity had come to be a central feature of the liberal movement, which combined in its program desires for political reform with the economic self-interest
of those most likely to gain from the creation of a new German
nation.

Before 1848, however, pressures for unity were overshadowed
by the power of those who defended the status quo: the various

dynasties who were jealous of their independent sovereignty and who feared nationalism's connection with demands for domestic political change; the landed nobility, whose power and privilege had become enmeshed with the institutions of the states; and a number of local elites, especially in the towns of the south and southwest, who viewed with suspicion any intrusion from the outside into the delicate balance of their local autonomy. It is worth noting that in most states the bureaucracy was deeply divided and ambivalent about the prospect of nationhood. Some officials viewed the nation as inexorably linked to the forces of political unrest and social disorder, but others recognized the enormous material and psychological power that was potentially contained in the idea and reality of nationalism. Throughout this period, therefore, we find bureaucrats acting as agents of political repression as well as taking the lead in creating those institutions, such as the *Zollverein,* which laid the foundation for future economic and political change.

In the spring and summer of 1848, the advocates of national unity seemed to win a sudden and convincing victory. In the face of widespread popular disorder, the defenders of the status quo retreated, national elections were held, and an all-German parliament met in Frankfurt to iron out the final details of the new Germany. Before long, however, it became clear that the task of nation-building was a great deal more difficult than it had appeared during the hope-filled springtime of revolution. The forces of order regrouped with surprising speed and, equally important, the advocates of nationhood divided into competing groups. As the debates at Frankfurt stretched into 1849, it became apparent that the *nation* meant rather different things to different people: to most Germans, it involved the necessary subordination of "lesser" nationalities such as the Poles and the Danes, whereas to these groups it meant freedom from all limitations on their rights to self-determination; even among the Germans there were deep divisions, especially between those who wanted the creation of a Protestant-dominated nation excluding Austria and those who wished a greater Germany in which the Hapsburg lands would continue to play a central role. A fragile compromise was finally achieved in support of a *kleindeutsch* Reich, that is, a German nation under Prussian rule excluding Austria. But although this solution was able to win a majority of the delegates at Frankfurt, it failed to attain the support of the Prussian monarchy, whose power was the necessary instrument of its realization. By the summer of 1849, the force of the revolution was spent, and in the reactionary decade that followed, the dreams of a united Germany remained unfulfilled.

Between 1866 and 1871, Bismarck's "revolution from above" attained what the revolution from below had sought in vain. Bismarck himself was a rather recent convert to the national cause. In 1848 he had been an outspoken enemy of the revolution and its national goals; in 1850 he had applauded the Olmütz Declaration in which Prussia formally abandoned any attempts to challenge Austria for leadership among the German states. But in the course of the fifties, Bismarck's ideas changed. First, he became convinced that a German nation was not incompatible with the maintenance of a Prussian state: as he put it, German interests were actually Prussian interests properly understood. Second, he came to believe that nationalism was not necessarily tied to political emancipation. Like his contemporaries Louis Napoleon and Disraeli, Bismarck saw that national enthusiasms might be turned toward a defense of established political and social hierarchies and that a pursuit of national goals could be used to deflect people's attention away from their domestic discontents.

The Bismarckian Empire, or Reich, was based on an attempt to combine national unity, Prussian hegemony, and the qualified independence of the most important middle-sized states created at the beginning of the nineteenth century. A national parliament, the Reichstag, was meant to serve as the expression of popular desires for a single nation. But the other national institutions were firmly in Prussian control: the Prussian king became German emperor, commander of the armed forces and spokesman of the nation in foreign affairs; the chief executive officer of the Reich, the chancellor (an office held by Bismarck himself until 1890), was appointed by the emperor and responsible only to him. Moreover, Prussia's size and constitutional position clearly es-

tablished its preeminence in the new nation: it had 60 percent of
the population and almost 65 percent of the territory; its votes,
together with those of its dependents, were sufficient to block any
constitutional revisions in the Bundesrat, an assembly of state
representatives that served as a kind of parliamentary upper
chamber. Nevertheless, the Reich was a federal structure, composed of twenty-five states (plus the conquered territory of Al-
sace and Lorraine, taken from France after the war of 1870).
Eight of these states were enclaves of Prussia and had only a
limited existence of their own, but others such as Bavaria, Baden, Württemberg, Saxony, and Hesse retained some measure of
independence, continued to have their own state parliaments
(Landtage), and controlled internal matters such as educational
and religious affairs.

II

Bismarck's Reich was also an attempt to resolve long-standing
political conflicts within the German states. Over the preceding
century, these political issues had sometimes paralleled and
sometimes intersected with the national questions we have just
considered. At the end of the eighteenth century, pressures for
popular political participation and constitutional government, like
those for national unity, were extremely weak. At that time, most
Germans were the rather docile subjects of one of two kinds of
political domination: in some regions, especially the south and
southwest, traditional elites ruled small entities in which social,
political, and economic power tended to intertwine and to be
regulated by custom and local usage; elsewhere—and here Prussia was the model—ambitious rulers had been able to build standing armies and administrative institutions that subordinated or
absorbed traditional institutions. The era of the French Revolution and the Napoleonic conquest affected this situation in two
important ways. First, the reorganization of Germany after 1806
spatially extended and institutionally deepened bureaucratic
power. Second, during this period modern representative institutions appeared for the first time on German soil. Significantly, the initiative for the creation of these institutions came from

the bureaucracy itself: the reform-minded bureaucrats who were the leaders of most states during the period between 1806 and 1820 viewed popular participation in public affairs as a valuable ally in the struggle to solidify their states—many of them newly created or enlarged under Napoleonic patronage—against the forces of localism and traditional authority.

Political life between 1815 and 1848 was dominated by the interaction among the defenders of traditional authority (chiefly the aristocracy and the towns of the south and southwest), the bureaucracies of the various states, and the representatives of the liberal movement who began to play a leading role in the state parliaments and local assemblies established after 1806. Although we cannot follow the complex story of their relationships, it should be noted that throughout the decades before 1848 the bureaucracy's attitude toward popular participation was roughly analogous to its views on nationalism: some officials were prepared to ally with traditional elites against any movement for greater popular representation, while others saw liberalism as a potential ally in the struggle to create a prosperous and powerful state.

Liberalism seemed to be the chief beneficiary of the revolution's stunning victory in the spring of 1848. Liberal delegates, many of them state officials, dominated the parliaments that met in Berlin and Frankfurt. But the same forces that emptied the liberals' dreams of national unity also doomed their efforts at constitutional innovation. By the fall of 1848, the rapid recovery of antirevolutionary forces had enabled the rulers of Prussia and Austria to reestablish their power. At the same time, divisions among the apparent victors of the revolution weakened their ability to impose their will. As was the case with the *nation* in 1848–1849, it quickly became apparent that *popular participation* meant very different things to different factions. Monarchy or republic, democratic or elitist suffrage, parliamentary power or subordinated representative assemblies—these were some of the political alternatives posed and contested during the Frankfurt parliament's long constitutional debates. The final compromise, which called for a hereditary monarch and a democratically elected parliament, won a majority at Frankfurt but, like the *klein-deutsch* Reich, the compromise collapsed under the weight of the states' opposition.

In some ways, as Heinrich Heffter once pointed out, the political situation after 1848 was less a continuation than a replication of the first half of the nineteenth century. The reactionary 1850s were followed by a brief "new era" in which liberal forces again seemed to triumph, and then by a period of struggle, centering in Prussia but involving other states as well, in which liberalism and the forces of reaction once again confronted one another in an intense if uneven conflict. In the course of this conflict Otto von Bismarck became minister president of Prussia in 1862, and it is against the backdrop of a struggle between liberalism and its enemies that his foreign political offensive must be viewed.

The Prussian victory over Austria at Königgrätz in 1866 not only was a turning point in the evolution of the national question but also marked a new stage in the relationship between liberalism and the state. In the wake of the enthusiasm generated by the victory of Prussian arms, Bismarck was able to split the liberal opposition in the Prussian parliament and win over a majority to support his constitutional arrangements for the new nation. Just as this constitution attempted to combine nationalism, Prussian power, and federalism, it also sought to reconcile pressures for popular participation and monarchical authority. We have already seen the powers of the crown: on the national level, the emperor retained the sole power to appoint the chief executive, and as king of Prussia, he continued to control the bureaucratic and military apparatus of the largest state. Nevertheless, the Reichstag did have the right to pass laws, which also had to be approved by the Bundesrat, and to vote on the budgets governing the Reich's sources of income. The most extraordinary element in the constitution was the provision that gave the vote for the Reichstag to all male, adult Germans. Bismarck's advocacy of democratic suffrage came from his conviction that the masses of the German people were basically conservative and could be counted upon to elect representatives loyal to the crown. By prohibiting any financial compensation for parliamentarians, he hoped to limit political activity to those propertied elites who social position and economic interests would make them amenable to cooperation with the government.

III

The national and political dimensions of the formation of the new Empire, the *Reichsgründung*, dominated the vision of most contemporaries between 1866 and 1871, as they have absorbed the attention of most historians. In the past few years, however, more and more scholars have begun to emphasize the way in which long-term social and economic developments provided the foundation and shaped the character of the new nation.

In the last third of the eighteenth century, the national and political lassitude we have just described had a clear socioeconomic analogue. In many parts of central Europe, guilds continued to limit the number of men allowed to practice a craft and to control the activities of those who did. Serfdom tied large numbers of peasants to the land and subjected them to a densely woven pattern of social, economic, and political restraints. Commerce was impeded by countless tariffs and tolls that raised the price of those few goods which moved across the tangle of boundaries separating the various states. Those towns that had not been reduced to sources of revenue for the bureaucratic states tended to be self-enclosed and self-protective, locking their gates against the intrusion of outsiders and thus excluding the possibility of acting as centers for economic growth.

If we look at the broad sweep of socioeconomic change that occurred in the century before 1871, the central theme is the gradual erosion of these various restrictions and restraints on the movement and use of human and material resources. But in order to grasp the significance of this process, two distinctive features must be kept in mind. First, social and economic emancipation in Germany was always linked to the expansion of the bureaucratic state. During the eighteenth century, in Prussia and the other territorial states, the bureaucracy began to undermine the power of the guilds and to replace them with administrative regulations. In the era of reforms after 1806, serfdom was abolished, restrictions on some forms of economic activity were reduced, and other kinds of restraints were weakened as the power of the state cut deeper into the sinews of traditional institutions. Between 1815 and 1848, the bureaucracies' relationship to the social and economic emancipation was roughly comparable to their attitudes toward national unity and political participation: to some officials, economic growth seemed like a dangerous threat to the established order, while others recognized that it could be a source of great power and well-being. This ambivalence was expressed in the complex blend of harassment and encouragement with which the state confronted those involved in the early stages of Germany's development as a major industrial power.

Second, although social and economic emancipation left few corners of German life untouched in the first two-thirds of the nineteenth century, its form and intensity varied greatly from one region to another; it was different in the cities than in the countryside; it affected some enterprises and trades more than others. For example, in Prussia, where bureaucratic institutions developed early, most guild restrictions were dismantled in the course of the eighteenth century, whereas in the south and west they persisted in some form until the 1860s. Similarly, in regions like East Elbian Prussia, where the state and the aristocracy established a compromise at the expense of the peasantry, the landed elite's power persisted, even in the face of legal emancipation; elsewhere, agriculture was carried on by a relatively free group of tenant farmers or small, independent producers. Moreover, throughout the nineteenth century the level of economic development varied enormously between, for example, the rather advanced economy of the Rhineland and the more locally oriented and traditionally controlled south.

The full force of Germany's socioeconomic diversity surfaced with unmistakable intensity during the revolution of 1848. In the 1840s, a series of economic difficulties produced widespread discontent in German society and provided the liberal movement with its popular base during the early stages of the revolution. But in 1848 and 1849 it quickly became clear that in socioeconomic affairs, no less than in their national and political goals, the enemies of the status quo were united in their discontent but deeply divided in their positive programs. The inability of the Frankfurt parliament to sustain popular support was due not only to the liberals' limited understanding of, and sympathy for, the desires of the masses of the population but also to the bewildering complexity and mutual incompatibility of the demands with which they were confronted.

The period between the revolution and the *Reichsgründung* was a time of great significance for Germany's social and economic development. In the 1850s, the communications network begun in the first half of the century was substantially enlarged. Technological innovations were introduced, new forms of industrial organization were adopted, and the volume and flow of capital and commodities were greatly increased. Within this context, Prussia's economic superiority acquired ever-greater political significance, not only by providing the foundation for Prussia's military hegemony over central Europe but also by broadening its appeal to "progressive" economic groups in the smaller German states. At the same time, the triumph of the Prussian-led *Reichsgründung* represented the culmination of the century-old process of social and economic emancipation. Among the first pieces of legislation passed by the new Reichstag were laws establishing the free movement of people and goods, a more unified currency, and a more relaxed attitude toward the formation of joint-stock companies. In these laws, as so often in the past, the destruction of restraints on social and economic activity was intimately tied to a victorious revolution from above and went hand in hand with an expansion of the state's power over traditional institutions.

Bismarck was not directly involved in the formulation of the measures that liberalized German social and economic life after 1866, but he accepted what was done for the same reasons that he advocated national unity and universal suffrage. He believed that these forces could be absorbed by, and in the end subordinated to, Prussian power, monarchical authority, and social inequality —those goals and values to which he remained firmly committed. Eventually, however, the economic and social dynamism that had provided the instruments for Prussia's triumph over Germany also generated the forces that would make the political system created between 1866 and 1871 increasingly fragile and crisis-ridden.

IV

Deeply rooted conflicts in the lives of nations are rarely solved. They may be reshaped, eased, or aggravated, but they almost never fully disappear. So it was with the conflicts addressed by the reforms and reorganization that occurred in the 1860s. Regional antagonisms, together with the social and ideological conflicts adhering to them, continued to plague the United States and Italy even after their victorious wars of unification. In Britain, it did not take long for new groups to attack the political accommodation underlying the suffrage reform of 1867. France's Third Republic, constructed in 1871 from the debris of the Second Napoleonic Empire, provided stability of a sort, but it was a stability that depended upon the adjournment of basic social and economic problems. In Japan, the process of modernization begun with the Meiji restoration of 1868 laid the basis for an extraordinary growth in national power, but this was attended by domestic violence and an ever more aggressive foreign policy. Most turbulent of all was the journey toward modernity begun in Russia with the emancipation of the serfs in 1861, a journey in which unrest would be an ever-present companion and revolution the unwanted destination.

The German Empire forged by the Prussian victories of 1866 and 1870 soon emerged as Europe's most formidable concentration of military and economic power. But Germany's ability to enjoy and exercise this power was persistently shadowed by the unresolved strains within her political and social structure. Prussian hegemony and national unity were never fully reconciled; there was a lasting dualism between state and nation and recurrent conflict between the interests of the Reich and those of its most important component. Regional rivalries, which coalesced in political Catholicism and the demands of the national minorities (Poles, Danes, French), persisted throughout the Imperial era. Even more formidable were the social and economic conflicts generated by the attempt to combine a dynamic industrial society with political authoritarianism and the power and privilege of traditional elites. Again and again between 1871 and 1914 these regional and socioeconomic conflicts intertwined to create an endemic sense of crisis in German political life and to render ever more problematical that synthesis between monarchical authority and parliament, between special privileges and democratic participation, upon which the Bismarckian political and social system ultimately rested. By the early 1890s, Heinrich von Sybel, whose joyous words of welcome to the Reich were quoted earlier, expressed a widely held feeling that the unity apparently attained in 1871 remained an elusive and distant goal. In 1891, Sybel wrote to a friend that Germany's future was filled with question marks:

> *Social reform, school reform, commercial policies, religious policies, and foreign policy—no prophet will be able to say in what direction we will be able to find our way in these matters; if we will be able to find our way at all is yet another question.*

Part I

Social and Economic Developments

One of the most unfortunate characteristics of traditional German historiography was a tendency to separate social, economic, political, diplomatic, and intellectual developments. Too often this methodological fragmentation obscured the interrelationship between these aspects of life and inhibited a critical analysis of both the past and the present. Almost all of the essays in this volume were written in reaction against this traditional view.

The purpose of this first section is to suggest the socioeconomic setting for the more specialized analyses that follow. Professor Karl Erich Born of Tübingen University provides us with a good general introduction to the social and economic changes that transformed German life after 1871. His essay first appeared in 1963 and is given here in a revised draft published in Moderne Deutsche Verfassungsgeschichte, *edited by E. W. Böckenförde (Cologne, 1973). The translation is by Paul Nicholas Pitz. Hans Rosenberg's pioneering work on the "Great Depression" was first published in 1943; it later provided the basis for a monograph entitled* Grosse Depression und Bismarckzeit *(Berlin, 1967). With this and several other seminal works on German social history, Rosenberg has had a powerful impact on three generations of postwar German historians. Rosenberg left Germany in 1933, taught for many years at Brooklyn College and then at the University of California in Berkeley, where he is now Shepard Professor of History, Emeritus.*

1

Structural Changes in German Social and Economic Development at the End of the Nineteenth Century

KARL ERICH BORN

In 1880, the elder Toynbee referred to the great economic and social changes of the nineteenth century as the "Industrial Revolution." This concept, borrowed from the language of science and politics, is still used, although it has long been obvious that what Toynbee called a revolution was not a sudden upheaval completed in a relatively short time, but rather a long-lasting evolution whose end is not in sight. We cannot, therefore, view the spread of technology, industrialization, urbanization, and the attendant social transformations as a unified whole or as a completed epoch. It is only possible to differentiate and explain various phases and partial developments within this protracted and still-unfinished process. Such a phase within the German economic and social development in the industrial age is the object of this investigation. In order to establish structural developments within the economy and society, the designation "end of the nineteenth century" cannot be conceived too narrowly. We use that phrase to refer to the decades from the 1870s to the beginning of World War I: the time of the rapid industrialization, of capital and business centralization, of increasing economic and sociopolitical organization, and of the rise of the German labor movement, which began with the *Gründerjahren* of the early seventies. In the political history of Germany, it is the epoch of the Empire. We will not be able to discuss the relationship between political-historical and economic-historical periodization, which is thereby implied; however, we will have to go into the interaction of socioeconomic and political structures.

Germany changed economically from an agrarian to a highly industrialized country. This is made clear by two characteristic facts: in 1870 the German raw iron production was 1.7 million tons, only one-fourth of Great Britain's; in 1913, however, the German production of 19.3 million tons was almost twice that of Britain's. The number of those employed in agriculture and forestry from the 1870s to 1913 dropped from 6 million to little more than 5 million, while the number of those employed in industry and mining almost doubled, rising from 5 to almost 9.5 million. Although in 1893 the output of British industry was still almost twice as much as the German, by 1913 German industrial production had overtaken the British and stood second only to the American.[1]

The rapid rise of Germany's industrialization was promoted by a number of factors that came into play at the beginning of the last third of the nineteenth century. Above all, the scientific-technological prerequisites should be mentioned here. Around 1870 Germany had caught up with Britain's technical head start in the raw material industries. By 1870 the last coal furnaces were replaced by coke furnaces, whose production capacity was five times as great. Around 1870 the German steel industry began using the Bessemer process that was discovered in Britain and had been in use there for over ten years. At the same time the foundations for the great upswing of the German optical, chemical, and electrotechnical industries were being laid with the beginning of systematic scientific-technical research in industrial laboratories and technical institutes.

The second factor that propelled German industry forward was the unification of the monetary system. This became possible with the founding of the Empire. In this regard it was not the unification of the currency or the transition from the silver to the gold standard that proved especially effective: long before the introduction of the deutsche mark as the German currency (1871), the various types of currency (tallers, guilders) were coined according to common guidelines set by currency agreements and had stood at a fixed rate of exchange to one another; the legal introduction of the gold currency in 1873 became fully effective only in 1907 because until then silver coins retained their value. The most important facet of the new monetary legislation was certainly the Federal Banking Law, which removed scattered paper currencies of uncertain legality and at the same time converted the Prussian bank into a National Bank. This made bank notes a valid medium of exchange and thereby allowed the flow of currency to match the fast-growing economy.

The third factor that increased the rate of German industrialization was the liberalization of German laws covering joint-stock companies through the *Aktienrechtsnovelle* passed by the North German Reichstag in the summer of 1870. This' law removed restrictions on the establishment of joint-stock companies, which previously had required the permission of the state. The mobilization, centralization, and coordination of scattered private capital for the financial outfitting of industry in grand style was thereby made possible. Thus the legal basis was provided for the development of large companies and for the centralization of enterprise, which usually are possible only in corporations. So the establishment of joint-stock companies began in great numbers after the summer of 1870. The economic upswing, continuous since 1867, the influx of 4.2 billion deutsche marks of French war reparations (between autumn 1871 and autumn 1873), as well as the insufficient regulatory provisions in the new legislation, unleashed wild speculation, coupled with frivolous, in part criminal, business practices. These *Gründerjahren* ended in 1873 with an economic depression, the *Gründerkrise*.[2] This was in fact only the German version of a general economic crisis, and the long depression that followed caused or at least prepared the way for profound structural changes in the German economy.

The most striking consequence of the *Gründerkrise* and the Great Depression was Germany's turning away from free trade to a policy of protective tariffs.[3] The initiative for protectionism came from the raw material industries in western Germany. Their total sales rose even during the crisis, in domestic as well as export products. But even with the growing sales, profits dropped sharply because of the catastrophic drop in prices. And in order to confront the drop in prices, heavy industry wanted protective tariffs. Until recently, it was believed that east German grain producers had taken up heavy industry's demand for a protective tariff and presented it with equal fervor. Certainly German agriculture was also in a state of crisis in the middle of the 1870s. Production costs rose sharply during the transition to intensive cultivation, and with these continuously rising costs went a decline in grain prices. Although it was once held that this situation was aggravated by the American grain imports and that therefore the German grain producers demanded a protective tariff against the American competition, Karl Hardach's recent work showed that in the 1870s only west German agriculture was in the protectionist camp, while the east German grain producers still rejected or were skeptical about protective tariffs.[4] The American hard wheat yielded good meal for the European consumer taste only when mixed with middle-European soft wheat, and was therefore still not formidable competition for the East Elbian landowners. Only when the Americans could after 1880 produce a better and competitive wheat meal through a change in their milling process and when a number of very rich grain harvests led to price drops did the East Elbian landowners become pro-tariff; indeed then they became extreme protectionists.

Just as free trade had not enjoyed the agreement of all branches of the economy before the early seventies, the protective tariff passed in 1879 did not fulfill the wishes and interests of all groups. Commerce, the credit institutions, and those industries which were interested in the importing of foreign raw materials (parts of the chemical and clothing goods industries), opposed a rigorous fulfillment of protectionist principles. This divergence of interests regarding trade policies led to divisions in political and economic organizations and to recurrent parliamentary debates on tariffs and trade agreements.

In addition to the turn to protectionism, the depression, with its many business failures—of 857 joint-stock companies that were started in Prussia after 1870, 160 were in liquidation or bankruptcy in 1874—gave new impetus to the movement toward concentration. This movement culminated in the founding of large enterprises, cartels, and syndicates. In the raw material industries the development of large-scale concerns had already begun in the 1850s because of the special technical requirements and the particular need for capital investments. But the main period when large concerns developed was during the *Gründerjahren* and in the time of the Great Depression. In the 1890s the trend toward large-scale enterprises also took hold in the consumer goods industry. In these years the number of independent businesses declined while production and the total number of employees increased. The formation of combines also began as the result of the crisis and depression. This process began in the mining industry during the 1880s among coal companies and iron works. It was followed in the 1890s by the further extension of vertical cartels in which the different production stages from the beginning to the finished product were put together in a single economic, but not legal, unit. Both developments—the founding of big businesses, rich in capital, and the start of combines—were promoted by the large German banks. After the experiences of the *Gründerkrise* and the depression the banks believed that they could reduce their own risk if they had debtors with a stronger capital basis and if the market could be made more manageable through the reduction of the number of competing enterprises.[5] And since the banks had noticed that during the crisis many businesses had entered into ruinous competition through price reductions, they also promoted the formation of cartels.

We can differentiate two periods in the development of German cartels before 1914. The cartels formed during the first period, from the end of the 1870s to the end of the 1880s, were still defensive measures against the effects of the crisis, what might be called "children of necessity." They were designed to hold off the flooding of the domestic market with goods through voluntary reductions in production. In most cases these cartels dealt with the merging of smaller and medium-sized enterprises; only in very few cases did large businesses join cartels. In general, these basically defensive cartels were transitory. As a rule they disappeared when the depression was over. In the second period, in the time of the industrial growth and extensive large-scale businesses after the mid-nineties, cartels were formed among big businesses. The cartel now no longer served as a defense against ruinous competition, but rather aimed at monopolistic domination of the market. In this period arose the contingency cartels of the raw material industries with their own sales organizations and the syndicates (among them the Rhine-Westphalian Coal Syndicate, the Steel Association, the Limestone Syndicate). In the end, cartelization included between 60 percent and 90 percent of production in the raw material industries. Through cartel arrangements the raw material industries took advantage of the protective tariff to keep the prices high on the domestic market and at the same time to conquer the foreign sales markets with lower export prices.[6]

Since in Germany, as in the United States and Japan, the invested capital of industry was raised almost entirely by the big banks, the ties between banks and industrial capital was very close, as in both these other countries. And this close relationship also produced the tendency toward consolidation in industry that was of particular importance in all three countries. In Japan and the United States the chief emphasis lay in the formation of trusts (despite the antitrust laws in the United States), while in Germany the main weight of the concentration lay in the development of syndicates and cartels.

Developments in industry and technology and the shift of the economic center of gravity from agriculture to industry resulted in significant internal migration and urbanization in Germany. Until about 1870, population growth, continuous since the middle of the eighteenth century, had still not led to any significant shift in the relative size of urban and rural populations. The migrations that are so characteristic of Germany's demographic history between 1880 and 1910 were limited prior to the *Reichsgründung* to the northwest and the southwest. Here early industrial cities in the Rhineland, Westphalia, and the Rhine-Main area received an increase in population from crowded neighboring rural areas. More striking than this movement to neighboring areas was emigration abroad, especially from those areas in southwestern Germany with traditional systems of land subdivision. The chief destination of this emigration was North America. Thus, in the five years from 1866 to 1870 alone, almost 500,000 Germans, mostly from the southwest, emigrated to America. The agrarian areas of eastern Germany were hardly touched by these population movements until about 1870. Up to that time the farm economy and the trade economy of the Prussian east provinces were able to absorb the growing population.

Several factors in the 1860s and 1870s provided the impetus for a rapid and extensive east-west inner migration. First, in the mid-sixties, the development of new land for cultivation in Prussia's eastern provinces stopped, thereby exhausting the ability of the east German agriculture and the trade economy dependent on it (grain trade, rural handicrafts and food industry) to accommodate a growing population.[7] Second, there was a change in the organization of agrarian labor. Since the transition from the three-field farming system to intensive rotation of crops, the master-serf relationship, which was by nature a work and profit community between estate owner and farm worker, was replaced by free hired workers and seasonal labor.[8] The third force was the agrarian crisis of the 1870s. In this crisis the great superiority of industrial over agrarian wages became apparent. Under the influence of these three forces the east-west inner migration started at the end of the 1860s. It flowed from East and West Prussia, Silesia, Pomerania, and Posen toward the industrial center, Berlin. In the 1870s it extended into central German industrial areas and in part into the Rhineland and Westphalia, and then after 1880 from the Prussian eastern provinces into the Ruhr area. Until 1893, this east-west inner migration was accompanied by emigration abroad, in which after the 1870s eastern Germans played a considerably larger role than those from the southwest. On the average, over 100,000 German emigrants, mostly farmers, left the German Empire annually until 1893. In 1893, when the free settlement of land in North America ceased and at the same time German industry began to expand, the emigration declined noticeably to 25–30 percent of its former size. Between 1893 and 1913 only 25,000 to 40,000 Germans emigrated each year. The emigration abroad was replaced by inner migration from east to west. And after 1900, the immigration of foreigners to Germany was greater than German emigration abroad: Germany had gone from an emigration to an immigration country. This was also a characteristic index of Germany's change from an agrarian to a highly industrialized country.[9]

Until 1914, inner migration from eastern Germany (East and West Prussia, Pomerania, Posen, and Silesia) involved over 2 million people, who departed for the Ruhr area, central Germany, and Berlin. The population increase of greater Berlin originated in this inner migration. A further result was a change in the relative size of the urban and rural population: in 1871 two-thirds of the German people still lived in rural communities, but on the eve of the First World War the urban population comprised almost two-thirds of the nation. This urbanization especially encouraged the growth of the large cities. In 1910 more than 21 percent of the German population lived in large cities; in 1871 it was not even 5 percent.[10]

Only a few effects of the urbanization can be pointed out here: the political representation of the German people in the Reichstag, which rested on general, equal, and secret suffrage and on the need for a majority within each district, became problematical, because the division into electoral constituencies was not adjusted with the population shift, and therefore the votes of the rural population, the main voting strength of the conservative parties, had a disproportionately greater weight. Since the 1880s, the German conservative parties needed fewer votes than any of the other parties in order to win a mandate. The Catholic Center Party was the second most advantaged party in this regard. In the parliamentary election of 1912 the smallest Reichstag constituency (Schaumburg-Lippe) had not quite 47,000 inhabitants, while the largest (Teltow-Charlottenburg) had almost 1.3 million inhabitants.[11] This discrepancy between political strength and population distribution, which was increasingly felt by the Social Democrats and the liberal parties, was one of the reasons that the Weimar Republic allowed the pendulum to swing in the opposite direction by adopting the system of proportional representation. The rapid population growth and the physical expansion of the cities also helped to produce "community socialism," i.e., local government control of the public utilities and transportation, which set in after the turn of the century.[12]

Furthermore, industrial inner migration became a significant force in the dissolution of Prussia, which began gradually after 1871. The migratory movement weakened the conservative, older Prussian areas. In combination with industrialization, it drained the economic and social power of Prussia out of the eastern provinces into the western provinces, which were much less tied to the traditions of the Prussian state; and the conservative-minded rural population of the eastern provinces, which respected the East Elbian nobility's claim to leadership, became a minority.[13]

Above all, inner migration was a social process, part of the development of an industrial society.[14] Only a few relics of the pre-industrial corporate society (*Ständegesellschaft*) remained intact; most of its major institutions had been destroyed at the beginning of the nineteenth century. Of these relics, the most manifest were the privileges—in part legal, in part de facto—of the aristocracy. These privileges involved the hereditary membership by the family heads of the higher nobility in the Upper Houses of the parliaments of the various German states; the entailment of estates against mortgaging, auction, and sale; and most important, the favoritism showed to aristocrats in the officer corps, the civil administration, and the diplomatic service. Thus in many respects the nobility still remained a *Stand*—a self-conscious social group—in spite of the great differences in wealth between rich landed-estate owners (the *Standesherren* and upper Silesian magnates), moderately well-off East Elbian landowners, and the impoverished nobility without land. The nobility could lay claim to this special status only as long as the monarchy existed. Nonetheless, the nobility was also affected by the social transformations of the nineteenth century. Thus the large rural estates were no longer exclusively controlled by the rural nobility. After the abolition of the nobility's exclusive right to own an estate, there was a high turnover of the rural properties and almost half of the "knightly estates" (*Rittergüter*) in eastern Prussia and Mecklenburg came into the possession of middle-class families. Only the largest landed estates (*Latifundien*) remained, with few exceptions, in the hands of the old higher nobility.[15]

After the onset of rapid industrialization, significant differences in the social, economic, and political interests and experiences of the bourgeoisie (*Bürgertum*) emerged, producing a striking fragmentation into various social groups. By 1900 the *Bürgertum* as a *Stand* or social stratum no longer existed as it still had in 1848.[16] The industrial upper-middle class (*Grossbürgertum*), which until the *Reichsgründung* had competed with the nobility for equality in the state, gained economic power, the likes of which had not been seen in Germany since the heyday of the Fuggers. In this *Grossbürgertum* the industrial entrepreneurs outnumbered the bankers and the big merchants. Through the development of large enterprise there arose a new type of entrepreneur. Along with the factory owners like Krupp, Thyssen, Stumm, and the private bankers like Mendelssohn, Warburg, Bleichröder, Bethmann, Oppenheim, there was a group of corporation directors and managers such as Jencke, Klupfel, Melcher, Kirdorf, Vögler and in the large banking corporations directors like Gwinner, Moritz Schultze, Dernburg, and Riesser. In the statistics of the German Empire, this group was counted as employees (*Angestellten*), but according to their function and significance, they belonged to the entrepreneurs, for in their hands lay the continuous leadership of the companies they represented in the various associations.

This upper *Bürgertum* was gradually "feudalized" at the end of the nineteenth century. In its attempt to climb to the top of the social pyramid, the upper *Bürgertum* searched for a way of life that would confirm its membership in the elite, and thought that this was to be found in the tradition-rich life-style of the nobility. We can see this adoption of aristocratic ways of living in the changing life-styles of the factory owners, in the development of the factory owner's home from a small house near the factory to the villa and then to the rural mansion. A further indication of this feudalization is to be seen in the fact that more and more sons of factory owners and merchants chose an army officer's career. Also, the struggle to attain awards and titles or even a patent of nobility must be seen in this connection. Nevertheless, this development was by no means uniform throughout Germany. There were historically conditioned differences among the individual states and even among the different Prussian provinces.[17]

The feudalization of the *Grossbürgertum* did not come merely from social ambition but also from a shared political interest.

This community of interests rested on the fact that the nobility and the upper-middle-class entrepreneurs had a common opponent in the labor movement. Against the labor movement they joined to defend the social and political status quo that corresponded to their interests. The conflict of economic interests between the upper-middle-class entrepreneurs and the nobility, insofar as they were large property owners, remained and culminated in the Reichstag's debates on Chancellor Caprivi's trade agreements (1892–1893) and in the debates of the Prussian Landtag concerning the building of the midland canal. But these economic conflicts receded in the face of common sociopolitical interests. And on the basis of these common interests the nobility and *Grossbürgertum* merged into one elite. This merger encouraged the approach of the National Liberals to the Conservatives (after the secession of the left wing of the National Liberals in the 1880s); moreover, the *Grossbürgertum*, with its worldwide economic involvements and interests, gave the German elite an impulse toward imperialism and naval expansion.[18]

The educated middle class (*Bildungsbürgertum*)—higher officials and professionals—was also carried along by the trend toward feudalization. Here the rank of the reserve officer became a kind of substitute ennoblement. The social view of the individual was influenced by whether or not he was a reserve officer.[19] Nevertheless, membership in the reserve officer corps played no role in an official's promotion.[20] The great social importance of the reserve officer's commission was the penetration of military thinking and values into the civilian life. In this way we can speak of a militarization of the German educated middle class. This phenomenon differentiated German militarism from militarism in other states.

Small business groups and the artisanal middle strata, despite Marx's gloomy prognosis, were able to assert their economic and social independence in the face of rapid industrialization. At the end of the nineteenth century, the new installation and repair crafts, created by industrialization, replaced those crafts which were displaced by industrial production.[21] And with industrialization there arose a new middle-class group, that of the white-collar employees. The growing scale of enterprise made the direction and administration of businesses increasingly complicated. This changed the relationship between the administrative and production sections and increased the importance and number of industrial management employees. Whereas in 1870 employees were numerically insignificant when compared to workers—there were 30 workers to 1 employee—they ranked with workers as a strong group among all employed persons on the eve of the First World War. The growth of the number of employees in these decades was relatively greater than that of the workers: the numerical relationship between them had shifted to 9:1 by 1913. Thus, in the decades when big concerns were formed, employees emerged as an important social group.[22] The fact that they were counted with the middle strata also shows that the middle class (*Bürgertum*) in the traditional sense no longer existed; for according to the classical bourgeois self-image only those who drew their income from an economically independent occupation were considered "middle-class"; even the membership of state officials had been questioned. If now a group of employees, who were dependent and in no way secure in their jobs, was labeled "middle-class" (this also had practical consequences because in addition to social insurance for workers, a special employees' insurance was created) then "middle-class" (*bürgerlich*) meant everything that did not belong to the nobility or proletariat.

The development of large enterprises also affected scientific and vocational training. The economic and organizational problems of these enterprises drew the attention of economists toward aspects of microeconomics. And so at the turn of the century, traditional commercial science was transformed into a scientific study of business economics. As long as enterprises remained of manageable size, practical commercial training had been sufficient. If an academic education was necessary, it was of a technical or scientific nature. Lectures on political science in German universities were held not for future entrepreneurs but rather for future higher administrative and financial officials. But experts schooled in economics were required for the commercial leadership of big concerns. Big business, therefore, led to the formalizing of commercial education. At the turn of the century, business schools (Leipzig, 1898; Cologne and Frankfurt, 1901;

Berlin, 1906; Mannheim, 1907) were founded for the academic education of the future business elite.[23]

The working class developed into the numerically strongest group during the Imperial era. Around 1870 it made up about one-fifth of the population, in 1882 one-fourth, and by 1901 one-third. Its material situation had steadily improved in the period of rapid industrialization. Wages in 1913 were on the average more than twice as high as those of 1871; on the average, real wages increased about 50 percent between 1871 and 1913.[24] Along with the increase in wages, the social insurance system, which was introduced in the 1880s and continually extended until 1914, contributed to the improvement of the workers' economic situation between the *Reichsgründung* and the First World War. This change in the situation of the workers was one of the most important reasons for the origin and success of reformism within German Social Democracy. If workers retained an antagonistic attitude not only toward the governments but also toward the political system, this was because they remained at a disadvantage in exercising their political rights. The municipal governments, the Prussian parliament, and after 1896 the Second Chamber of the Saxon parliament were elected according to class election laws that gave greatly added weight to the votes of the wealthy. Above all, however, restrictions on their right to organize embittered the working class. In paragraph 153 of the Empire's Industrial Code, which forbade compulsory organization, the scope of the punishable actions was wider than in the criminal code. According to this paragraph, actions punishable under criminal law only in quite specific, narrowly described situations became illegal as soon as they were committed in order to force someone to participate in a strike or join a union. These legal sanctions were on the side of the employer and directed against compulsory organization (*Koalitionszwang*); however, that had no practical meaning, since the compulsory organization could be practiced legally. When these legal conditions were worked out in the years from 1865 to 1869, the government and the legislators were not yet confronted by mass unions or by a politically significant socialist party. Therefore the need for antisocialist measures had also not been the most important motive for the enactment of the special criminal regulations against the compulsory organization; more important was the individualistic concept of the constitutional state that sought to protect the individual from group pressure. The model for these measures was the Le Chapelier law of the French Revolution, which had sought to avoid the development of the new privileged corporations after the abolition of the guilds. But with the growth of Social Democracy and the socialist union movement, this part of the Industrial Code was not implemented in the spirit in which it was issued. The authorities regarded and used it much more as a substitute for the antisocialist law that expired in 1890. The government and the conservative parties viewed the unions as recruiting offices for the Social Democratic party and therefore tried to undermine the political labor movement by limiting the sociopolitical representation of labor's interests. So governmental social policies remained restricted to what was for that time a very active and expanded welfare system, but the emancipatory components of social policy, the realization of the free and equal representation of workers' interests, was left untouched. And the more the economic situation of the workers improved and moved away from the misery of early industrialization, the more important political discrimination became. Thus the labor question became a constitutional question.[25]

Within the rural population there were still those great differences in property which had become more acute after the agrarian reforms at the beginning of the nineteenth century. In 1882, 76.6 percent of the German farmers had small farms with up to 5 hectares of arable land; only 15.7 percent of the total arable land belonged to this 76.6 percent of the farmers. Another 17.6 percent were "middle-class," with farms between 5 and 20 hectares; 29.8 percent of the total arable land belonged to them. Big farmers with property from 20 to 100 hectares made up 5.3 percent of the independent farmers, but their share of the total arable land was 30.1 percent. Almost 25 percent of the total farmable land was landed estates, but they made up only 0.5 percent of all agricultural enterprises. This distribution by size and ownership changed little in the years before 1914. Nevertheless, the trend was reversed in the 1880s because of the crisis in agriculture.

Until then, large farms and landed estates had increased in size at the expense of the middle-sized and small farm enterprises; thereafter both the number of large agricultural enterprises and their share of the total arable land dropped somewhat, while the number of middle-sized and small farmers increased, as did their share of the land. Nevertheless, in 1907 51.3 percent of the total arable land was in the hands of estate owners and big farmers (5 percent of all farmers).[26]

With the change from an agrarian to a highly industrialized nation, from an agrarian to an industrial society, large pressure groups developed to represent differentiated social and economic interests. The first of these were the trade unions formed by the new stratum of factory workers at the end of the 1860s. Until the 1890s, unions were not mass organizations but rather were composed of small, activist elites of skilled workers who were tied to political parties—the Social Democrats and left-wing liberals. Unions did not become mass movements until after the expiration of the antisocialist law, which also restricted unions, and after the end of the long depression that followed the economic crisis of the 1870s. Unions had 3 million members in 1913, almost one-third of those employed in industry and mining. The Socialists' Free Unions with 2.5 million members were far and away the strongest and actually the most representative labor organization, while the liberal Hirsch-Duncker unions, and the Christian unions (founded in 1894–1895 and patronized by the Center), remained minorities. The political orientation of the unions declined as they became mass movements. There were hardly any differences among the organizational structures and the practical activity of the three parties' unions.[27] There were even some local trade associations that belonged to more than one central organization.

This transformation of unions from small, politically and ideologically oriented elites to economically and socially oriented mass organizations and pressure groups caused a persistent conflict between the Social Democrats and the Free Unions and also tensions in the Catholic Center party between 1903 and 1914.[28] The dispute about the use of mass political strikes provided the impetus for the conflict in the socialist camp; in the Center party it was the dispute about religious versus nonsectarian unions.

Both disputes involved conflicts between union pragmatism and ideological rigidity. In both cases union pragmatism eventually won. At the same time, the unions influenced and altered the character of the parties under whose political patronage they remained. The victory of reformism in Social Democracy was prepared by the activities of unionists in the party leadership. In the Center, the Christian unions strengthened those who worked for the reform of the constitution toward a parliamentary system.[29]

Employers' associations began a few years after the first unions. Economic associations had been formed in the decade before the *Reichsgründung*, but they had very limited goals. Their main activity lay in gaining public support for better transportation systems, such as the building of roads and canals. In the early 1870s these associations were both supplemented and replaced by tightly organized groups that sought direct influence on political decisions. Among these the Association for the Protection of Common Economic Interests in the Rhineland and Westphalia, the so-called *Langnamverein* (founded in 1871), and the Confederation of German Iron and Steel Industrialists (*Verein Deutscher Eisen- und Stahlindustrieller*) (founded in 1874) were the most important. The Central Association of German Industrialists (*Centralverband Deutscher Industrieller*) was founded in 1876. These organizations were not established as opponents of the then still insignificant unions. At first they represented those in favor of protective tariffs.[30] Later these associations began to advance all the economic interests of their members. The Central Association of German Industrialists included branch associations (like the Confederation of German Iron and Steel Industrialists), regional associations (like the *Langnamverein*) and Chambers of Commerce (until 1922 Chambers of Industry and Commerce were called Chambers of Commerce even though they included representatives of industry). In addition, individual large firms were direct members of the Confederation of German Iron and Steel Industrialists. At first this organization was the common representative of entrepreneurs from all industries. However, since a firm's influence in the association depended upon the number of its employees, heavy industry, which had developed large enterprises first, quickly gained predominance. But the economic and tariff policy interests of the other industries were not always in complete accord with those of heavy industry. Therefore in 1895 some chemical and textile firms formed their own organization, the Industrialists' League (*Bund der Industriellen*). In trade politics, the league was a counterweight to the protectionistic Central Association of German Industrialists. In questions about the economic system and in general political questions there were no noteworthy differences between them. They maintained good relations with the German Conservative party and the Free Conservatives, and especially with the National Liberals. They also had connections in the Center party.

These interest groups could become politically effective by influencing the composition of the parliamentary factions of those parties close to them. After the 1870s most candidates in parliamentary elections were no longer able to finance their own campaigns as they had previously. That was because of the intensification of election campaigns. Interest groups became involved in financing campaigns and thereby were able to participate in the selection of candidates. This changed the structure of the parties. From loose alliances of dignitaries, they became well-organized parties strongly influenced by economic and social interests. This development manifested itself for the first time in the Reichstag elections of 1878. During the autumn after the election, a suprafactional Political-Economic Alliance (*Volkswirtschaftliche Vereinigung des Reichstages*) was formed by delegates from the Conservative, National Liberal, Center, and Free Conservative factions. This alliance was an organization of those in favor of protective tariff from four parliamentary factions. In addition to the direct and indirect influence on the parties by entrepreneurs, directors, and associational officials (such as Stresemann), the employers' organizations could acquire political impact by presenting their views in regular personal contacts with the highest officials of the Empire and the individual states.[31] However, one should not overestimate the influence they exerted on government policies. For example, the government instituted those social reform measures which they considered necessary despite the entrepreneurs' opposition. On the other hand, the government's opposition toward Social Democracy, the Free Unions, and efforts at constitutional reform did not need to be inspired by entrepreneurs. From the beginning, opposition to the Left provided a community of interests among the bureaucracy, nobility, and upper-middle class and the interest groups. Nor was the foreign policy of the Empire decisively influenced by interest groups. This is shown most clearly by the fact that the strongest economic involvement through trade, capital investments, and cartels existed with the greatest rivals and opponents of the Empire after 1900: Britain, France, and Russia.[32]

The one-sidedly upper-middle-class and industrial orientation of the Central Association of German Industrialists was opposed after 1909 by the *Hansabund*, which was also led by entrepreneurs. The *Hansabund* was especially opposed to the social and political cooperation of the Central Association of German Industrialists with Conservatives and Junkers. According to the intention of its founder, the banker Jacob Riesser, the *Hansabund* was to represent the interests of all middle-class groups: industry, trade, banks, craftsmen, and white-collar employees. The banks and their interest group, the Central Association of German Banks and Banking Enterprises (*Centralverband des deutschen Bank- und Bankiersgewerbe*) dominated the *Hansabund*.[33] Their chief opponents were the Conservative agrarians. Because of the multiplicity and diversity of interests represented in the *Hansabund*, it was not nearly so influential as the Central Association of German Industrialists or the Industrialists' League.

For a long time, interest groups also attempted to influence government social policies on behalf of their members. But then it proved to be more effective to have special employers' associations to promote the particular social and economic interests of the entrepreneurs as employers. Toward the end of the nineteenth century, therefore, regional branch employers' associations were founded. During the long-lasting strike of the textile workers in Crimmitschau in 1904, the employers' associations acted together to support and thereby strengthen the firms involved in the strike. This ad hoc cooperation was institutionalized that same year by the creation of central employers' organizations. These organizations—the Central Office of German Em-

ployers' Associations, (*Hauptstelle Deutscher Arbeitgeberverbände*) and the Unions of German Employers Associations
(*Verein deutscher Arbeitgeberverbände*)—differed only in their
membership. The union, unlike the central office, also took in
employers' associations of craftsmen. In their sociopolitical orientation, they were both close to the Central Association of
German Industrialists.[34]

In the same period in which entrepreneurs and workers established interest groups, agricultural interests did the same. In the
last third of the nineteenth century three types of agrarian interest groups were formed: religiously oriented Catholic farmers'
unions; an interest group dominated by eastern German landed
elites; and liberal farmers' associations. The Catholic farmers'
unions were the first to be established. They began after 1862 in
Westphalia, the Rhineland, and southern Germany. They tended
to be led by the Catholic landed nobility or the clergy. Their
purpose was to influence the economic policy on behalf of the
preservation of agricultural property holders. They leaned
strongly toward the Center party and therefore formed no nation-
wide organization of their own.[35]

In 1868 large landholders in eastern Germany established the
Congress of North German Farmers (*Kongress Norddeutscher
Landwirte*) in order to represent commercial interests of the East
Elbian grain producers who still favored free trade. In the crisis
in 1876 a new, moderately protectionist group of eastern German
agrarians, the Union of Tax and Economy Reformers (*Vereinigung der Steuer- und Wirtschaftsreformer*) was founded alongside
the free-trade-oriented congress. Both existed side by side into
the 1880s, since only some of the agrarians favored protective
tariffs. Only with the price drop and the now serious competition
of the Americans during the 1880s did protectionist tendencies
dominate East Elbian landowners. And when grain tariffs were
reduced by the Caprivi trade treaties of 1891–1893, the Farmers'
League (*Bund der Landwirte*), an extremely protectionistic and
radical organization of the East Elbian landowners, was established. Its founders were a middle-class farm agent (Ruprecht-
Ransern) and a middle-class estate owner (Dr. Gustav Roesicke)
—another sign of the shift from landed aristocracy to a landowner class. The Farmers' League was able to win many support-

ers among the big and middle-sized farmers through a skillful blend of propaganda and business connections (for example, it arranged the cheap use of farm machines and fertilizers for its members). Since its leadership was dominated by the large eastern German estate owners, it remained limited spatially to northern and eastern Germany. This was also the area in which the German Conservative party had its electorate and its "secure" constituencies. And since large landowners occupied most of the leading positions in the German Conservative party, the party became the political arm of the Farmers' League.[36]

Those farmers who rejected the Conservative large landowners who dominated the Farmers' League, as well as the religious and political party affiliation of the Catholic farmers' unions, joined farmers' unions that leaned mostly toward the liberal parties. Their impact was small since they lacked the resources of a great party.

Let us summarize our survey of the structural changes involved in Germany's transition from an agrarian to a highly industrialized nation, from an agrarian to a highly industrialized society: after traditional corporate social and economic institutions (estates, guilds, mercantile, political-economic organizations) were abolished at the beginning of the nineteenth century, they were not replaced by permanent social and economic organizations until the last third of the century. Each individual stood alone. Thus one can speak of a middle-class–individualistic era. In the period of rapid industrialization at the end of the nineteenth century, big businesses, conglomerates, cartels, and large interest groups provided the organizational foundation for the new industrial age. There is a striking parallel between the development of these economic and social organizations and the increase in participation in the parliamentary elections during the Empire: the stronger the interest groups and the more their membership increased, the higher the rate of electoral participation. This parallelism may be coincidental. It may, however, point to the fact that with the mobilization and organization of the economic and social interests in these institutions, the participation of the individual in political life was awakened. To test this hypothesis would be a worthwhile goal of a project based upon the cooperation of political, economic, and social historians.

NOTES

[1] There are good statistical compilations on the history of German industrialization in W. G. Hoffmann, F. Grumbach, and H. Hesse, *Das Wachstum der deutschen Wirtschaft seit der Mitte des 19. Jahrhunderts* (Berlin, 1965) and W. G. Hoffmann and J. H. Müller, *Das deutsche Volkseinkommen 1851 bis 1957* Tübingen, 1957).

[2] See K. E. Born, "Wirtschaftsentwicklung und Wirtschaftsstil im ersten Jahrzehnt nach der Reichsgründung," in *Wissenschaft, Wirtschaft und Technik: Festschrift für Wilhelm Treue* (Munich, 1969), 173–89.

[3] I. N. Lambi, *Free Trade and Protection in Germany, 1868–1879* (Wiesbaden, 1963) and H. Boehme, *Deutschlands Weg zur Grossmacht: Studien zum Verhältnis von Wirtschaft und Staat während der Reichsgründungszeit 1848–1881* (Cologne, 1966).

[4] K. Hardach, *Die Bedeutung wirtschaftlicher Faktoren bei der Wiedereinführung der Eisen- und Getreidezölle in Deutschland 1879* (Berlin, 1967).

[5] There is a great deal of material on the concentration movement in German industry and its relationship to the banks in J. Riesser, *Die deutschen Grossbanken und ihre Konzentration* (Jena, 1912). Riesser was director of the Darmstadt Bank and founder of the *Hansabund*.

[6] E. Maschke's *Grundzüge der deutschen Kartellgeschichte* (Dortmund, 1964) offers a good survey of the development of German cartels before 1914. There is a useful compilation of the literature on cartels in Arnold Wolfers, "Das Kartellproblem im Lichte der deutschen Kartell-Literatur," in *Schriften des Vereins der Sozialpolitik*, vol. 180:3 (Berlin, 1931). For some contemporary material provided by the Imperial government, see *Deutscher Reichstag, 11. Legislatur-Periode, II. Session 1905/06, Drucksache No. 4.*

[7] G. Ipsen, "Die preussische Bauernbefreiung als Landesausbau," *Zeitschrift für Agrargeschichte und Agrarsoziologie*, II (1954).

[8] Max Weber, "Die Verhältnisse der Landarbeiter im ostelbischen Deutschland," in *Schriften des Vereins für Sozialpolitik*, vol. 55:3 (Leipzig, 1892).

[9] On demographic developments, see: H. Haufe, *Die Bevölkerung Europas: Stadt und Land im 19. und 20. Jahrhundert* (Berlin, 1936); G. Mackenroth, *Bevölkerungslehre: Theorie, Soziologie, und Statistik der Bevölkerung* (Berlin, Göttingen, and Heidelberg, 1953). The following works treat German population movements: E. Keyser, *Bevölkerungsgeschichte Deutschlands* (Leipzig, 1943); H. Haufe, "Die nordostdeutsche Bevölkerungsbewegung 1817–1933," *Archiv für Bevölkerungswissenschaft und Bevölkerungspolitik*, V (1935); K. Keller, "Umfang und Richtungen der Wanderungen zwischen der preussischen Provinzen in den Jahren 1871 bis 1925," *Zeitschrift des Preussischen Statistischen Landesamts*, LXX (1931). A short summary of the most important demographic data for Germany between 1860 and 1914 can be found in Part III of the "Bevölkerungs-Ploetz," Kirsten, Buchholz and Köllmann, *Raum und Bevölkerung in der Weltgeschichte*, vol. 2 (Würzburg, 1956), 218–29.

[10] The historical impact of population growth is analyzed in Peter Rassow's penetrating essay on "Die sozialgeschichtlichen und allgemeingeschichtlichen Wirkungen der Bevölkerungsvermehrung Europas und Deutschlands im 19. Jahrhundert," published in P. Rassow, *Die geschichtliche Einheit des Abendlandes* (Cologne and Graz, 1960). W. Brepohl's *Der Aufbau des Ruhrvolkes im Züge der Ost-West-Wanderung* (Recklinghausen, 1948) shows how a new population group was produced by internal migration. The connection between migration and the labor question has been examined by W. Köllmann in "Industrialisierung, Binnenwanderung, und 'Soziale Frage,' " *Vierteljahrschrift für Sozial- und Wirtschaftsgeschichte*, XLVI (1959).

[11] E. R. Huber,, *Deutsche Verfassungsgeschichte seit 1789*, vol. 3 (Stuttgart, 1963), pp. 871ff.

[12] K. Bücher, *Die wirtschaftlichen Aufgaben der modernen Stadtgemeinde* (Leipzig, 1898) and H. Lindemann, *Arbeiterpolitik und Wirtschaftspflege in der deutschen Stadverwaltung*, 2 vols. (Stuttgart, 1904).

[13] K. E. Born, "Preussen und Deutschland im Kaiserreich," *Tübinger Universitätsreden*, vol. 28 (Tübingen, 1967), pp. 13ff.

[14] L. Beutin, "Die Massengesellschaft im 19. Jahrhundert," in Beuten's *Gesammelte Schriften*, ed. H. Kellenbenz (Cologne and Graz, 1963).

[15] H. Rosenberg, "Die Pseudodemokratisierung der Rittergutsbesitzerklasse," in *Zur Geschichte und Problematik der Demokratie: Festschrift für Hans Herzfeld* (Berlin, 1958).

[16] The analysis of the.social history of the German *Bürgertum* in the industrial age has been started by Hans-Joachim Henning's work on *Das westdeutsche Bürgertum in der Zeit der Hochindustrialisierung (1860–1914)*, vol. 1 (Wiesbaden, 1971).

[17] See the material in Henning, *Das westdeutsche Bürgertum.*

[18] See in particular E. Kehr, *Schlachtflottenbau und Parteipolitik 1894–1901* (Berlin, 1930); H.-U. Wehler, *Bismarck und der Imperialismus* (Cologne, 1969); D. Stegmann, *Die Erben Bismarcks* (Cologne, 1970). These studies present a great deal of material and are basic for the problem. In their interpretations the authors are occasionally misled by their strong partisanship into making one-sided, exaggerated judgments.

[19] E. Kehr, "Zur Genesis des Königlich Preussischen Reserveoffiziers," in *Der Primat der Innenpolitik*, ed. H.-U. Wehler (Berlin, 1965).

[20] See Henning, *Das westdeutsche Bürgertum.*

[21] W. Wernet, "Das gewerblich-kleinbetriebliche Element im modernen Industrialismus," *Schmollers Jahrbuch*, LXXIV (1954).

[22] A. Killat, *Die Angestellten* (1952) and S. Kracauer, *Der Angestellter* (1928).

[23] K. E. Born, *Geschichte der Wirtschaftswissenschaften an der Universität Tübingen 1817–1967* (Tübingen, 1967).

[24] These statements on wages represent averages and approximations. There were very marked differences among various branches and occupations as well as among regions.

[25] On the government's *Sozialpolitik*, see H. Rothfels, *Theodor Lohmann und die Kampfjahre der staatlichen Sozialpolitik* (Berlin, 1927); W. Vogel, *Bismarcks*

Arbeiterversicherung (Braunschweig, 1951); K. E. Born, *Staat und Sozialpolitik seit Bismarcks Sturz* (Wiesbaden, 1957).

[26] H. Haushofer, *Die deutsche Landwirtschaft im technischen Zeitalter,* vol. 5 of *Deutsche Agrargeschichte* (Stuttgart, 1963) gives a well-informed survey of the problems and developments in German agrarian history between the freeing of the serfs and the Second World War.

[27] For a reliable history of the German unions, see D. Schuster, *Die deutsche Gewerkschaftsbewegung* (Düsseldorf, 1969).

[28] H. J. Varain, *Freie Gewerkschaften, Sozialdemokratie und Staat, 1890–1920* (Düsseldorf, 1956); G. A. Ritter, *Die Arbeiterbewegung im Wilhelminischen Reich 1890–1900* (Berlin, 1963); H. Langerhaus, "Richtungsgewerkschaft und gewerkschaftliche Autonomie 1890–1914," *International Review of Social History,* II (1957).

[29] R. Morsey, *Die deutsche Zentrumspartei 1917–1923* (Düsseldorf, 1966).

[30] Henry Axel Bueck's tendentious but detailed work *Der Centralverband Deutscher Industrieller 1876–1901,* 3 vols. (Berlin, 1902–1905) is still an essential source for the origins of the Central Association of German Industrialists. On other associations, see C. Klein, *Aus der Geschichte des Vereins Deutscher Eisen- und Stahlindustrieller* (Düsseldorf, 1924) and J. Winschuh, *Der Verein mit dem langen Namen* (Berlin, 1932).

[31] There are now two well-informed studies on interest groups and politics after 1890: H. Kaelble, *Industrielle Interessenpolitik in der Wilhelminischen Gesellschaft: Centralverband deutscher Industrieller 1895–1914* (Berlin, 1967) and D. Stegmann, *Die Erben Bismarcks* (Cologne, 1970).

[32] These economic connections are usually overlooked by those who study the relationships between interest groups, the state, and the parties. The picture one gets from this, however, must be supplemented by research on the actual economic situation, such as the flow of commodities and rate of investment. The best documentation for this is in the firms' own archives and in statistical data on economic life.

[33] J. Riesser, *Der Hansabund* (Jena, 1912).

[34] The origins of Employers' Organizations is best described in G. Kessler, *Die deutschen Arbeitgeberverbände* (Leipzig, 1907). For a survey, see G. Erdmann, *Die deutschen Arbeitgeberverbände im sozialgeschichtlichen Wandel der Zeit* (Berlin, 1966).

[35] K. Schade, *Die politische Vertretung der deutschen Landwirte seit 1867* (Bonn diss., 1956); F. Jacobs, *Von Schorlemer zur Grünen Front* (Stuttgart, 1957); S. R. Tirrell, *German Agrarian Politics after Bismarck's Fall: The Formation of the Farmers' League* (New York, 1951).

[36] Hannelore Horn makes this point in an interesting case study on *Der Kampf um den Bau des Mittellandskanals* (Cologne and Opladen, 1964).

2

Political and Social Consequences of the Great Depression of 1873–1896 in Central Europe[1]

HANS ROSENBERG

I

Recurrent long-time alternations of prosperity and depression affecting the physical volume and the rate of growth, or at the least the movement, of the value of economic goods and services have been detected throughout the history of modern exchange economies.[2] Empirical observations of this kind are distinctly different from the theoretical claims which have grown out of Kondratieff's study of 'long waves'.[3] The nature of 'long waves', sometimes called 'secondary trends', 'major cycles' or 'trend cycles', is still as controversial and problematical as the intricate question of their causation.[4] The data at our disposal are still too inadequate to verify the theses advanced by some economists. 'Long waves', we are told, are more than historical episodes of 'accidental' regularity resulting from a unique conjuncture of historical circumstances; they are a permanent, inherent characteristic of the cyclical life process of mature capitalism, produced systematically and rhythmically in accordance with the immanent laws of that economy.

But whatever the status of long-term economic fluctuations in the lofty realm of economic metaphysics, from a pragmatic viewpoint they can be useful descriptive devices of historic periodization which help to establish fairly distinct units for investigation. By 'long waves' we shall mean alternating long-run periods of economic acceleration and retardation superimposed on shorter cyclical and non-cyclical fluctuations, and to illustrate their significance and usefulness attention will be drawn to some of the political and social consequences of the downgrade of the long wave of 1849–96 in central Europe.

In the economic history of England the downswing of 1873–96 is sometimes referred to as 'The Great Depression'.[5] Actually, it was a trend of world-wide scope which, despite sharp national, regional, and local differences, displayed in its fundamental tendencies, and also in many of its particular features, a far-reaching degree of unity.[6] Initiated in some countries, above all in Austria, Germany, and the United States, by a crash, violent panics and dramatic 'crises', in others, as for instance in England and France, by milder and much smoother forms of 'recession', this Great Depression was not accompanied by economic retrogression or by a spectacular breakdown. On the contrary, total output, commercial turn-over, and national wealth continued to increase, though at a distinctly lower rate of growth than between the trend prosperities of 1849–73 and 1897–1914. Any textbook on economic history shows that it was this period which witnessed great additions in the efficiency of plant and the productivity of labour, creative innovations in business methods, and a wholesale adoption of improvements in technology and organization.

The quantitative record appears to be less impressive when the increase in population and the resumption of large-scale emigration after 1879 are taken into account. Moreover, quantitative growth of production and the expansion of trade, coupled with relatively little unemployment save in a few particular recession years, may be a symptom either of prosperity or of depression. In certain circumstances the swelling of quantities may, from the entrepreneur's and the investor's angle, appear as a manifestation of economic distress. In this technical sense, the years from 1873 to 1896 do indeed mark a period of 'great depression' in central Europe. The unsteady upward tendency of physical production and of economic services coincided with an unsteady and steep downward tendency of values.[7] The trend of the price level continued to fall throughout the whole period. Interest and discount rates, commodity and stock prices, profit margins and money wages, save again in particular years, failed to recover and to regain the level of 1849–73, or to anticipate the standards of 1897–1914. Vast quantities of capital remained idle or found a refuge in foreign investments in non-capitalist and semi-capitalist countries, or at home in government securities, initiating an era of cheap public borrowing.[8]

The behaviour of the 'time series' and the fact that short-term cycles of producers' prosperity between 1873 and 1896 were mild and brief, vanishing again and again into thin air, account for the gloom and the feeling of tension, insecurity, and anxiety prevalent throughout the period. Economic pessimism appeared to be deep-rooted and firmly entrenched. Business men, big and small, voiced their complaints about the short duration of recovery and the long periods of relapse, the 'commercial paralysis', the 'deplorable state of trade', the 'continuous distress', the 'dullness and disheartening monotony' of the general market situation. With tiresome persistence they pointed to unprofitable business, with its detrimental effects on public welfare, and to the great risks they had to face in the struggle for survival.

The search for a determination of the causes of the 'depression of business' produced a voluminous literature which enriched the social sciences, found expression in poetry and fiction,[9] and widened the domain of 'crackpot' writing. The explanatory comments ranged from an emphasis on 'overproduction', 'unfair competition', 'the abrupt transformation in the production and circulation of the whole world', 'the inflammable conditions of international affairs' and the like, down to 'the excessive expenditures for alcoholic beverages, and the general improvidence of the working classes', 'the low price of German vinegar', and 'the immigration of Polish Jews'. The psychological exaggeration of economic difficulties and antagonisms created an atmosphere in which the economic depression seems to be taken for granted.

Since sinful capitalist Babylon seemed to be faced with collapse, apocalyptic horsemen appeared on the horizon. It was a golden opportunity for prophets of disaster. Most of them followed in the footsteps of Karl Marx who already, in January 1875, had predicted the approach of the 'universal crisis', which, as the crowning point of a series of periodic cycles, 'by the universality of its theatre and the intensity of its action will drum dialectics even into the heads of the mushroom-upstarts of the new, holy Prusso-German empire'.[10] It was left to his fellow-workers and disciples to draw a challenging picture of the 'chronic' and 'permanent' character of the depression, which allegedly reflected the antinomy between productive power increasing in a geometric, and the extension of markets proceeding at best in an arithmetic ratio. It was proclaimed to signify a crisis not in, but of the economic system, with the world revolution already around the corner, 'when the unemployed, losing patience, will take their own fate into their own hands'.[11]

In actual fact, the Great Depression produced a redistribution of national incomes which, through alterations in price relationships, proved in the long run to be beneficial to most consumers and employees. It witnessed a remarkable advance in the material conditions and real wage income of the industrial and agricultural workers. Moreover, it was not marked by an unbroken sequence of 'bad' years, even for the vast majority of entrepreneurs, investors, and independent self-employers. In the case of Germany, annual business measurements reveal[12] three cyclical downswings—1873–9, 1882–6, 1890–4—and two intervening rises— 1879–82, 1886–9.

II

The slump of 1873–9 transformed political parties and ideologies. It was the opening phase of a long-run depression which involved important alterations or innovations in the economic structure, and in part a decisive break with previous trends. Thus, for instance, it first brought to a standstill and then reversed the old secular tendency toward concentration of landownership at the expense of peasant holdings,[13] and it helped to establish and to maintain a political alliance between big agrarians and peasants. In Germany and Austria, the direct and indirect response to the economic trend depression consisted of a transition to a kind of 'neo-mercantilism'. Attempts at political emancipation by uprooted handicraftsmen and by petty traders formed part of the processes of accommodation to the changed economic setting. The survivors of the pre-capitalist era, on the look out for effective mechanism for self-defence, adopted an attitude of growing belligerency toward the superior strength of 'mobile capital' and to the competition, real and imaginary, of capitalist industry and large-scale retail trading. In the name of the 'protection of the weak', the artisan and shopkeeper class began, as it had done before in the crisis situation of 1848, to assail the principle of economic individualism and to agitate for a curtailment of freedom of trade through the direct intervention of the state. Their demands for a restoration of compulsory gild organizations and for special laws against 'usury' and against peddling trades found at least partial recognition in the German legislation of 1881, 1883, and 1897, and more drastically in the revision of the Austrian trade codes in 1883 and 1885.[14] But the search for economic security through political pressure paved the way also for the formation of new and wider fronts among the peasants and farmers. The vast majority of them manned the bandwagons of the conservatives and clericals in the hope of obtaining under their leadership cheap credit, reduced taxes, higher agricultural prices and protection against the middle-man, and were thus gradually turned into a first line of defence for the big agrarians.

Last but not least, the intensified social and political mobility of the 'common man' manifested itself in the rapid numerical growth of the social-democratic working-class movement, first in Germany and later in Austria. The Gotha Programme of 1875 was formulated in the midst of the storm and stress of the very intense first cyclical slump of our period. The much more challenging Erfurt Programme of 1891 was drafted while the third cyclical depression was in full swing. No wonder that, in accordance with common human inclinations to review present-day developments *sub specie aeternitatis,* it emphasized the increasingly 'universal' and 'devastating' character of recurrent economic 'crises', which seemed to make 'general insecurity' a normal condition of capitalist society. On the other hand when, with the anti-socialist law out of the way, German economy experienced between 1895 and 1900 a boom unprecedented in magnitude since 1854–7 and 1871–3, the time seemed to be ripe for a less pessimistic and a less emotionally distorted diagnosis of the economic situation. The emergence of revisionism signified a more realistic perception of the long-term tendencies and of the actual economic and social results of the Great Depression. Thus we find, for example, recognition of the changing character of the economic process as a whole through a gradual attenuation of cyclical fluctuations; of the reduced danger of violent ruptures and of 'anarchy' in production and distribution in consequence of the more intensive rather than extensive expansion of the world market and of the use of new social machinery of regulation making for more stable market conditions. Acknowledgement was now also made of the sectional character of industrial concentration; of the tenacity of small-scale landownership and cultivation, the handicrafts and retail trades; of the wider diffusion of national wealth and income, passing on some of the material benefits of the depression to the working classes.[15]

The struggle for material gains, or at least against material losses, through political activity from below gradually changed the whole character and social significance of the political party system. The liberal parties were made the scapegoats for the slump.[16] They were above all accused of being responsible for the economic policies hitherto pursued, which were now blamed for the 'frustration of the national economy'. *Ressentiments* found concrete expression in the spotlight now thrown on prominent liberal parliamentarians, who were indicted as leading, and often fraudulent, promoters, acting in close alliance with Jewish speculators and paving the way for the collapse of 1873 and its disastrous effects.[17] Dissatisfactions, enmities, jealousies, in competition with the socialist onslaught, gave rise to various Christian-social and anti-Semitic party groupings. They thundered their invectives against the 'immorality' of 'mobile capital' under the control of the Jews, and at the same time denounced them as the brains trust of the liberal parties and the ringleaders of socialist 'anarchism' blocking the road to prosperity.

Jewish emancipation and assimilation had advanced by leaps and bounds in central Europe during the upgrade from 1849 to 1873. Anti-Semitism, while it lasted, had on the whole manifested itself in the mild form of social boycott, defended by its practitioners primarily on religious grounds. After 1873, 'anti-Semitism rose as the stock market fell'.[18] Hand in hand with its growth went its qualitative transformation. It developed more and more into an economic and political mass movement, ideologically founded on the theory of race and blood. In an era loaded with tension, violent competition and nationalistic emotionalism, the new force proved to be such a valuable weapon in the fight for survival or domination that even conservative and clerical parties began to use it on a grand scale.[19]

The long-run results of these political processes of adaptation began to be effective by 1878, when the majority over the anti-liberal parties was reversed in the German Reichstag, the Prussian Landtag, and the Austrian Reichsrat. Constitutionally and ideologically this meant a strengthening of the power and prerogative of the established monarchical governments. Vested interests of whole groups of producers were becoming directly dependent on government support and intervention, and all attempts aiming at the inauguration of a genuine parliamentary system met with defeat.

The growth of physical production and trade in our period functioned as an instrument of compensation for the continued decline of prices. It proceeded in waves and was made possible by a greatly accelerated 'mass mobilization' of consumers, which reduced the inequalities in consumption habits and had a levelling influence on social distinctions. This had its political counterpart in the broadening of the social base of the political party system. Contrary to the traditions of the prosperous *laissez-faire* age of 1849–73, the political aloofness of the common man was slowly breaking down. Politics in the Great Depression era ceased to be a concern of small groups, privileged by social status, wealth or education. The centre of gravity of political agitation shifted from issues of political policies, from national unification and constitutional reconstruction problems most characteristic of the fifties and sixties, to a crude emphasis on economic objectives. Instead of controversies about political freedom, the fight for economic security became the focus of public discord.[20] Exposed to the pressure of an electorate in a state of uproar, all political parties had, in order to maintain and fortify their position, to become mass parties, to put into motion and get hold of the indifferent non-voter, and to overhaul their leadership, platforms and propaganda techniques. Decades of relative stability in party alignments, with secure and steady majorities, gave way to erratic fluctuations in party strength as well as in party coalitions and combinations.[21] The variations in the composition, duration, vigour and efficiency of these party alliances and counter-alliances remain largely unexplainable unless they are linked up with the changing economic tendencies. To some extent they are to be explained as attempts to turn to advantage the ups and downs of cyclical oscillations.

This long-range process of transformation crystallized first in the fight for tariff protectionism, which brought about the reconciliation of the hitherto antagonistic interests of the big industrialists and agrarians.[22] The new alliance in 1878–9 was facilitated by the fact that some of the traditional grievances of the agrarians against large-scale industry had become pointless. As a result of the shrinkage of industrial production and the steep decline of emigration after 1873, the rural labour supply was no longer depleted. Agricultural money wages, which under the pressure of industrial demand for labour had risen very intensely in the boom years of the early seventies, now ceased to advance. The virtual cessation of industrial investments and the fall in interest rates had cheapened agricultural credit. The political effectiveness of the new coalition was ultimately guaranteed by securing the support of Bismarck and of a parliamentary majority which cut across the established party lines. The connecting link was furnished by the Catholic Centre, which combined in its ranks industrial and agricultural protectionist interests. It was prepared, by virtue of its social philosophy, for a crusade against atomistic *laissez-faire* individualism.[23] Having its geographical base in western and southern Germany and in Silesia (that is, in the strongholds of the iron and textile industries and of medium-scale agricultural production, where agitation for protectionism was, or could be made, most popular) the Centre used the tariff issue as a springboard for political conquests, and above all for the termination of the *Kulturkampf*.

III

The Great Depression marked the decisive turning-point in the nineteenth-century history of the relationship between the state and the economy. The crash of 1873 was a death-blow to that kind of state interventionism which had endeavoured to destroy mercantilist hangovers and to build a new framework of economic life on the 'natural rationality' of the market mechanism. After 1873 governments, on their own initiative or through pressure from below, began to liquidate the short-lived episode of internal and external free trade which, though primarily determined by political power calculations,[24] had been conditioned by the upgrade economic trend between 1849 and 1873. The social character of the economic processes of production, distribution and consumption became officially recognized. From this time onwards it tended to be the destiny of the state to function as the supreme agent of economic co-ordination and integration on a national scale. Not natural law but a 'New Deal' was to establish order in the realm of economic society by forcing the government to reassume old functions and usurp new ones.

The reorientation of government policies was not the offspring of farsighted, long-range planning, but the unforeseen result of haphazard emergency measures inspired by expediency and designed to restore confidence and to overcome short-run dislocation. The Austrian government in 1873 proclaimed its right and duty 'to guard economic activity against enduring disturbances'.[25] The recovery policy and the modest economic reforms which it initiated, however, were based upon the optimistic assumption that prosperity had given way to 'one of those recessions as they usually occur with elementary violence in the economic life of the nations from time to time, due to an overestimation of capital resources and an over-expansion of credit'.[26] Thus government action between 1873 and 1878 remained chiefly confined to the extending of credit facilities to large-scale private enterprises such as railroads and industrial joint-stock companies faced with financial collapse. In addition, a few public work and relief schemes were launched, and the building trade was encouraged through tax exemptions. Laws were passed which curtailed fraudulent promotion and speculation on the stock market and provided for a reconstruction of the *Nationalbank*.[27] On the other hand, the policy of 'restoring confidence' consisted in the dissolution of numerous labour associations and the imprisonment of their leaders.[28] Driven underground, the more uncompromising elements of the young Austrian labour movement gained the upper hand, and, as in Germany, the 'Marxians' gradually ousted the disciples of Lassalle.

More important historically than the emergency schemes were the enduring changes in the structure and functions of the state that grew out of them: the advance of the Leviathan state, the growing dependence of economic agencies on state aid, and the intensification of nationalism. When, for instance, the Austrian government after 1876 began to take over some of the virtually bankrupt private railroad companies in response to the crash of 1873 and its immediate aftermath (which was then interpreted as a protracted cyclical and not yet as a trend-depression) it could not be foreseen that this would lead to a lasting break with tradition and to the displacement of private by public railroads during the eighties and nineties. Nor was it easy to anticipate that after 1879 the new policy of nationalizing the railroads and of providing capital for new construction (chiefly in the economically under-privileged areas, the strongholds of the subject Slavonic peoples) would accelerate the centrifugal rather than the centripetal effects of rising mass nationalisms. Economically fortified, the subject nationalists used the railroad issue as a political battleground for pushing their claims for administrative and institutional decentralization, or autonomy on national lines.[29]

In Germany a policy of vigorous state intervention was not adopted before 1878. This meant a radical reverse in basic attitudes, since the government up to 1877 had adhered to the gospel of automatic adjustments from within the economic mechanism, and had watched with Olympian aloofness 'one of those stagnations as they periodically recur in course of time'.[30] Some emphasis, however, was at that early date put on the extension of public work projects to be carried out by private enterprise, whereas at the height of the boom the policy of withholding orders had been pursued.[31] The first cyclical slump of the Great Depression touched its bottom by 1876–7. Bismarck had by that time become sufficiently alarmed by the persistence of the industrial and commercial slumps and by the widening discrepancy between productive capacity and effective demand. Moreover, he was strongly impressed by the beginning of agricultural distress, which affected him personally since he had burnt his fingers in speculative land purchases.[32] It sharpened his understanding of the grievances of hard-pressed producers and debtors, of the dangers inherent in the spread of unemployment, labour unrest, socialist agitation and the growing militancy and tension in all party camps. He no longer found consolation in the fact that the downgrade was of world-wide scope.[33]

The economic crisis had produced a fiscal crisis which, as in Austria, manifested itself in what in those days were considered to be grave budgetary difficulties. The unbalanced deficit in the Reich budget increased from year to year after 1872. In these circumstances the Imperial government was forced to demand larger annual subsidies from the states. The financial position of the latter deteriorated steadily between the years 1873–9, as the French war indemnity was spent and the slump reduced the yield from direct taxation and the revenues from state enterprises. State governments grudgingly realized that a solution of their own fiscal troubles presupposed a strengthening of the financial status of the Reich. Bismarck began by 1877 to respond actively to the acute fiscal plight by launching a programme which asked for a comprehensive reform of indirect taxation, the introduction of a tobacco monopoly for the Reich, and the nationalization of the German railroad system at a time when public credit was cheap and the prices of railroad shares low. He met with defeat, and his attempt to shelter public finance against the disrupting effects of economic oscillations resulted in a growth of political disharmony. The crystallization of a strong protectionist front among industrialists and agrarians in 1878, combined with the weakening power of resistance on the part of the state governments, created a new situation. Grasping the fresh opportunities inherent in the situation, Bismarck, by a series of masterful tactical manoeuvres and demagogic tricks, linked up the pressing

need for fiscal stabilization in an unbalanced national economy
with the new panacea of 'solidarity protectionism' in such a way
that both became interdependent.

The Imperial government's recovery policy for the 'protection
of national labour'[34] promised a renewed advance of business
under more favourable conditions by the building of new tariff
walls, and by government control of the transport system, which
was to accompany the piecemeal nationalization of the Prussian
railroads after 1879. Government intervention was not, however,
to be identical with a surrender to the pressure of severely hit
groups of large-scale producers. On the contrary, it was to be a
mere instrument of general policy and was to function as a vehi-
cle for the strengthening of governmental authority and the sovereignty of the Reich. The political power vested in the Reich
executive was to be used to help overcome short-run economic
contraction and stagnation, but in exchange for its services the
state was to make durable political conquests, which would inci-
dentally also serve Bismarck's own aggrandizement.

Vast schemes loomed before Bismarck's eyes; the establishment, for instance, of the unassailable financial independence of
the Reich and its military machine, beyond the reach of parliamentary control, by manipulating the producers' demand for tariff protection and by reforming taxation so as to reduce overhead
costs. Or the political exploitation of economic and fiscal malad-
justments so as to secure a new balance of power between the
Reich and the states: to destroy the remnants of particularism
which had hitherto found their stronghold among south German
protectionists, and to complete the national unification by ce-
menting it with unbreakable economic ties. Or the 'cashing in' on
the 'red menace'; on big industry's dependence on government
support; and on the chronic agricultural distress which grew more
severe during the eighties. The harvesting of the crop sown in
1878–9 required patience, skill and time. But the *Kartell* Reichstag of 1887 and the *Sammlungspolitik* inaugurated in 1897 showed
an ultimate yield which, in the light of the objectives aimed at,
was far from unsatisfactory.

A planned political by-product of the Tariff Law of 1879 was
the solidifying of Prussian-German militarism as a state within

the state. As almost all the regular expenditure of the Empire was devoted to the army, the grant of tariffs and indirect taxes, voted under the pressure of an economic emergency, practically nullified the Reichstag's constitutional right to make annual budget grants. There was to be no repetition of the constitutional conflict of 1862–6, which had grown out of the liberal Landtag's unwillingness to back up a costly armament programme at a moment when the country was still suffering from the aftermath of the world's economic crisis of 1857, aggravated by the war of 1859. The new alliance, formed in 1879, between the militarists and protectionists was, from Bismarck's viewpoint, designed to give stability and financial security to the military machine. It greatly facilitated long-term planning of defence as embodied in the renewal of the septennates in 1880 and 1887, each of which accidentally coincided with the shift from cyclical depression to recovery.

State support of large-scale producers had been preceded by, and was up to the Caprivi régime accompanied by, a labour policy which was originally launched as an instrument of the economic recovery policy. But from the very beginning the attempt to turn economic contraction into expansion, and to neutralize the most dangerous social tensions, was merely a subordinate phase of a policy of political power. The ups and downs of the economic curve had to be acted upon in such a way that the 'red menace' was kept under control. The way for the necessary action was paved by the rapid growth and aggressiveness of the social-democratic movement, primarily a consequence of widespread unemployment and slump conditions between 1873 and 1878. The anti-socialist law of 1878 and its successors asked for 'that degree of dictatorship' necessary to fight with success 'a hostile army living in our midst', which was alleged to deepen the depression by undermining confidence, by scaring off investments and by creating a general atmosphere of disheartening instability and uncertainty.[35] Recovery or an increase in wages and security of employment was, according to the official view, unattainable unless public confidence was restored by a forceful defence of private property; by the encouragement of individual initiative; and by the maintenance of the entrepreneur as 'master in his own house', unhampered by government intervention into hours, wages and working conditions in general.[36]

The alliance between labour and socialism was to be rendered ineffective by a state policy which made political persecution the complement of material protection. Bismarck's insistence on compulsory workers' insurance against illness, accidents, invalidity and the insecurity of old age, with the financial aid of the state, was under Caprivi supplemented by the regulation of working conditions through the Industrial Code of 1891, aimed at the establishment of a manageable social equilibrium. The power of the state was to be made serviceable not only to the vested interests of the government's most useful supporters, but also to its most dangerous and potentially strongest enemies. To strengthen national cohesion and morale the government had to function as an arbiter and guardian of social welfare and a defender of the economic security of those classes which were exposed more immediately and more intensely than others to the pressure of cyclical oscillations, and at the same time were more decisive in determining the balance of power.

IV

The vibrations of the economic system between 1873 and 1896 had their repercussions not merely in domestic politics and social relations but also in the realm of foreign policy. The sharp contrast between Bismarck's hazardous war policies of the sixties and, after the middle of the nineties, the ambitious pursuit of *Weltpolitik* on the one hand, and on the other the pacific and exceedingly cautious and moderate foreign policy of the seventies, eighties and early nineties is hardly adequately explained in psychological or ideological terms, or by pointing to an inner break in Bismarck's conception of power politics, reaching saturation point with the founding of the Empire. From the seventies onwards, Bismarck adjusted his aims and strategy in the field of international relations to the changing historical conditions, and among them to the strains and irritations, some sporadic and some more permanent in character, which resulted from the downgrade of the long wave.

Bismarck in 1879 summed up the international experiences of

1875–8 by referring to the uncertainty about the stability of European peace, resulting in a continued lack of confidence and in prolonged economic stagnation. The preservation of peace and the restoration of a more lasting belief in the pacific future of Europe were, he considered, prerequisites for a world recovery.[37] Bismarck's persistent emphasis on the vital need for stabilization in an unbalanced world continued to be motivated to a great extent by the imperative desire to solidify the gains of 1866 and 1871. At the same time, however, a moderate and unadventurous foreign policy presented itself as an inescapable political necessity in the light of domestic affairs.[38] With economic dislocation and discontent, social unrest and class conflicts at home; with national unity, the future of authoritarian monarchical government and the position of the propertied and conservative elements in the country jeopardized by the growth of a socialist movement, the risk of foreign war had by all means to be avoided. War, even among other nations, must be prevented, because of 'the inevitable repercussions on our economic interests, and also because we never can foresee to what extent we might become involved in foreign entanglements'.[39]

It is, therefore, much more than a coincidence that the year 1879, the decisive turning-point in German and Austrian internal politics and in the domestic balance of power, also involved a reorientation of the foreign policies of both countries. The building of a conservative domestic front found its parallel in the international field in the attempt to lay the foundation of a conservative bloc among the Great Powers. The search for an enduring political and social equilibrium between the classes at home corresponded with the drive for the establishment of a balanced order between the states, by reconciling competitive interests and by strengthening the dynastic solidarity of the monarchical idea against the democratic revolutionary principles of the west and against the rising dangers of 'Slavonic Napoleonism'. The Austro-German defensive alliance was founded as a guarantee of peace against Russian pressure and belligerency. It was signed at a time when the appeasement of the Centre Party through the break with liberalism and the liquidation of the *Kulturkampf* accompanied the overtures to Catholic Austria. To Bismarck it promised to be a safe instrument with which to isolate France, to compromise the conflicting power interests of Austria and Russia, and to defeat the aggressive intentions of the pan-Slav forces in Russia. It was to serve as a basis for a renewal of the Three Emperors' League and for shifting 'the centre of gravity in the Russian Empire back to the conservative and propertied classes'.[40]

The Austro-German alliance of 1879 turned out to be the beginning of a new technique in international relations, of a system of alliances, replacing the system of separate states acting individually. The tendency was in line with one of the most outstanding and permanent economic results of the Great Depression, affecting business organization, business methods and the business spirit. The desperate drive to overcome the risks of cut-throat competition and to establish a more even level of business security and stability was in the direction of combination, co-operation and joint action through the formation of trade associations, collective lobbying agencies, cartels, syndicates, amalgamations, co-operative societies, and trade unions. The tendency had already manifested itself to some extent during the upgrade from 1849 to 1873. It receded into the background between 1875 and 1877, when the search for an escape from bankruptcy bred disharmony and disruption, and translated into immediate action rugged individualism of a *sauve qui peut* nature. However, the more general waning of faith in the effectiveness of individual action, accelerated by the emergence of 'solidarity protectionism' in 1878, altered the setting. After years of experimentation, the trend toward cartellization in industry, banking transport, trade, insurance and the professions was much intensified from the middle of the eighties onwards.[41] As a device aiming at longtime stabilization it began to exert an universal appeal. The method of collective action now found widespread application in both its political and economic aspects. This issue symbolizes the parallelism and the correlationship of economic, social and political trends which mark the unity and inherent synthesis of central European developments between 1873 and 1896.

To the student interested in the more general historic impact of business variations, cyclical and non-cyclical, it would be a tempting task to analyse the history of Austro-German-Russian diplomatic manoeuvres up to Bismarck's anti-Russian credit prohibition of 1887 and the German-Russian tariff war of 1893, in relation to and in terms of grain prices, harvest cycles, cattle plagues, veterinary police measures, tariff and currency fluctuations and railroad and shipping freight rates.[42] Such a study would not only deepen the understanding of the European alignments and alliances; it would also reveal more clearly the internal contradictions of Bismarck's policy. The predominantly pro-agrarian tendency of his protectionist economic policy, accelerated in 1885 and 1887, accounts largely for his domestic difficulties as well as for the growing alienation of German-Russian relations. It thus undermined the ultimate objectives of his defensive peace policies, which in their final outcome were further endangered by the combination of a policy of national self-sufficiency with one of world-wide expansion.

Up to the Congo Conference, official German colonial policy retained its originally conceived character as a modest instrument of the government's protectionist recovery policy. The subsequent shift from economic to political considerations was facilitated by the meagre economic returns of Germany's colonial possessions. Colonial gains of some sort, even if economically valueless, became a vital concern for the position of the government in its fight to keep its supporters satisfied and to weaken the Reichstag opposition.[43] However, even short-run insistence on the right to *Weltpolitik* in defiance of England's policy made for international complications. It helped to lay the foundation for the bolder and more aggressive and reckless political and economic imperialism of the Wilhelmian era, eager for expansion, taking its risks and bursting forth in spurts of self-assertion under the impetus of the prosperity of 1897–1914.

V

The pressures, tensions and energies released and the ruptures caused by the trend depression of 1873–96, which were interrupted but not broken by cyclical rises and random fluctuations, appear to have been compelling enough to upset the traditional balance of political and social forces and ideas. Restless economic mobility, though merely a part in a single cultural whole, carried sufficient weight of its own to enforce numerous political adjustments and legislative and administrative measures. Their express purpose was to develop expedient defence mechanisms, to alleviate adverse business conditions and social frictions, to preserve old and to open up new economic outlets, and, through the use of the power of the state, to build up an institutional setting better able to turn depression into prosperity, confusion into a controllable balance. Here lies the great historical significance of the crisis situation of 1878–9, 'when something had to be done'.

The Great Depression not merely *caused* alterations in the political and social framework, it also *conditioned* shifts in social values and political influence and furnished a general background for institutional innovations and changes in policy by setting new limits to political objectives, tactics and strategy. For individual or group action, whatever its subjective motivation and underlying wishful thinking, there was no promise of success unless it adjusted itself to the changing processes of the economic system, but chance situations were also created for opportunists who felt called upon to capitalize economic disharmony and stringency, real or imaginary, and to use the insecurities of a discouraged citizenry as a springboard for political conquests.

NOTES

[1] Based on a paper read at the annual meeting of the American Historical Association on 27 December 1940.

[2] See for instance W. Abel, *Agrarkrisen und Agrarkonjunktur in Mitteleuropa, vom 13. bis zum 19. Jahrhundert* (Berlin, 1935); M. J. Elsas, *Umriss einer Geschichte der Preise und Löhne in Deutschland* (Leyden, 1936), vol. I; with special regard to the seventeenth and eighteenth centuries, the suggestive study by J. Griziotti Kretschmann, 'Ricerche sulle fluttuazioni economiche di lunga durata', *Giornale degli economisti e rivista di statistica* (1933), pp. 461–508.

[3] N. D. Kondratieff, 'Die langen Wellen der Konjuntur', *Archiv für Sozialwissenschaft und Sozialpolitik* (1926), pp. 573–609; an abridged English version in the *Review of Economic Statistics*, XVII, 105–15.

[4] See W. C. Mitchell, *Business Cycles. The Problem and its Setting* (New York, 1927), pp. 226–30; C. A. R. Wardwell, *An Investigation of Economic Data for Major Cycles* (Philadelphia, 1927); S. S. Kuznets, *Secular Movements in Production and Prices* (Philadelphia, 1930), pp. 259–66; W. Woytinsky, 'Das Rätsel der langen Wellen', *Schmollers Jahrbuch für Gesetzgebung* (1931), pp. 577–618; F. Simiand, *Les fluctuations économiques à longue période et la crise mondiale* (Paris, 1932); J. Lescure, *Hausses et baisses des prix de longue durée* (Paris, 1933); L. H. Dupriez, 'Einwirkung der langen Wellen auf die Entwicklung der Wirtschaft seit 1800', *Weltwirtschaftliches Archiv* (1935), pp. 1–12. The only comprehensive attempt made so far to apply systematically the 'long-wave' concept to the writing of economic history from the end of the eighteenth century onwards is by J. Schumpeter, *Business Cycles, A Theoretical, Historical, and Statistical Analysis of the Capitalist Process* (New York, 1939), 2 vols. See my critical comments in the *American Historical Reivew*, XLVI, 96–9.

[5] G. D. H. Cole, *British Trade and Industry* (1932), pp. 77–99; H. L. Beales, 'The "Great Depression" in Industry and Trade', *Economic History Review*, v, 65–75; W. W. Rostow, 'Investment and the Great Depression (1873–96)', *ibid.* VIII, 136–58.

[6] Clear consciousness of this international parallelism and some notion of the economic unity of the period under discussion are to be found in contemporary literature. See F. X. v. Neumann-Spallart, *Uebersichten der Weltwirtschaft* (Berlin, 1879), II, 20 ff.; v, 83–9; F. v. Juraschek, *Uebersichten der Weltwirtschaft* (Berlin, 1896), pp. cxvii ff.; F. C. Huber, *Fünfzig Jahre deutschen Wirtschaftslebens* (Stuttgart, 1906), pp. 34, 78 f.; Viscount Goschen, *Essays and Addresses on Economic Questions, 1865–1893* (1905), pp. 189–216; D. A. Wells, *Recent Economic Changes* (New York, 1889), pp. v f., 1–26, 82–113, and *passim*; H. Denis, *La dépression économique et sociale et l'histoire des prix* (Brussels, 1895), *passim*.

[7] For the statistical details see E. Wagemann, *Economic Rhythm; A Theory of Business Cycles* (New York, 1930), p. 265; R. Wagenführ, *Die Industriewirtschaft. Entwicklungstendenzen der deutschen und internationalen Industrieproduktion*

1860–1932 (Berlin, 1933), pp. 13 ff.; A. Jacobs and H. Richter, *Die Grosshandels-preise in Deutschland von* 1792 *bis* 1934 (1935), pp. 45, 74–83; E. Varga (ed.), *World Economic Crises*, 1848–1935 (Moscow, 1937), vol. I, 'Comparative Data for the Leading Capitalist Countries', pp. 178 f., 200–4, 230–3, 258–61; vol. III (1939): J. Trachtenberg, *Monetary Crises* (1821–1938), pp. 695, 703–8, 718 f., 724 f.

⁸ Juraschek, *op. cit.* pp. lxix, lxxv ff.; H. Stuebel, *Staat und Banken im preussischen Anleihewesen von* 1871 *bis* 1913 (Berlin, 1935), pp. 23, 41 ff.

⁹ See L. Niemann, *Soziologie des naturalistischen Romans* (Berlin, 1934), pp. 13–18, 28–40, 51 f., 95 f.; E. Kohn-Bramstedt, *Aristocracy and the Middle-Classes in Germany*, 1830–1900 (1937), pp. 231–42.

¹⁰ In the preface to the second edition of *Capital*, vol. I.

¹¹ F. Engels, in 1886, in the editor's preface to the first English translation of *Capital*, vol. I. See also 'Zur Jahreswende' (anonymous), *Die Neue Zeit*, IX, 433–6; A. Bebel, *Unsere wirtschaftliche und politische Lage* (2nd ed. Zürich, 1893), pp. 13–18; K. Kautsky, *Bernstein und das sozialdemokratische Programm* (Stuttgart, 1899), pp. 136–42.

¹² For descriptive annual data see Neumann-Spallart and Juraschek, *op. cit. passim*; Huber, *op. cit.* pp. 40–88; W. L. Thorp, *Business Annals* (New York, 1926), pp. 207–12, 223–7.

¹³ Figures in M. Sering, *Deutsche Agrarpolitik auf geschichtlicher und landeskundlicher Grundlage* (Leipzig, 1934), p. 30.

¹⁴ An excellent body of material on the actual economic conditions and development of the handicrafts throughout our period is collected in 'Untersuchungen über die Lage des Handwerks in Deutschland mit besonderer Rücksicht auf seine Konkurrenzfähigkeit gegenüber der Grossindustrie', *Schriften des Vereins für Sozialpolitik*, vols. LXII–LXX (Leipzig, 1895–7). Vol. LXXI deals with the corresponding problems in Austria. See also vol. LXXXVII on 'Hausindustrie und Heimarbeit in Deutschland und Oesterreich'. The political implications, anticipating the long-run consequences, are very revealingly outlined by F. Perrot, *Das Handwerk, seine Reorganization und seine Befreiung von der Uebermacht des Grosskapitales* (Leipzig, 1876). For Austria see H. Waentig, *Gewerbliche Mittelstandspolitik* (Leipzig, 1898), pp. 94–100, 108, 150 ff., 206 f.

¹⁵ The classical formulation in E. Bernstein, *Die Voraussetzungen des Sozialismus und die Aufgabe der Sozialdemokratie* (Stuttgart, 1899). It is interesting to note that Bernstein turned back to a more 'orthodox' evaluation of the trends of economic development during the depression years which followed the cyclical slump of 1907. See his *Der Revisionismus in der Sozialdemokratie* (Amsterdam, 1909).

¹⁶ See H. v. Poschinger, *Bismarck und die Parlamentarier* (Breslau, 1895–6), II, 326 ff., III, 19 ff.; H. Oncken, *Rudolf von Bennigsen* (Stuttgart and Leipzig, 1910), II, 373 ff., 402–12, 417 f.; J. Heyderhoff and P. Wentzcke (ed.), *Deutscher Liberalismus im Zeitalter Bismarcks. Eine politische Briefsammlung* (Bonn and Leipzig, 1926), II, 150–2, 212–15, 219, 230–4, 242, 248–53, 268–71, 280, 378 f., 383; L. Bergsträsser (ed.), *Der politische Katholizismus* (Munich, 1923), II, 86–94, 121.

For Austria see G. Kolmer, *Parlament und Verfassung in Oesterreich* (1902–3), II, 270, 279–82, 308, 473; III, 47, 62, 223; R. Charmatz, *Deutsch-österreichische Politik. Studien über den Liberalismus und über die auswärtige Politik Oesterreichs* (Leipzig, 1907), pp. 45–7.

[17] Rudolph Meyer, *Politische Gründer und die Korruption in Deutschland* (Leipzig, 1877), *passim*, especially pp. 88 ff.; O. Glagau, *Der Bankerott des Nationalliberalismus und die 'Reaktion'* (8th ed., Berlin, 1878), *passim*.

[18] R. J. Sontag, *Germany and England. Background of Conflict, 1848–1894* (New York, 1938), p. 146.

[19] O. Glagau, *Deutsches Handwerk und historisches Bürgertum* (Osnabrück, 1879), pp. 44 ff., 54, 79; W. Frank, *Hofprediger Adolf Stoecker und die christlich-soziale Bewegung* (Berlin, 1928), pp. 75–102, 191, 296, 307–13, 321; K. Wawrzinek, *Die Entstehung der deutschen Antisemitenparteien* (Berlin, 1926); F. Salomon (ed.), *Die deutschen Parteiprogramme* (Leipzig, 1924), II, 57–65. For Austria see Kolmer, *op. cit.* III, 178, 203, 217; IV, 158–66; V, 235–8; Charmatz, *op. cit.* pp. 90–102; Waentig, *op. cit.* pp. 136–68; P. Molisch, *Geschichte der deutschnationalen Bewegung in Oesterreich* (Jena, 1926), pp. 95–7, 118 f., 143.

[20] See Bismarck's comments in his *Gesammelte Werke* (Amsterdam, 1924–8), VIII, 455; XII, 424 f.

[21] A statistical summary of the six Reichstag elections between 1877 and 1898 in *Statistisches Jahrbuch für das Deutsche Reich*, XXII, 161; for Austria see Kolmer, *op. cit.* III, 12; IV, 4; V, 10, 12.

[22] For the more technical details and a chronological narrative of events the reader is summarily referred to the monographic treatment of central European tariff policies by W. Ashley, J. v. Bazant, A. Beer, W. Gerloff, J. Grunzel, L. Lang, A. v. Matlekovits, A. Peez, and A. Zimmermann. Far superior in quality and more fully aware of the effects of economic fluctuations in these crucial years are W. Lotz, *Die Ideen der deutschen Handelspolitik* (Leipzig, 1892), and the practically forgotten but excellent book by M. Nitzsche, *Die handelspolitische Reaktion in Deutschland* (Stuttgart and Berlin, 1905). For the parliamentary aspects see J. Ziekursch, *Politische Geschichte des neuen deutschen Kaiserreiches* (Frankfurt, 1927), II, 309–75; H. Oncken, *op. cit.* II, 297–307, 317–475; L. Maenner, 'Deutschlands Wirtschaft und Liberalismus in der Krise von 1879', *Archiv für Politik und Geschichte*, IX, 347–82, 456–88. In regard to Austria see Kolmer, *op. cit.* vols. II and III, *passim*, and Charmatz, *op. cit. passim*. Charmatz's analysis is mainly based on the source material collected by Kolmer.

[23] See Windthorst's Reichstag speech of 1879, proclaiming the Centre as the 'liquidator' of the 'bankruptcy' of 'liberal economy' ('Der Politische Katholizismus', *op. cit.* II, 116–130).

[24] H. Rosenberg, *Die Weltwirtschaftskrisis von 1857–1859* (Stuttgart, 1934), pp. 202–10; and *Die nationalpolitische Publizistik Deutschlands* (Munich and Berlin, 1935), II, 559–632.

[25] Emperor Francis Joseph's address to the Reichsrat, 5 November 1873 (Kolmer, *op. cit.* II, 285).

[26] *Ibid.*

[27] Details in Kolmer, *op. cit.* II, 470–509.

[28] Waentig, *op. cit.* pp. 174 f.

[29] Kolmer, *op. cit.* III, 76; IV, 318.

[30] Bismarck, *Die Gesammelten Werke*, XI, 405.

[31] H. v. Poschinger (ed.), *Aktenstücke zur Wirtschaftspolitik des Fürsten Bismarck* (Berlin, 1890), I, 186 f.; Bismarck, *op. cit.* XI, 579.

[32] Bismarck, *op. cit.* VIII, 463.

[33] Bismarck, *op. cit.* XI, 405, 467, 486.

[34] For the official motivation, see Bismarck, *op. cit.* XII, 19, 52–7, 67 ff., 84, 288 ff., 433 ff., 618; XIII, 324 f.

[35] Bismarck, *op. cit.* XII, 1–15.

[36] *Ibid*, p. 438.

[37] *Die Grosse Politik der Europäischen Kabinette* 1871–1914, ed. J. Lepsius, A. Mendelssohn-Bartholdy, F. Thimme (Berlin, 1922), III, 58.

[38] *Ibid.* III, 162 f., 175, 407; Bismarck, *op. cit.* XII, 433.

[39] *Die Grosse Politik*, IV, 17.

[40] *Ibid.* III, 52–9, 80 f.; IV, 19.

[41] F. Kleinwächter, *Die Kartelle* (Innsbruck, 1883), pp. 126–206; L. Brentano, *Ueber die Ursachen der heutigen Not* (Leipzig, 1889), pp. 23–8; 'Ueber wirtschaftliche Kartelle in Deutschland und im Auslande', *Schriften des Vereins für Sozialpolitik*, vol. LX (Leipzig, 1897); see also K. Bücher, *ibid.* LXI, 142 ff.

[42] Valuable hints in this direction will be found in the monographs of R. Ibbeken, E. Kehr, A. Vagts, W. Hallgarten, R. J. Sontag, and P. R. Anderson.

[43] *Die Grosse Politik*, IV, 96 f.

Part II

Elites and Institutions

The following selections seek to illuminate the problem of political and social change in Germany by examining some key leadership groups. The first essay, which originally appeared in Modern European Social History *(edited by Robert J. Bezucha, Lexington, Mass., 1972), provides a general introduction to those leadership groups that supported the existing system. Werner T. Angress's analysis of Jewish reserve officers approaches the critically important military establishment from an unusual direction, but his work underscores a persistent problem faced by conservative elites: how to reconcile the need for institutional efficiency with a defense of traditional social values. John Röhl's study shows how this same tension existed in the bureaucracy. Werner Angress is Professor of History at the State University of New York in Stony Brook; his article first appeared in the Yearbook of the* Leo Baeck Institute *(London, 1972). John Röhl teaches at the University of Sussex; his article is reprinted from* The Journal of Contemporary History *(Vol. 2, 1967).*

3

Conflict and Cohesion among German Elites in the Nineteenth Century

JAMES J. SHEEHAN

This essay seeks to provide a rough sketch of the changing character and relationships of certain elites in nineteenth-century Germany.[1] In order to deal with some very complex issues as concisely as possible, I have had to limit the focus in two important ways: first, I have not tried to confront Germany's regional diversity, but rather I have emphasized Prussian developments in the period before national unification and Prussia together with the Reich after 1871; second, I have concentrated on the landed aristocracy, the bureaucracy, the army, and on the relationships of these institutions to propertied and educated elites. To have tried to include an account of other institutions, such as political parties, local government, universities, business enterprises, and the like, would have raised more analytical and evidential problems than can be handled in one historian's lifetime, let alone in one brief essay.[2]

Before we begin to consider the historical dimensions of our problem, it may be useful to recall the distinctions about social stratification offered by Max Weber.[3] There are, Weber maintained, three distinct hierarchies in the modern social system: first, there is an economic hierarchy, which is determined by individuals' relationship to the market and defines what Weber called "class"; second, there is a prestige hierarchy, which is based on the possession of social power and defines status; third, there is a political hierarchy, which is based on the possession of power.

In the pre-modern era, which in German central Europe lasted until the second half of the seventeenth century, these three hierarchies tended to coincide, especially at their upper levels. The nobility possessed the most important economic resource, the land, and also held a near monopoly on prestige and power. In fact, as Otto Brunner and others have pointed out, pre-modern political and social concepts do not clearly distinguish between economic, social, and political power.[4] In what Brunner has called the world of *Herrschaft,* the key authority relationship was that between the lord (*Herr*) and his dependents, a relationship that was based on a fusion of the lord's mastery over the means of production, his unchallenged role as social leader, and his preeminence in the political system. In this social setting, the state as an exclusively political institution did not exist, nor did a market economy based exclusively on economic factors.

Brunner's image of the world of *Herrschaft* is, of course, an ideal type. In practice, economic, social, and political power were never entirely fused. But they were closely linked and when, in the course of the eighteenth century, men began to sense that they were drifting apart, the proper relationship between wealth, status, and power became a central theme in German social thought and literature.[5] By the first decades of the nineteenth century it had become conventional for the defenders of the old aristocracy to lament the passing of wealth and power into the hands of baseborn individuals who were ill prepared to lead society. These laments were answered by those who regarded the nobility's residual privileges as anachronisms and called for the assumption of power and status by men who represented the "productive forces" in social and economic life.

During the middle decades of the nineteenth century, many of those who identified with the forces of "progress" believed that a new synthesis of class, status, and power was emerging. These men were confident that economic growth and social progress were inexorably intertwined. For them, the spread of cities, the modernization of the economy, and the increasing level of education would provide the basis for a new economic, social, and

political elite. As the industrialist Friedrich Harkort put it in the
1840's: "The locomotive is the hearse which will carry absolutism and feudalism to the graveyard."[6]

The obituary proved premature. By the end of the nineteenth
century, Germany had locomotives aplenty, indeed the German
economy was the most advanced in Europe, but there had not
been congruent changes in a number of important social and political institutions. Pre-modern social groups continued to occupy
key positions in the political system and their values continued to
flourish. The result was that in a number of German institutions
there was a mixture of modern and pre-modern groups and values. We can now follow the development of this situation among
German elites, where—in Robert Michels' concise phrase—"we
find less a replacement of the old ruling groups by new groups
coming to power than an amalgam and fusion of the two."[7]

I

When Harkort spoke of the demise of "feudalism" he had in
mind the social and political power of the landed nobility. It
seemed to him, and to many of his contemporaries, that just as
aristocrats had been the chief beneficiaries of traditional social
institutions, so they would be the chief casualties when these
institutions gave way to an urban, industrial world. Indeed, an
observer in the 1840's could not overlook the important ways in
which the power of the aristocracy had declined: the expanding
institutions of the state had cut into the nobility's control over
local institutions, while the growth of commerce and industry had
threatened both the economic position of many estateowners and
their unchallenged monopoly of social status.[8] In retrospect we
can see that the decline of the aristocracy was neither as complete nor as irreversible as many hoped or feared in the middle of
the century. To be sure, many nobles did collapse in the face of
change, lost their ancestral homes and slipped into the shadowy
world of the déclassé. Others maintained their social standing by
accepting the dependent status of a landless bureaucrat or officer.
But the aristocracy as a privileged and powerful group in German
society did not disappear. Many nobles were able to acclimate
themselves to the new world and bend its forces to their will. For
these men, who could augment the residual privileges of their

caste with an understanding of new techniques of political and economic exploitation, the path to power was broad and the rewards of power were great. The history of the landed nobility east of the Elbe river, that group conventionally called the "Junkers," provided the most striking example of challenge and response in the German aristocratic community.[9]

Until the second half of the seventeenth century, the Junkers enjoyed that economic, social and political preeminence which belonged to the landed elites in the world of *Herrschaft*. They ruled their peasants with most of the powers of a sovereign, they staffed the diffuse organs of local administration and they controlled the *Stände*, corporate representative institutions which limited the financial autonomy of the ruling Hohenzollern. Beginning in the 1640's, the Junkers' position began to be challenged from two directions. First, the Hohenzollern rulers gradually developed administrative and military institutions which freed them from the fetters imposed by the *Stände* and created independent centers of political power. Second, in the course of the eighteenth century economic pressures on the estateowners drove many nobles off the land. Although until 1807 it was impossible for a commoner to own an estate legally, by the end of the eighteenth century the relentless logic of the market had seriously eroded the economic position and social power of many old families.[10]

During the opening decades of the nineteenth century pressures from both the state and the market increased. During the reform era (1806–1819), some of the most important legal foundations of noble privileges were removed by progressive bureaucrats eager to expand their own power and modernize Prussian society. At the same time, an increasingly fluid economic situation increased the dislocation of the aristocratic estateowners. In 1847, for example, commoners owned 1,100 estates in Silesia, while aristocrats owned 1,856.[11] Nevertheless, despite the erosion of their privileges, despite the growing social heterogeneity of the estateowning class, despite the dangers of political heterodoxy, the Junkers managed to survive as a self-conscious social group whose power and prestige in German society was in no way proportionate to its size, collective talents, or relative economic importance.

In the next two sections of this essay we will consider in some detail how the evolution of the state's bureaucratic and military institutions at first threatened, but eventually came to reinforce the Junkers' position in the state and society. For the moment it is sufficient to call attention to one general feature of the Junkers' relationship to the state that influenced their ability to accommodate themselves to the challenges they faced. As the state evolved in Prussia, it reduced the political autonomy of the Junkers on both the national and local levels, but it also provided them with new avenues to power and influence. In the course of the eighteenth century, many Junkers made their career in the bureaucracy and it became customary for most of them to spend at least a brief period in military service. These experiences gave them access to new forms of political power denied to those aristocratic groups that remained outside of the nexus of state institutions. Moreover, state service may have instilled in the Junkers a certain respect for efficiency, a kind of "rationality" which was often so conspicuously absent among aristocratic groups which lived in idle but diminishing grandeur or became ceremonial appendages to a princely court. In the long run, therefore, the growth of the Prussian state gave the Junkers opportunities and a taste for power that remained among their most prominent characteristics as a social group.

The same combinations of short-run danger and long-run opportunity obtained in the Junkers' relationship to the economic market. To understand this relationship it is necessary to keep in mind that the income the Junkers derived from their estates was not in the form of rents, but rather was the profit they earned as agricultural entrepreneurs.[12] This gave them a direct and powerful relationship to their peasant dependents, and it also involved them directly in the struggle to defend their economic self-interest. In the second half of the nineteenth century the Junkers became the chief spokesmen for agrarian interests in Germany; they were able to identify themselves and their values with the good of German agriculture as a whole. This process helped the Junkers to absorb the "new men" who bought estates and to make them part of a group with a strong sense of collective purpose and self-interest, a group whose tone and direction was set by the representatives of the Junker class. The result was a new social group, composed of old families and recent arrivals, of nobles and commoners, but a group whose political uniformity represented the persistence of old values in the face of growing social heterogeneity.[13]

The Junkers' survival, therefore, depended on their ability to deflect the impact of both economic and political challenges to their position. By becoming the spokesmen for German agriculture they were able to turn the economic conflicts of the late nineteenth century to their advantage. And by becoming part of the expanding state institutions they were able to attenuate, or at least to delay, the erosion of the substance of their political power. We can now follow this latter theme more closely by turning to the growth of administrative institutions in Prussia and their highly complex relationship to the landed elite.

II

As we have seen, the growth of a bureaucratic apparatus in Prussia can be traced to the mid-seventeenth century when a series of energetic Hohenzollerns, beginning with the so-called "Great Elector" Frederick William (1640–1688), began to build a powerful set of central administrative institutions. These institutions were meant to help the ruler extract resources (mainly human and financial support for the army) from his territory and to enable him to employ these resources without interference from the landed nobility. Princely ambitions for power and independence conditioned the character of the emerging bureaucracy: the ruler's desire for efficiency led him to consider an official's ability and performance as well as his lineage for recruitment and promotion; similarly, the ruler's desire for independence often led him to encourage the ambitions of able commoners, who tended to be more responsive to the royal will than the less dependent nobility.[14]

From the first, therefore, the bureaucracy was directed against the landed aristocracy's autonomy and traditional authority. Especially in the century between the reign of the Great Elector and that of Frederick II ("the Great," 1740–1786) clashes between the nobility and the central power were frequent and often bitter. However, the relationship was never one of unremitting hostility.

The enmity between monarch and noble was always qualified by the knowledge that they belonged to the same social world and that neither could destroy the other and survive. Moreover, aristocratic and bureaucratic institutions tended to overlap and coexist. Prominent noblemen often held high administrative posts, while successful commoners in the bureaucracy were frequently ennobled and absorbed into the aristocracy. The mixed character of the administrative elite is suggested by the term *Amtsaristokratie* which came to be used to refer to the leaders of the bureaucracy. This group was defined by both office (*Amt*) and by high social status, it embodied both bureaucratic and aristocratic values, and it was recruited and judged according to a blend of ascriptive and achievement standards.[15]

On the local level, the overlapping of bureaucratic and aristocratic institutions was even more apparent. The Hohenzollerns were always more interested in securing their own freedom of action at the head of the state than in interfering with the nobles' domination over their dependents. Even during the reign of the Great Elector, therefore, nobility and prince forged a fragile but significant compromise by which noble acquiescence in princely ambitions was exchanged for the central government's support for the persistence of the nobles' control over their peasantry.[16] The institutional expression of this arrangement became the office of *Landrat,* the chief administrative officer in rural Prussia, who was at once an agent of the state and a part of the local aristocratic establishment.[17] Until the end of the Prussian monarchy in 1918, the *Landrat* served as a boundary figure between the central government and the local interests of the nobility. His appointment was never simply a bureaucratic decision, as this account of the *Landrat*'s role in Silesia around 1900 makes clear:

> *The selection of a* Landrat *involved many considerations in addition to personal ability: political views, connections in his district, and family ties to influential people who could facilitate and enrich the fulfillment of his duties but also could limit his absolutely necessary freedom of action.*[18]

The final phrase is worth noting because it hints at the tension inherent in the *Landrat*'s role: appointed by the state, but tied to the local elite, he could face some difficult choices when the interests of these two forces came into conflict. This tension continued to emerge again and again through the life of the Prussian state.[19]

The role conflict built into the *Landrat*'s position was felt to some extent by other eighteenth-century bureaucrats whose function as instruments of the royal will did not always coincide with their interests and loyalties as members of the aristocracy. This problem was complicated during the second half of the eighteenth century when bureaucrats began to develop a sense of institutional self-esteem and self-interest that transcended their earlier self-image as agents of the king. During this period officials gradually came to regard themselves as "state servants" instead of "royal servants," a shift in terminology that reflected their conviction that they were the proper guardians of the public interest.[20] In the reigns of the weak kings who followed Frederick II the bureaucracy increased its autonomy from its royal master and began to function more and more as an independent center of political power.

Many of the same men who began to view the bureaucracy as the proper center of political power also became convinced that the administration should play an active role in the modernization of Prussian politics and society. These officials became the advocates of a "revolution from above" which was of great significance for the history of modern Germany.[21] From the outset, there was a latent ambivalence in the work of these bureaucratic reformers: on the one hand, they wanted to release "the inexhaustible power that slumbers unused and undeveloped in the nation;"[22] but on the other hand, their own position depended on the existence of an essentially authoritarian system of bureaucratic control. This ambivalence shaped the experience of modernization in Prussia, a process which combined the loosening of traditional inhibitions of economic growth and social mobility with the tightening of bureaucratic control over political power.

The connection between reform and bureaucratic power was apparent in the Prussian Legal Code, which was formulated under the influence of progressive officials during the last decades of the eighteenth century,[23] and it remained a prominent feature of the political, social, and economic changes introduced after 1806, when the defeat of Prussia by Napoleon gave reform-minded officials an opportunity to dominate the Prussian administration. Taken together, these reforms made some significant steps towards economic and social emancipation, but they also bolstered the power and independence of the bureaucratic apparatus.[24]

During the era of reform the conflict between the leading reformers in the bureaucracy and the majority of landed aristocrats once again reached crisis proportions. The Junkers objected both to the social and economic emancipation being pushed by the reformers and to the steps being taken to increase the bureaucracy's political power. It was with considerable relief, therefore, that the aristocracy viewed the waning of the reform impulse which followed the defeat of Napoleon in 1815. Some of the high-ranking reformers were forced from office, while the influence of men with ties to the landed nobility increased within the administration.[25] However, despite the name conventionally given to the era following 1815, these years did not see a "restoration" of pre-reform institutions. Bureaucratic power was not significantly weakened, nor were the social and economic reforms undone. There was, however, a new set of tensions built into the administration by a continuing conflict over reform. After 1815 the conflicts already apparent within the administration—between loyalty to the state and to the nobility, between obedience to the king and institutional self-interest—were overlaid by conflicts between those who wanted to continue the "revolution from above" and those who saw the bureaucracy as a dike against the further spread of economic change, social dislocation, and secular culture into Prussia.[26]

This conflict within the bureaucracy was reflected in the extremely ambiguous relationship between the state and society which was one of the central themes in the period 1815–1848. In some respects, the state played a clearly repressive role, censoring news, inhibiting political organization, and interfering in economic and social life. But in other ways the state was a source of progress and enlightenment: bureaucrats encouraged the growth of schools, steered government investment towards productive enterprises, built highways and railroads, and so on. This ambiguity helps to explain why the state was attacked from both the left and right before 1848, when Junkers like the young Bismarck viewed the state as too liberal and liberals like the Rhenish businessman David Hansemann viewed it as too reactionary. In a sense, both were right, because in the period following the great reforms both tendencies coexisted within the administrative establishment.[27]

The revolution of 1848 significantly changed both the relationship between the state and society and the alignment of forces within the bureaucracy itself. In the first place, the outbreak of revolution greatly strengthened the hands of those officials who had long maintained that to sponsor social and economic change was to undermine political stability. Second, the political movements and parliamentary institutions that began in 1848 provided a new set of competitors for the bureaucracy and thereby an impetus for greater political conformity within it. Finally, leading bureaucrats were deeply shaken by the degree to which men from their own institution had joined opposition movements during the revolution. Taken together these developments convinced officials that the relative tolerance of political diversity within the bureaucracy might have been possible when officials' political authority had been unchallenged, but that such tolerance was a luxury they could not afford in the turbulent political world born in 1848.[28]

Beginning in the 1850's, therefore, the pressures for political conformity within the bureaucracy increased significantly. These pressures did not bring about a sudden destruction of the progressive impulse within the administration, but this impulse was quickly blunted, and there was a clear shift of the initiative into the hands of the more conservative elements. Fewer and fewer officials now regarded the administration as a kind of "quasi-parliament" in which a variety of opinions could be expressed and synthesized, nor was there much talk of the need for "intellectual freedom in order to create what is needed" for the state.[29] Instead, the primary task of the official was now seen as the loyal and unquestioning defense of the status quo.

The struggle against independence and progressive views in the bureaucracy was intensified when Otto von Bismarck became

Minister President of Prussia in 1862. Bismarck took vigorous action against those officials who joined the liberal opposition during the constitutional conflict in the 1860's.[30] After national unification in 1871, he moved against those men who seemed to endanger his own personal authority as well as against those who did not fit into the emerging conservative coalition he was attempting to create.[31] Even some of his admirers regretted the changes in the character of the administration that resulted from Bismarck's ruthless demands for obedience:

> . . . the domination of this Jupiter has meant that independence increasingly disappears. Every day men assume the highest offices who are undoubtedly efficient, but from whom no one expects an independent opinion or action. Rather, these men belong to the most subserviently obedient cohorts of Prince Bismarck.[32]

By the time Bismarck was forced from office in 1890, therefore, the Prussian and the imperial bureaucracies had become obedient but largely directionless institutions. His successors could not match his mastery of the administration, nor could they provide it with energy and direction. By 1914, the bureaucracy of both Prussia and the Reich was governed by a persistent inertia, a lack of positive goals, a tendency to break down into conflicting departments each with its own particular interests and orientation.[33] These structural weaknesses of the administration inhibited the government's ability to respond to the needs of a rapidly-growing industrial society. At the lower levels of the administration, honesty, a relatively high degree of efficiency, and adequate technical skills helped to compensate for the failures in the upper ranks, but these virtues could at best postpone a confrontation with the major problems of German society.

It is important to emphasize that the weaknesses of the bureaucracy during the Imperial era came less from individual failings than from institutional training and recruitment policies that aimed at finding reliable defenders of the established order and were only secondarily interested in finding men who might grapple with the problems of a complex society. The training of politically-important bureaucrats, for example, was meant to ensure that only conservatively-oriented men could gain access to significant positions of power. The content of an official's education put emphasis on legal studies, which had a predominantly conservative cast in German universities. This was reinforced by the conservative ideology of the university community, as well as by the prevailing values in the student fraternities which played a central role in both the social and professional life of many bureaucrats.[34]

Even more explicitly than the form of training, modes of recruitment were designed to avoid both social and political heterodoxy. In the face of a steadily expanding state apparatus and an increasingly insistent need for technically competent personnel, the leaders of the bureaucracy after 1870 could not avoid recruiting from a wide range of social groups. Nevertheless, there was a concerted effort made to keep the most important positions in the hands of "reliable" individuals from establishment backgrounds. In view of the overall growth of the bureaucracy in the course of the nineteenth century, this effort at frustrating the bureaucratic "tendency towards leveling" was surprisingly successful.[35] The recruiting mechanism for leading positions screened out men with inferior social credentials or questionable political views since after candidates had passed the necessary examinations they could still be rejected by the responsible district governor (*Regierungspräsident*) if he felt that the candidates did not fit in. Otto Hintze, who was not one to dwell on the bureaucracy's shortcomings, pointed out that this system opened the way for personal as well as political prejudices. In fact, it formalized what Max Weber called a system of "unofficial patronage" by which family ties, personal influence, fraternity membership, and a reserve officer's commission influenced appointment and promotion.[36] The results of this system are made clear if we consider the social composition of the upper ranks of the administration, the majority of whom came from social groups traditionally tied to the political and social order. In 1910, for example, seventy-five percent of the leading officials in Prussia were the sons of army officers, landowners, or other officials. Equally apparent is the tendency to maintain the identification of ascriptive status and political power. The number of titled individuals was disproportionately high in the upper ranks of the administration, a dispro-

portion which suggests the degree to which a "von" before one's
name could help to level the climb up the ladder of success.
Indeed it is remarkable to consider that the percentage of nobles
among district and provincial governors declined less than ten
percent in the century before 1914 despite the transformation of
German society which occurred in that period.[37]

Although, as has been mentioned, the tensions between the
bureaucracy and the landed nobility were by no means totally
dissolved in the late nineteenth century, the cooperation between
these two elites was tightened by the common danger posed by
forces for social and political democratization. The careful nur-
turing of conservative ideology within the administration and the
continued association of rank and aristocratic title tended to buttress the nobility's position, as well as to block the way for political reform. "How would it be possible for us to have a liberal
government?" asked one official in 1910. "We are caught in an
iron net of conservative administration and local government
[Selbstverwaltung]."[38]

III

Like the bureaucracy, the Prussian army originated as part of the
Hohenzollerns' efforts to widen the circle of their own power
over Prussian society.[39] After the middle of the seventeenth century, the army played a key role in the process of state building,
absorbed a large part of the state's income, and, to a degree,
shaped the civil administration. Until about 1700, the army was
an instrument of the central power. In the early eighteenth century, however, two developments turned the army into a key institution for the Prussian social system. First, during the reign of
King Frederick William I (1713–1740) the officer corps began to
be recruited largely from the Prussian nobility since that monarch
was convinced that military service would inculcate obedience to
the state and sovereign. By the middle of the century a rather
large percentage of the landed nobility spent some time in the
officer corps, where their loyalty to the king as feudal overlord
was reshaped into the obedience owed by an officer to his com-
mander-in-chief. Second, the introduction of the so-called Canton System greatly increased the army's role in the life of the

Prussian peasantry. By this system, rural Prussia was divided into Cantons which were held responsible for the recruitment and maintenance of a certain number of troops. In order to avoid a shortage of agricultural labor, eligible peasants spent part of the year on active duty and then returned home to take part in planting and harvesting the crops. The local military authority controlled not only those in military service, but also aspects of social and economic life in the Canton. Since the military authorities were often estateowners or the relatives of estateowners, this system reinforced the obedience of the peasant for his lord with the obedience of the soldier for his military superior. In effect, therefore, during the first half of the eighteenth century both the relationship between the monarch and the aristocracy and the relationship between the aristocracy and peasantry tended to take on a military cast.[40]

During the reign of Frederick II the domination of the officer corps by the aristocracy was firmly established. In the 1780's at least ninety percent of the corps had titles; commoners were usually relegated to unfashionable branches which required some kind of technical training.[41] Unfortunately, hereditary privileges and family connections are usually not the best way to select military leaders. After Frederick's death the Prussian military establishment became ossified and a little senile, combining, in disastrous proportion, ineptness and overconfidence. These frailties were revealed with painful clarity on the battlefield of Jena in 1806, when Napoleon's army reduced the Prussian forces to a disorderly and retreating mob.

In the army, as in the bureaucracy, the defeat of 1806 opened the way for a progressive minority of officers to effect reforms. In the next few years, aristocratic privilege was formally removed, educational requirements were tightened, and competence was made an important criterion for promotion.[42] However, the power of the army's traditional leadership was not broken during the era of reform. In some ways the officer corps was modernized, but aristocratic status continued to play an important role in recruitment and advancement, while pre-modern aristocratic ideals continued to set the tone for military life.[43]

After the middle of the nineteenth century, new pressures for modernization were generated by the need to expand the military establishment into a mass army and by the increasingly technical character of modern warfare. These demands had to be met if the army was to be an effective instrument of foreign policy. However, the army had another, equally important role to play. It had to be not only the defender of the state against foreign enemies, it also had to defend the established order against domestic unrest.[44] This duality of its functions meant that the army, to an even greater degree than the bureaucracy, faced the need to synthesize operational efficiency and political reliability; it had to be able to put together modern skills and pre-modern values; it had to prevent social heterogeneity from generating political heterodoxy.

In their attempt to escape the dangers attendant upon institutional expansion and technical modernization, the leaders of the army used many of the same techniques employed by the bureaucracy for similar purposes. For example, when it became clear that the officer corps was simply too large to be recruited solely from the nobility, the military leadership made sure that the expansion of the corps involved only those commoners from "reliable" social and political backgrounds. The results of this policy are clear when we consider that in the 1860's, although more than half of the newly-commissioned officers were commoners, eighty percent were from families whose social position as landowners, officers, and officials tied them to the old social order.[45] Even after a candidate had passed the formal requirement for a commission, he had to be elected by the officers of the regiment to which he aspired. This mechanism—which was the military analogue to the power of the district governor in the administration—insured that socially and politically "unacceptable" individuals were excluded. After an individual joined the corps, everything was done to ensure that he conformed to the army's traditional values. Even the mildest form of political opposition was prohibited, and officers were encouraged to center their social life within the corps, lest they become infected with the dangerous ideas prevalent in the civilian world.[46]

As in the bureaucracy, the continued importance of aristocratic status in the officer corps was one result of the need to maintain political reliability in the face of rapid social change. The Prussian nobility continued to set the tone for the corps. They dominated the "best" regiments and their values informed the semi-feudal code of military honor. Moreover, although the aristocracy was no longer formally advantaged, their names appear with increasing frequency at each step up in the military hierarchy. The data on the social composition of the corps leaves no doubt that the possession of a "von" greatly facilitated professional success: thus in 1886 thirty-five percent of the corps were non-noble, in 1895 sixty-six percent and in 1913, seventy percent; however in 1866 eighty-six percent of those with the rank of colonel and above had titles, in 1900 sixty-one and in 1913 fifty-two percent.[47] Therefore, despite a growing emphasis on technology, despite more stringent educational requirements, and despite the increasingly mixed social composition of the military elite, aristocratic status continued to be associated with high rank and traditional social values continued to be cherished in the corps.

The social significance of the army as a bastion of aristocratic values and power was increased by the fact that the army's influence extended beyond those who served on active duty. The key institution in this was the reserve officer corps. In the reserves, as in the regular army, regimental officers controlled the selection of their colleagues. Moreover, reserve officers were subject to many of the same pressures for social and political conformity that existed in the army as a whole. The impact of these pressures after 1871 was considerable because membership in the reserves became a highly-valued sign of social status and, in some professions, almost a prerequisite for a successful career. As one father advised his son in the 1890's: "To be a successful German these days, one must be a successful soldier."[48] During the Imperial era, therefore, the officer corps helped to institutionalize the reconciliation of the *Bürgertum*[49] and the established order, as in the eighteenth century it had furthered the reconciliation of the landed nobility and monarchical authority.[50]

IV

In each of the elites which we have discussed, the process of modernization produced a marked social heterogeneity. This was true of the Junkers, whose social diversification was caused by

the subjection of estateowning to the demands of the economic
market. In the army, and to a lesser degree in the bureaucracy,
the need to expand in size and technical competence opened the
way for a variety of social groups. However, as we have noted,
all three of these elites were at least partially successful in maintaining traditional social and political values in the face of this
increasing social diversification. The prestige of the nobility and
the economic interests common to all estateowners enabled the
Junkers to absorb the new arrivals. Indeed, after 1871 many of
these new men played an active role in the political movements
which developed to defend the privileges and powers of the landed elite. In the army and bureaucracy, carefully-established
modes of recruitment and well-nourished corporate ideals accomplished analogous results. We must now attempt to put this process of social fusion into its proper historical setting by examining
the shift in values which occurred among the propertied and educated strata of German society during the last third of the nineteenth century.

Before considering the shift in the attitudes of the German
Bürgertum we must make the obvious but often forgotten point
that the values of social groups do not change like soldiers on
parade, suddenly and with uniformity. Throughout the Imperial
period, many German burghers did not participate in the process
which we will describe, but remained faithful to the ideals of
freedom and equality which had characterized the best of the
liberal movement. Others participated, but in subtle and elusive
ways, which are difficult to measure and document. Still others
wavered according to specific issues and changing interests. The
following pages, therefore, seek only to illuminate the most
prominent features of a diverse social landscape, a landscape still
insufficiently explored by sustained historical research.

The clearest expression of a shift in attitudes among the
Bürgertum was their reconciliation with the Prussian monarchy
after the military victories of 1866 and 1871. This reconciliation
involved an enthusiastic acceptance of the Imperial political system and a retreat from the political ambitions articulated by the
liberal movement during the middle third of the century. The
changing political behavior of the *Bürgertum* was part of a broad-

er change in values which included a basic shift in the relationship between propertied and educated commoners and the aristocracy. Among many burghers, acceptance of the Imperial political system was accompanied by a desire to share in the traditional prestige of the landed nobility. Such ambitions were not new in German society, but after the formation of the Reich they became notably more widespread and intense. Rhenish manufacturers, Berlin bankers, even proud Hamburg patricians rushed to buy estates, less as an investment than as an attempt to acquire the environment within which the habits of the aristocracy might gracefully be emulated.[51] Some of these men were able to marry into noble families, usually those families in need of financial resuscitation. The more perceptive members of the government viewed this process with some satisfaction and furthered it by catering to the *Bürgertum*'s appetites for titles and honors. Bismarck, for example, came to regard ennoblement not as a reward for service, but as a political means of widening the base of the conservative coalition in German society.[52]

The ambition to emulate and even to be absorbed into the world of the aristocracy could only be sustained by the upper stratum of the *Bürgertum,* which tended to become—in Robert Michels' words—"merely the threshold to the nobility."[53] However, we can trace the effects of this attitudinal shift in circles beyond the relatively small group which could acquire titles and estates. Thus, many who could not presume to a patent of nobility could still hope for one of the many decorations granted by the monarch, which carried some patina of traditional prestige. Also, membership in a fashionable regiment, a prestigious student fraternity, or the reserve officer corps broadened the range of opportunity for men to bask in the reflected glory of the aristocratic establishment.[54] For those denied the chance to wear the king's coat as an officer or to acquire a facial scar in a dueling fraternity, there remained the vicarious satisfaction of following the affairs of the court and aristocracy in literature and periodicals. Our knowledge of this diffusion of values among the lower strata of the *Bürgertum* is very slim, although E. K. Bramstedt's work on the popular magazine *Die Gartenlaube* is a suggestive beginning.[55]

The most obvious cause for the redirection of the *Bürgertum*'s sociopolitical attitudes was the effect of the unification of Germany under Prussian leadership in 1871. The victories of Bismarck's diplomacy and Moltke's army earned the admiration of many who months before had been vowing undying enmity to the reactionary regime of Junkers. The events of dramatic years of the *Reichsgründung* crystallized a sense of insecurity and uneasiness which had been part of the German *Bürgertum*'s self-image for decades, and which were deepened by the failure of the revolution of 1848 and the inconclusive course of the Prussian constitutional conflict. The achievements of the 1860's possessed such psychological power over the *Bürgertum* because these triumphs contrasted so sharply with German liberalism's lame efforts at political action. For many, this contrast induced a permanent rejection of political opposition and an unwavering allegiance to Bismarckian politics. For some, the *Reichsgründung* called into question not only the political goals of liberalism, but the social values upon which these goals had rested. Herman Baumgarten, for example, drew from the events of 1866 the lesson that "it is a ruinous error . . . to believe that any competent scholar, lawyer, merchant, or official, who is interested in public affairs and who reads the newspapers carefully, has the ability to become actively involved in politics. . . ."[56]

If the triumphs of the *Reichsgründung* played on the *Bürgertum*'s sense of inferiority, the formation of the German Social Democratic Party and the example of the Paris Commune deepened their fear of social unrest.[57] Once again, the events of the period 1866–1871 tended to crystallize long-term developments: the deep-seated social and cultural cleavages in German society and the *Bürgertum*'s longstanding anxiety about the threats to social order from the lower classes. By the 1870's, many burghers saw royal power and even aristocratic influence as necessary allies against the dangers of social and political democracy. For these men, the danger of radical change converted the nobility from a rival into an ally in the defense of property and order, agrarian Germany from a bastion of backwardness into a necessary source of stability, the Prussian army from an instrument of tyranny into the most reliable guarantee of domestic tranquility.[58]

The third element which helped to forge new ties between sectors of the *Bürgertum* and the conservative forces in the Empire was produced by the growing sense among these groups that they shared certain common economic interests. One aspect of this was the increasing interrelationship of the state and some industrial enterprises—especially in the field of armaments—that made it economically essential for industrialists to have close and amicable ties to the bureaucratic and military establishments. Moreover, beginning with the period of economic dislocation following the depression of 1873, agricultural and industrial interests found that they shared a common need for state help in the form of tariff protection. These common interests, reinforced as they were by closer social ties and by a sense of common threat from the left, helped to provide the basis for a discontinuous, tension-filled, but enormously significant alliance between heavy industry and landed wealth.[59]

These three elements—a common commitment to the new Reich, a sense of common peril, and an awareness of mutual economic interests—helped to close the political and social gap between the old aristocracy and the *Bürgertum* and to forge a conservative coalition between the representatives of economic "progress" and those forces of "absolutism and feudalism" that Friedrich Harkort had consigned to an early extinction. The defenders of the status quo recognized that this coalition of forces provided the best defense for the Imperial social and economic system. It was from this coalition that the most reliable parliamentary support for the government was to be found and it was from the social groups that composed this coalition that the leaders of the bureaucracy and army were recruited.[60]

This is not the time to give a detailed picture of how this sociopolitical alignment shaped German history between the *Reichsgründung* and the war. It is enough for our purposes to recall that in 1878–1879 Bismarck presided over its first great parliamentary manifestation in a series of moves that included the adoption of a protective tariff policy and the passage of vigorous laws against Social Democracy. During the 1880's Bismarck added an element which was to become increasingly important in the persistence of the conservative coalition: the support for an expansionist foreign policy. Under Bismarck's successors after

1890, economic protection, anti-socialism, and imperialism continued to serve as the political focus for the cooperation of the defenders of the Reich.[61] Throughout the Imperial period, in the parliaments and in other key institutions, these factors mobilized some of Germany's most vigorous and powerful social groups against meaningful reform and in the process facilitated the persistence of aristocratic ideals and influence until well into the twentieth century.

V

In conclusion, let us return briefly to the Weberian distinction between class, status, and power with which we began. On the preceding pages we have traced how the fusion of these hierarchies in the landed aristocracy was shattered by the growth of a bureaucratic state and the development of a modern economy. And yet, as we have seen, a new progressive synthesis did not emerge. The modernization of Prussia did not bring to an end the forces of "feudalism and absolutism," as men like Harkort hoped and expected. Instead, Germany before 1914 was hallmarked by a pervasive institutional incongruence: the German economy was the most dynamic and innovative in Europe, but pre-modern elites and values continued to be important in German political and social life. The great estates east of the Elbe, the bureaucracy, and the army continued to provide institutional support for those who defended the need for a hierarchical social system and the virtues of an authoritarian polity.

The persistence of these values is even more striking when we consider that they were defended not merely by remnants of the old aristocracy, but by a fusion of the traditional nobility and significant sectors of the propertied and educated *Bürgertum*. Indeed, this fusion of old and new elites into a conservative coalition was the key element in the persistence of pre-modern values in the political and social systems. This coalition was able to play such a formidable role in the defense of the status quo only because the Junker landowners, bureaucrats, and officers were joined by a significant number of bankers, industrialists, and professors. Knitted together by common fears and common interests, these forces, and the institutions they dominated, formed an almost irresistible barrier to substantial social and political reform.

It would, of course, be a mistake to overestimate the cohesion of this conservative coalition and to overlook the conflicts that continued to erupt both within and between its components. In the fast-changing social and economic world of the late nineteenth and early twentieth centuries, industrialist and landowner, civilian and officer, aristocrat and burgher frequently found their interests in conflict. But these conflicts were always attenuated by the common interests and dangers which we have described. The same complex of social, economic, and political forces which created the sources of conflict within the conservative coalition also produced the common perils that kept the alliance together. The threat of social and political democratization to the entire system of privilege, property, and power always overshadowed the intramural struggles within the ranks of the privileged, the propertied, and the powerful.

On the eve of the war in 1914, there were signs that this blend of conflict and cohesion was becoming unstable. Labor unrest, the growing strength of Social Democracy, and a widespread sense of political frustration combined to provide an impetus for considering new solutions to Germany's discontents. On the one hand, there were those who argued for a broad reformist coalition including progressive elements in the *Bürgertum* as well as moderate Social Democrats. On the other hand, there were those who saw no way out of the Reich's political problems but an authoritarian regime to be produced by a right-wing coup.[62] The war gave both of these groups opportunities undreamt of before 1914. By 1917 they had begun to coalesce into the moderate and rightwing movements whose long struggle for power conditioned the course and sealed the fate of Germany's democratic experiment after 1918.[63]

However, if we look back from 1914 rather than ahead into the turmoil unleashed by the war, the conservative coalition emerges as impressively adept in its struggle to contain pressures for social and political change. But we should not forget that the cost of their success was high: the alienation of lower income and status groups from the Imperial system; the persistence of anachronistic groups and values in key positions of power; the loss of a creative impulse at the heart of the political apparatus; and the recurrent need to use foreign political antagonisms for domestic political purposes. The prosperous and powerful Reich of 1914 was able to defer payment of these costs, but in the decades following a bill of great magnitude would come due.

NOTES

[1] I use the term *elite* here in the ordinary-language meaning of a group at the top of either the social, economic, or political hierarchies. For further information and analysis of the concept, the following books and articles can be consulted: G. D. H. Cole, *Studies in Class Structure* (London, 1955); R. Aron, "Social Structure and the Ruling Class," *British Journal of Sociology*, I (1950), 1–16 and 126–43; S. Langer, *Beyond the Ruling Class* (New York, 1963); T. Bottomore, *Elites and Society* (New York, 1965); U. Jaeggi, *Die gesellschaftliche Elite* (Bern, 1960); and H. Dreitzel, *Elitebegriff und Sozialstruktur* (Stuttgart, 1962). R. Bendix and S. M. Lipset have collected some important essays on elites in *Class, Status, and Power* (2nd ed., New York, 1966).

[2] Wolfgang Zapf has attempted to analyze the whole elite structure of twentieth-century Germany in his *Wandlungen der deutschen Elite, 1919–1961* (Munich, 1965). There are some articles on a variety of elites in *Führungsschicht und Eliteproblem, Jahrbuch der Ranke Gesellschaft*, III (1957). A guide to statistical material on elites may be found in my article "Quantification in the Study of German Social and Political History," in *Dimensions of the Past*, ed. by Val Lorwin and Jacob Price (New Haven, 1972).

[3] There is a convenient summary of Weber's views in Part II of *From Max Weber: Essays in Sociology*, ed. by H. Gerth and C. W. Mills (New York, 1958).

[4] Brunner's concept of *Herrschaft* is given in the conclusion of his *Adeliges Landleben und europäischer Geist* (Salzburg, 1949), 313–39, and in his essays collected under the title *Neue Wege zur Sozialgeschichte* (2nd ed., Göttingen, 1968). An astute critique of Brunner's work can be found in David M. Nicholas, "New Paths of Social History and Old Paths of Historical Romanticism. An Essay Review on the Work and Thought of Otto Brunner," *Journal of Social History*, III (1970), 277–94.

[5] For an introduction to this problem see J. Schultze, *Die Auseinandersetzung zwischen Adel und Bürgertum in den deutschen Zeitschriften der letzten drei Jahrzehnte des 18. Jahrhunderts* (Berlin, 1925) and R. Pascal, *The German Sturm und Drang* (Manchester, 1955). The impact of social conflict between aristocracy and new social groups on progressive theologians can be seen in the useful monograph by Alexandra Schlingensiepen-Pogge, *Das Sozialethos der lutherischen Aufklärungstheologie am Vorabend der Industriellen Revolution* (Göttingen, 1967).

[6] Quoted by F. Zunkel, *Der Rheinisch-westfälische Unternehmer 1834–1879* (Cologne and Opladen, 1962), 89–90. For some interesting remarks on the cultural impact of the railroad, see M. Riedel, "Vom Biedermeier zum Maschinenzeitalter. Zur Kulturgeschichte der ersten Eisenbahnen in Deutschland," *Archiv für Kulturgeschichte*, XLIII (1961), 100–23.

[7] *Umschichtungen in den herrschenden Klassen nach dem Kriege* (Stuttgart, 1934), 39. For some stimulating ideas on the origins and implications of Ger-

many's peculiar mixture of modern and pre-modern forms see T. Veblen, *Imperial Germany and the Industrial Revolution* (New York, 1954); T. Parsons, "Democracy and Social Structure in Pre-Nazi Germany," an essay first written in 1942 and reprinted in *Essays in Sociological Theory* (Glencoe, Ill., 1954); G. Lukács, "Einige Eigentümlichkeiten der geschichtlichen Entwicklung Deutschlands," in *Die Zerstörung der Vernunft* (Neuwied, 1962), 37–83; and R. Dahrendorf, *Society and Democracy in Germany* (New York, 1967).

[8] For a contemporary statement of the dangers facing the aristocracy, see the quotation from von der Marwitz in F. von Oertzen, *Junker. Preussischer Adel im Jahrhundert des Liberalismus* (Berlin, 1939), 68. Ferdinand Toennies has a brief but incisive introduction to the problem of the nobility in "Deutscher Adel im 19. Jahrhundert," *Neue Rundschau*, XXIII (1912), 1041–63.

[9] For an introduction to the Junkers in the eighteenth century see the essay on Prussia by A. Goodwin in the volume he edited on *The European Nobility in the Eighteenth Century* (London, 1953). A rather sympathetic picture of this social group can be found in W. Görlitz, *Die Junker* (Glücksburg/Ostsee, 1956). My account has been most influenced by the writings of Robert Michels, Otto Hintze, and especially, Hans Rosenberg: R. Michels, "Zum Problem der Zeitlichen Widerstandsfähigkeit des Adels," *Probleme der Sozialgeschichte* (Leipzig, 1914); Hintze, "Die Hohenzollern und der Adel," *Regierung und Verwaltung, Gesammelte Abhandlungen* vol. 3 (Göttingen, 1967) and *Die Hohenzollern und ihr Werk* (Berlin, 1916); Rosenberg, "The Rise of the Junkers in Brandenburg-Prussia, 1410–1653," *American Historical Review*, XLIX (1943–44), 1–22 and 228–42 and "Die Pseudodemokratisierung der Rittergutsbesitzerklasse," in *Moderne Deutsche Sozialgeschichte*, ed. by Hans-Ulrich Wehler (Cologne, 1966).

[10] On this point see J. Ziekursch, *Hundert Jahre schlesischer Agrargeschichte* (Berlin, 1927), and F. Martiny, *Die Adelsfrage in Preussen vor 1806 als politisches und soziales Problem* (Stuttgart and Berlin, 1938). For the economic situation of the Junkers in the early nineteenth century, see E. Jordan, *Die Entstehung der Konservativen Partei und die preussischen Agrarverhältnisse von 1848* (Munich and Leipzig, 1914).

[11] Reinhart Koselleck, *Preussen zwischen Reform und Revolution* (Stuttgart, 1967), 347. Johannes Ziekursch studied 355 Silesian estates and found that in the 1850's only 59 of them had been in the same family for more than 40 years. Ziekursch, *Agrargeschichte*, 385.

[12] The classic statement on this issue is in the work of Georg Friedrich Knapp. See, for example, his *Grundherrschaft und Rittergut* (Leipzig, 1897). See also Max Weber's famous article on "Capitalism and Rural Society in Germany," reprinted in *From Max Weber*, 363–85. For some useful data on the concentration of land in Prussia see Weber's "Agrarstatische und sozialpolitische Betrachtungen zur Fideikommissfrage in Preussen," *Gesammelte Aufsätze zur Soziologie und Sozialpolitik* (Tübingen, 1924).

[13] This point is made forcefully in Rosenberg's article on "Die Pseudodemokratisierung"; see also the excellent monograph by Hans-Jürgen Puhle, *Agrarische Interessenpolitik und preussischer Konservatismus im wilhelminischen Reich* (Hanover, 1967). Ursula Lindig's dissertation on "Der Einfluss des Bundes der

Landwirte auf die Politik des wilhelminischen Zeitalters, 1893–1914'' (Hamburg, 1954) is greatly inferior to Puhle, but has some useful data. The best account in English is S. Tirrell, *German Agrarian Politics after Bismarck's Fall* (New York, 1951).

[14] The best introduction to the process of bureaucratic state-building in Prussia is Hans Rosenberg, *Bureaucracy, Aristocracy, Autocracy: The Prussian Experience, 1660–1815* (Cambridge, Mass., 1958). Those who know Rosenberg's profound contribution to Prussian history will recognize the extent of my debt to his work in this section and indeed throughout this essay. The classic formulation of a definition of bureaucratic authority can be found in Max Weber, *The Theory of Social and Economic Organization* (Glencoe, Ill., 1947), 329ff. Hanns Hubert Hofmann has edited a most useful collection of essays on the emergence of the state, *Die Entstehung des modernen souveränen Staates* (Cologne and Berlin, 1967).

[15] Rosenberg, *Bureaucracy*, 70ff., 107, and 139ff.

[16] Hintze, "Die Hohenzollern und der Adel," 39.

[17] For an account of the specific development of the office in one region see Hintze, "Der Ursprung des preussischen Landratsamts in der Mark Brandenburg," in *Gesammelte Abhandlungen*, vol. 3, 164–203.

[18] Georg Michaelis, *Für Staat und Volk: Eine Lebensgeschichte* (Berlin, 1922), 187.

[19] For a dramatic example of this conflict in the 1890's, see H. Horn, *Der Kampf um den Bau des Mittellandkanals* (Cologne and Opladen, 1964).

[20] O. Hintze, "Das preussische Staatsministerium im 19. Jahrhundert," in *Gesammelte Abhandlungen*, vol. 3, 534.

[21] On the "revolution from above" see Koselleck, *Preussen, passim*, and also L. Krieger, *The German Idea of Freedom* (Boston, 1957), especially 139ff.

[22] The phrase is from the military reformer Gneisenau, as quote by Friedrich Meinecke, *Das Zeitalter der deutschen Erhebung* (Göttingen, 1957), 70.

[23] The best account of the Legal Code is in Koselleck, *Preussen zwischen Reform und Revolution*. See also Hintze's essay "Preussische Reformbestrebungen vor 1806," in *Gesammelte Abhandlungen*, vol. 3, 504–29; Rosenberg, *Bureaucracy*, 190f.; and two recent articles by Günter Birtsch, "Zum konstitutionellen Charakter des preussischen Allgemeinen Landrechts von 1794," *Politische Ideologien und Nationalstaatliche Ordnung (Festschrift für Theodor Schieder)* (Munich and Vienna, 1968) and "Gesetzgebung und Repräsentation im späten Absolutismus," *Historische Zeitschrift*, CCVIII (1969), 265–94.

[24] There is an enormous literature on the Prussian reforms, which included fundamental changes in the legal position of serfs, structural changes in the educational system, shifts in the legal restrictions on trade and commerce, as well as administrative and military reforms. The best introduction to what the reformers did is in E. R. Huber, *Deutsche Verfassungsgeschichte*, vol. 1 (Stuttgart, 1957). Huber is much less help in explaining the motives of the reformers and the implications of their reforms. On these problems see Koselleck, *Preussen*; Rosenberg, *Bureaucracy*, 202ff.; E. Kehr, "Zur Genesis der preussischen Bürokratie und des Rechtsstaats," *Der Primat der Innenpolitik*, ed. by Hans-Ulrich Wehler

(Berlin, 1965), 31–52; and H. Heffter, *Die Deutsche Selbstverwaltung im 19. Jahrhundert* (Stuttgart, 1950).

[25] See the data on the social composition of the bureaucracy in Koselleck, *Preussen,* 434–35, n. 155.

[26] A good example of this conflict can be seen in Thomas Nipperdey's interesting account of educational policy in early-nineteenth-century Prussia, "Volksschule und Revolution im Vormärz," *Politische Ideologien und Nationalstaatliche Ordnung (Festschrift für Theodor Schieder)* (Munich and Vienna, 1968), 117–42. There are some excellent essays on this and related problems in *Staat und Gesellschaft im deutschen Vormärz,* ed. by W. Conze (Stuttgart, 1962).

[27] For a characteristic critique of the bureaucracy see the memorandum written in 1840 by Hansemann and reprinted in *Rheinische Briefe und Akten,* ed. by J. Hansen, vol. 1 (New edition, Osnabrück, 1967), 197ff. The ambivalent character of the state, especially in its relationship to economic development, is reflected in the debate over whether the state promoted or retarded economic growth. For the former view see W. O. Henderson, *The State and the Industrial Revolution in Prussia* (Liverpool, 1958), and for the latter, R. Tilly, *Financial Institutions and Industrialization in the Rhineland, 1815–1870* (Madison, 1966). It seems to me that to some extent both Henderson and Tilly are correct, since government policy did both impede and encourage economic development.

[28] On the Prussian bureaucracy at mid-century see the monograph by John Gillis, *Bureaucracy in Crisis* (Stanford, 1971). For some remarks on the reasons for discontent within the bureaucratic ranks, see L. O'Boyle, "The Problem of an Excess of Educated Men in Western Europe, 1800–1850," *Journal of Modern History,* XLII (1970), 471–95.

[29] The phrase is Leopold von Ranke's and is quoted in H. Holborn, "Der deutsche Idealismus in sozialgeschichtlicher Beleuchtung," *Moderne Deutsche Sozialgeschichte,* ed. by Hans-Ulrich Wehler (Cologne, 1966), 92.

[30] See E. Anderson, *The Social and Political Conflict in Prussia, 1858–1864* (Lincoln, Neb., 1954) and A. Hess, *Das Parlament das Bismarck widerstrebte* (Cologne and Opladen, 1964).

[31] The classic account of the conservative shift in Bismarckian Germany and its relationship to the bureaucracy is E. Kehr, "Das soziale System der Reaktion in Preussen unter dem Ministerium Puttkamer," *Der Primat der Innenpolitik,* ed. by Hans-Ulrich Wehler (Berlin, 1965), 64–86. For an account of Kehr and his contribution to German historiography, see Wehler's introduction to this volume and James J. Sheehan, "The Primacy of Domestic Politics: Eckart Kehr's Essays on Modern German History," *Central European History,* I (1968), 166–174.

[32] Karl Oldenburg, *Aus Bismarcks Bundesrat. Aufzeichnungen des Mecklenburg-Schwerinschen Bundesrats-Bevollmächtigten Karl Oldenburg aus den Jahren 1878–1885* (Berlin, 1929), 10.

[33] For some remarks on this tendency in bureaucracies in general see G. Almond and C. B. Powell, *Comparative Politics: A Developmental Approach* (Boston, 1966), 156. In the German case the situation was aggravated by the problems arising from the unclear division of powers between the Prussian and the Imperial administrations. On this problem see R. Morsey, *Die oberste Reichsverwaltung*

unter Bismarck 1867–1890 (Münster, 1957), and E. Klein, "Funktion und Bedeutung des Preussischen Staatsministerium," *Jahrbuch für die Geschichte Mittel- und Ostdeutschlands* IX/X (1961), 195–261.

[34] For the importance of fraternity membership in a bureaucrat's career, see Ernst von Ernsthausen, *Erinnerungen eines preussischen Beamten* (Berlin and Leipzig, 1894), 32ff. and 54ff. and H. Holborn, ed., *Aufzeichnungen und Erinnerungen aus dem Leben des Botschafters Joseph Maria von Radowitz* (reprinted edition, Osnabrück, 1967), I, 24.

[35] Max Weber argued that bureaucratic institutions produced a "tendency towards leveling" because they were forced to seek competent individuals from all sectors of society. See *Theory of Social and Economic Organization*, 340. For some data on the overall growth of the bureaucracy, see John Cullity, "The Growth of Governmental Employment in Germany, 1882–1950," *Zeitschrift für die gesamte Staatswissenschaft*, CXXIII (1967), 201–17.

[36] See O. Hintze, *Der Beamtenstand* (*Vorträge der Gehe-Stiftung*, vol. 3) (Dresden, 1911), 48, and M. Weber, "Parlament und Regierung im neugeordneten Deutschland," *Gesammelte Politische Schriften* (Tübingen, 1958), 355. L. Schücking claimed that in 1903–1905 almost 750 candidates for a bureaucratic post in Prussia were refused and that the majority of them were rejected because their backgrounds did not give sufficient guarantee of conservative views: *Die Reaktion in der inneren Verwaltung Preussens* (Berlin, 1908), 44.

[37] On the social composition of the Prussian bureaucracy see the figures released by the Minister of the Interior in 1910 and reprinted in W. Koch, *Volk und Staatsführung vor dem ersten Weltkriege* (Stuttgart, 1935), 78. The problem has been analyzed in more general terms in the following works: F. von Schulte, "Adel im deutschen Offizier- und Beamtenstand. Eine soziale Betrachtung," *Deutsche Revue*, XXI (1896), 181–92; N. von Preradovich, *Die Führungsschichten in Österreich und Preussen (1804–1918)* (Wiesbaden, 1955); R. Morsey, *Die oberste Reichsverwaltung*; J. C. G. Röhl, "Higher Civil Servants in Germany, 1890–1900," *Journal of Contemporary History*, II (1967), 101–21 (republished in this volume); and L. Muncy, *The Junker in the Prussian Administration under William II, 1888–1914* (Providence, R.I., 1944).

[38] As quoted in J. Bertram, *Die Wahlen zum deutschen Reichstag vom Jahre 1912* (Düsseldorf, 1964), 131.

[39] As on so many problems of Prussian institutional history, the best place to begin a study of the army and Prussian society is the work of Otto Hintze. See, for example, Hintze's essay "Staatsverfassung und Heeresverfassung," *Staat und Verfassung, Gesammelte Abhandlungen*, vol. 1 (2nd ed., Göttingen, 1962), 52–83. There is a great deal of information in Curt Jany, *Geschichte der königlich-preussischen Armee*, 4 vols. (Berlin, 1928–33). Also useful is Gordon Craig, *The Politics of the Prussian Army, 1640–1945* (New York and Oxford, 1956), and the first volume of Gerhard Ritter's *Staatskunst und Kriegshandwerk* (Munich, 1954), which has recently appeared in an English translation.

[40] These developments are skillfully analyzed in O. Büsch, *Militärsystem und Sozialleben im alten Preussen 1713–1807* (Berlin, 1962).

[41] Karl Demeter, *The German Officer-Corps in Society and State, 1650–1945*

(New York and Washington, 1965), 3ff. This is an abridged translation of *Das deutsche Offizierkorps in Gesellschaft und Staat 1650–1945* (2nd ed., Frankfurt, 1962).

[42] On the military reforms see Ritter, *Staatskunst*; Craig, *Politics of the Prussian Army*; W. O. Shanahan, *Prussian Military Reforms, 1786–1813* (New York, 1954); and P. Paret, *Yorck and the Era of Prussian Reform, 1807–1815* (Princeton, N.J., 1966).

[43] See the data in Koselleck, *Preussen*, 434–35, n. 155.

[44] For an intelligent treatment of the general problem of armies' foreign and domestic functions, see A. Vagts, *A History of Militarism* (rev. ed., n.p., 1959).

[45] Demeter, *The German Officer-Corps*, 20ff. See also the following for the army in late-nineteenth-century Germany: E. Obermann, *Soldaten, Bürger, Militaristen* (Stuttgart, 1958); G. Ritter, *Staatskunst und Kriegshandwerk*, vol. 2 (Munich, 1960); F. Endres, "Soziologische Struktur und ihre entsprechende Ideologien des deutschen Offizierkorps vor dem Weltkriege," *Archiv für Sozialwissenschaft und Sozialpolitik*, LVIII (1927), 282–319; and the essays on the army by Manfred Messerschmidt and Wilhelm Deist in *Das kaiserliche Deutschland: Politik und Gesellschaft 1870–1918* (Düsseldorf, 1970).

[46] M. Kitchen, *The German Officer Corps, 1890–1914* (Oxford, 1968), 115ff.

[47] Demeter, *German Officer-Corps*, 22ff. and Schulte, "Adel im deutschen Offizier- und Beamtenstand." On the value of a title see the remark by Leopold von Ranke cited in Vagts, *Militarism*, 195, and B. von Hutten-Czapski, *Sechzig Jahre Politik und Gesellschaft* (Berlin, 1936), I, 146.

[48] *Bürgermeister Mönckeberg. Eine Auswahl seiner Briefe und Aufzeichnungen*, ed. by Carl Mönckeberg (Stuttgart, 1918), 25 and 97–99.

[49] I have decided to use the German term *Bürgertum* here because to substitute *Bourgeois* or *middle class* is to imply a set of social similarities that do not exist. *Bürgertum* has a rather more traditional and somewhat more exclusive connotation than either the French or the British term. I will use it to mean nonaristocratic groups with a comfortable income and a secure place in an economic, cultural, or governmental institution.

[50] See E. Kehr, "Zur Genesis des königlich-preussischen Reserveoffiziers," in *Primat der Innenpolitik*, 53–63. The works cited in note 45 are also useful on the social significance of the army.

[51] F. Zunkel, *Der Rheinisch-westfälische Unternehmer*, 128ff. and P. E. Schramm, *Hamburg, Deutschland, und die Welt* (Munich, 1943), 615ff.

[52] On Bismarck's views of ennoblement see R. Morsey, *Die oberste Reichsverwaltung*, 247. Lamar Cecil has done a statistical study of ennoblement that emphasizes the continued importance of traditional considerations such as service at court, and so on. L. Cecil, "The Creation of Nobles in Prussia, 1871–1918," *American Historical Review*, LXXV (1970), 757–95.

[53] Michels, "Zum Problem der zeitlichen Widerstandsfähigkeit des Adels," *Probleme der Sozialphilosophie* (Leipzig, 1914), 151. See also Werner Sombart, *Die deutsche Volkswirtschaft im neunzehnten Jahrhundert* (2nd ed., Berlin, 1909), 508.

[54] Note the novelist Theodor Fontane's remark on the occasion of his receiving a Hohenzollern order in 1889: "If I were a man with a social position . . . this distinction would have practically no meaning for me. But in view of the fact that in Germany, and particularly in Prussia, you count for something only if you are 'government-graded' such a medal has some real practical value: people look at you with great respect and treat you decently." Quoted by J. Remak in *The Gentle Critic: Theodor Fontane and German Politics, 1848–1898* (Syracuse, 1964), 67. It was generally recognized that a title was helpful in most careers as well as in elevating one's social position. See, for example, Robert von Mohl, *Lebenserinnerungen 1799–1875* (Stuttgart and Leipzig, 1902), I, 64.

[55] E. K. Bramsted, *Aristocracy and the Middle Classes in Germany: Social Types in German Literature 1830–1900* (rev. ed., Chicago and London, 1964), 203ff.

[56] H. Baumgarten, "Der deutsche Liberalismus: Eine Selbstkritik," *Preussische Jahrbücher*, XVIII (1866), 472. Heinrich von Treitschke wrote about the same time that "if you watch our middle class at close range . . . you can't help seeing that as a rule only aristocrats (of birth or mind) make good statesmen." Quoted in A. Dorpalen, *Heinrich von Treitschke* (New Haven, 1957), p. 114. For a useful analysis of the impact of the *Reichsgründung* on German politics see Karl Georg Faber, "Realpolitik als Ideologie: Die Bedeutung des Jahres 1866 für das politische Denken in Deutschland," *Historische Zeitschrift*, CCIII (1966), 1–45.

[57] For the impact of the Commune, see J. J. Sheehan, *The Career of Lujo Brentano: A Study of Liberalism and Social Reform in Imperial Germany* (Chicago and London, 1966), 46ff. and the literature cited there.

[58] For a provocative interpretation of the relationship between German Socialism and society, see G. A. Ritter, *Die Arbeiterbewegung im wilhelminischen Reich* (Berlin/Dahlem, 1959).

[59] The interaction of economic interests and political alignment has recently become a central issue in the historiography on the Empire. Much of this new work builds on some classic accounts on political developments that had, until a few years ago, been on the fringes of German scholarship: E. Franz, *Der Entscheidungskampf um die wirtschaftspolitische Führung Deutschlands (1856–1867)* (Munich, 1933); E. Kehr, *Schlachtflottenbau und Parteipolitik 1894–1901* (Berlin, 1930); and Hans Rosenberg, "Political and Social Consequences of the Great Depression in Central Europe, 1873–1896," *Economic History Review*, XII (1943), 58–73 (reprinted in this volume). Especially noteworthy among the recent works are: H. Böhme, *Deutschlands Weg zur Grossmacht* (Cologne and Berlin, 1966); Ivo Lambi, *Free Trade and Protection in Germany, 1868–1879, Beiheft 44, Vierteljahrsschrift für Sozial- und Wirtschaftsgeschichte* (Wiesbaden, 1963); Karl Hardach, *Die Bedeutung wirtschaftlicher Faktoren bei der Wiedereinführung der Eisen- und Getreidezölle in Deutschland 1879* (Berlin, 1967); H. Rosenberg, *Grosse Depression und Bismarckzeit* (Berlin, 1967); W. Steglich, "Beitrag zur Problematik des Bündnisses zwischen Junker und Bourgeoisie in Deutschland 1870–1880," *Wissenschaftliche Zeitschrift der Humboldt Universität Berlin*, IX (1959–60), 323–40; H.-J. Puhle, *Agrarische Interessenpolitik*; H. Kaelble, *Indus-*

trielle Interessenpolitik in der Wilhelminischen Gesellschaft (Berlin, 1967); D. Stegmann, *Die Erben Bismarcks. Parteien und Verbände in der Spätphase des Wilhelminischen Deutschlands* (Cologne and Berlin, 1970). For additional citations and an excellent summary, see H.-J. Puhle, "Parlament, Parteien und Interessenverbände 1890–1914," in *Das Kaiserliche Deutschland*, ed. by M. Stürmer (Düsseldorf, 1970), 340–77.

[60] For two striking examples of this process, see the material on the Hansemann family in Böhme, *Deutschlands Weg* 203, 426, and 429, and the career of Johannes Miquel described by Hans Herzfeld in *Johannes von Miquel*, 2 vols. (Detmold, 1938).

[61] On the domestic uses of foreign policy see Kehr's essays in *Primat der Innenpolitik* and *Schlachtflottenbau*; Hans-Ulrich Wehler, *Bismarck und der Imperialismus* (Cologne and Berlin, 1969); V. Berghahn, "Flottenrüstung und Machtgefüge," in Stürmer, *Das Kaiserliche Deutschland* (Düsseldorf, 1970), 378–96; Stegmann, *Erben Bismarcks*; F. Fischer, *Krieg der Illusionen. Die deutsche Politik von 1911 bis 1914* (Düsseldorf, 1969); K. Wernecke, *Der Wille zur Weltgeltung* (Düsseldorf, 1970); and Pauline Anderson, *The Background of Anti-English Feeling in Germany, 1890–1902* (Washington, 1939).

[62] For the political situation on the eve of the war see Fischer, *Krieg der Illusionen*; Stegmann, *Erben Bismarcks*; Hans-Ulrich Wehler, *Krisenherde des Kaiserreiches. Studien zur deutschen Sozial- und Verfassungsgeschichte* (Göttingen, 1970); G. Schmidt, "Deutschland am Vorabend des Ersten Weltkriegs," in Stürmer, ed., *Das kaiserliche Deutschland*, 397–433. For additional literature and a brief statement of the alternatives facing the Reich in 1914 see J. Sheehan, "Germany, 1890–1918: A Survey of Recent Research," *Central European History*, I (1968), 345–72.

[63] On the relationship between Imperial and republican politics see G. A. Ritter, "Kontinuität und Umformung des deutschen Parteisystems, 1918–1920," in *Entstehung und Wandel der modernen Gesellschaft. Festschrift für Hans Rosenberg* (Berlin, 1970), 342–84. On the formation of the radical right-wing movement during the war see Stegmann, *Erben Bismarcks*, 449ff.; F. Fischer, *Griff nach der Weltmacht* (Düsseldorf, 1961), pp. 419–620; and G. Feldman, *Army, Industry and Labor in Germany, 1914–1918* (Princeton, N.J., 1966). On the moderates see K. Epstein, *Matthias Erzberger and the Dilemma of German Democracy* (Princeton, 1959), and the documents on *Der Interfraktionelle Ausschuss 1917/18*, ed. by E. Matthias and R. Morsey, 2 vols. (Düsseldorf, 1959).

4

**Prussia's Army and the
Jewish Reserve Officer Controversy
before World War I**

WERNER T. ANGRESS

Shortly after the turn of the century Germany's
Jews, acting through their organisations,
launched an extended campaign designed to secure once again the promotion of unbaptised
Jews to reserve officer status.* Such promotions
had been withheld from them since 1885, although they were legally entitled to this right under the constitutions of Prussia and the Empire.[1]
Efforts to this effect were sustained until the
summer of 1914 when war compelled the military
to discontinue its discriminatory practices. While
this particular complaint reflected but one of
many Jewish grievances with regard to discrimination in state employment,[2] it attracted public
attention, aroused strong emotions on all sides
and thus lent itself particularly well to highlight
the ceaseless Jewish efforts for attaining equal
rights, in practice rather than only on paper, with
their fellow citizens. The main thrust was directed at the Prussian army, partly because most
German Jews resided in that state,[3] but chiefly
because the Prussian King, as German Emperor
and *Oberster Kriegsherr,* nominally appointed all
officers in the Prussian army and in the army
contingents of most other German states.[4] In
these, Jews were likewise unable to secure reserve commissions, except for the Bavarian army which, in peace time, remained under the
exclusive command of its own king.

The question of officer status for Prussia's

Jews during the nineteenth century, although complex and vicis-
situdinous, must be briefly sketched as it provides the background essential for an understanding of the Jewish efforts during
the twentieth. The Emancipation Edict of 11th March 1812 granted to the Jews in Prussia citizenship and equal rights with all
other Prussians regarding choice of occupation and place of dom-
icile.[5] But whereas Article 16 of the Edict ruled them eligible for
military service, Article 9 barred them from becoming army officers.[6] Although this restriction, which applied equally to all but
the lowest menial jobs in the Prussian bureaucracy, judiciary and
other state-connected civilian employment, contained vague references to future review and possible revision,[7] no substantial
changes materialised for another thirty-six years. To be sure,
Prussian Jews took part in the wars of liberation, many of them as
volunteers, and over twenty became officers.[8] But when political
reaction descended upon Central Europe after the Vienna settlement, the question of appointing Jews to higher posts in the bureaucracy and to officer status in the army was reviewed by King
Frederick William III and his cabinet, who rejected the proposi-
tion. This was done with the justification that in a Christian state
Jews could not be allowed to serve in any position of authority
over Christians, a dictum which remained for decades the basic
argument of Prussian officials against the appointment of Jews to
officer's rank. A royal cabinet order of 18th August 1822 merely
legitimised an already existing practice.[9] Only one unbaptised
Jew, Meno Burg, received a commission during the *Vormärz*
period, rising to the rank of a major of artillery on active service.
However, his was an isolated and utterly unrepresentative case.[10]

With the Revolution of 1848 and the end of Prussian absolutism
the legal basis of the situation changed. As early as 6th April,
Frederick William IV adopted as Article 5 of his "Decree about
some fundamentals concerning the future Prussian constitution"
the wording: "The enjoyment of civil and political rights
[*staatsbürgerliche Rechte*] is henceforth to be independent of the
religious denomination." The essence of this clause was retained
in the Constitution of 5th December 1848 (Article 12), and was
supplemented by Article 4 which declared all Prussians equal
before the law, and all public offices open to every qualified citi-

zen. Both Articles were included in the revised Constitution of
31st January 1850, and remained in force until November 1918—
on paper.[11]

Although a few Jews became medical officers during the years
1848/9, the period of reaction that followed was not conducive to
tolerance, and during the following fifteen years they remained
barred from holding public office and receiving commissions.[12]
How this was done despite the law, then and in years to come,
will be subsequently related.

In the wars of unification a number of Jews served once again as
officers, including in the Prussian army.[13] On 3rd July 1869 the
Reichstag and *Bundesrat* of the North German Confederation
had passed the law which established the principle of equal opportunity for all qualified citizens throughout the Confederation,
regardless of their creed, to hold public and political office.[14] The
law was subsequently incorporated into the Constitution of the
Empire. Its passage, but also the impact which the so-called liberal seventies had on the administrative policies of Prussia and the
Empire, may account for the fact that throughout the first decade
following the *Reichsgründung* a number of Jews were able to
secure commissions, albeit only as reserve officers, in the Prussian army and the contingents under its jurisdiction. But by the
end of the decade the practice was discontinued. The last time a
Jew received a reserve commission outside Bavaria prior to 1914
was in 1885, and there seem to have been virtually no appointments during the five preceding years.[15]

The question is, why? As we are dealing here with intangibles
rather than with officially documented decisions, the answer must
be sought, not in governmental files, but in the changing political
and social climate of the period. The years 1878/9 saw the termination of Bismarck's liberal alliance. By forging an economic tie
between the agrarian and industrial interests, Bismarck laid the
foundations for what a little less than two decades hence came to
be known as *Sammlungspolitik* of all *staatserhaltende* segments
of German society. Besides its obvious economic rationale in the
midst of a severe and lingering depression, Bismarck's move
served the additional purpose of fashioning an essentially con-

servative front against what he saw as threatening forces of sub-
version, notably the Social Democrats, but also the Progressives
with their democratic objectives and their open opposition to the
neo-absolutist Bismarckian establishment.[16] The onset of conservatism in the eighties, highlighted throughout the Reich by the
repressive anti-Socialist laws, was accompanied in Prussia by the
appointment, in 1881, of the stalwart conservative Robert v. Puttkamer as Minister of the Interior. Though dismissed again by
Emperor Frederick III in 1888, Puttkamer's influence left a lasting imprint on Prussia, especially its bureaucracy. The liberal
Geheimräte of yore were replaced by strictly conservative officials, many of whom came from the middle class. But unlike their
predecessors of an earlier generation, the new men made their
way to positions of authority via the exclusive duelling student
fraternities (*Korpsstudenten*) and the reserve officer corps to the
Assessor examination and onward, up the ladder—dutiful, obedient, loyally patriotic men whose political views and social values did not substantially differ from those of the Junkers after
whom they modelled themselves. The feudalisation of the Prussian bureaucracy, predominantly aristocratic in the provinces,
bourgeois in Berlin, was reinforced during this period by a renewed emphasis on Christian virtues, embedded in the Christian
(Lutheran) Church, that was nurtured by Puttkamer.[17]

The revival of conservative views extended also to the Prussian army officer corps. Its members had always regarded themselves as the first estate of the realm and the principal bulwark
against the nation's foreign and domestic foes.[18] During the period in question, the *Reichsfeind* at home constituted to them a
greater danger than the French or Russians, and against this internal foe, in the words of a military spokesman writing in 1882, the
army was pitted as "the only fixed point in the whirlpool, the rock
in the sea of revolution that threatens on all sides, the talisman of
loyalty and the palladium of the prince".[19] Thus in the face of
profound social and economic changes, and an equally changing
Zeitgeist—the nature of which the army neither appreciated nor
tried to understand[20]—Prussia's leadership, civilian and military,
was particularly intent on safeguarding the homogeneity of the
officer corps against the new and alien forces begotten by a rapid-

ly industrialising age. And since the nobility was no longer able to supply a sufficient number of applicants to satisfy the army's need for officers, it became necessary to turn to the reservoir of the educated bourgeoisie. In doing so, the military was determined to select only men from families of proper social standing and impeccable political views.[21] While this had been the army's attitude ever since the 1860s, it became more pronounced during the last two decades of the century. Thus it was hardly coincidental that the military reorganisation of 8th March 1883, among other changes, transferred the administration of all personnel matters—which included officer appointments and promotions—from the War Ministry to the Chief of the Military Cabinet who, unlike the War Minister, was not subject to parliamentary interpellation. The change reflected the army's desire to remove military affairs, and especially personnel matters, as much as was constitutionally possible from an inquisitive Reichstag.[22] The principal architect of the reorganisation was Emil v. Albedyll, until 1887 Chief of the Military Cabinet, who shared the ultraconservative views of his former mentor, General Edwin v. Manteuffel. So did Albedyll's friend, General Alfred Count v. Waldersee, since 1882 General Quartermaster in the General Staff. Nor was War Minister Paul Bronsart v. Schellendorff, appointed in 1883, a man of liberal leanings.[23]

Neither the Prussian bureaucracy nor the army had ever been favourably disposed towards Jews. In the 1880s, political distrust reinforced these sentiments. For besides harbouring a traditional prejudice against Jews *qua* Jews, Prussia's governing hierarchy, from the "All Highest" quarters and Prince Bismarck down to the bureaucracy and army, could not fail to notice that the Jews, who in the past had been by and large overwhelmingly loyal supporters of politics and parties in favour with the government, were beginning to change their attitude. More and more Jewish voters, until 1879 generally staunch National Liberals and even Free Conservatives, switched their support to the oppositional Progressives. Liberal newspapers, some of them owned, many of them widely staffed by Jews, espoused political views which official circles considered critical, hence oppositional, hence subversive. Even in the proscribed SPD Jews could be found in leading

positions, and a few represented that party in the Reichstag.[24]
The reason behind this slow but perceptibly shifting attitude
among German Jewry was the increase of antisemitism.

This phenomenon is well known by now and need only be
sketched very briefly.[25] Antisemitic agitation, in contrast to mere
anti-Jewish prejudice, made its appearance in the mid-seventies,
during the heyday of the Empire's liberal era. But it did not gain
real momentum until the close of the decade when Adolf Stoecker's Christian Social movement got its start. Largely a by-product
of the economic depression which prevailed between 1873 and
1896, antisemitism in its crassest manifestations affected above
all the lower middle class which was particularly vulnerable, both
to the effects of the economic crisis and to the arguments of
antisemitic agitators that their plight was largely the fault of the
Jews.[26] But this orgy of hate did not remain confined for long to
artisans, small shop-keepers, and peasants. Heinrich von
Treitschke's university lectures and learned articles made anti-
semitism respectable among the young generation of Germany's
educated bourgeoisie.[27] The rapid urbanisation of Germany's
Jewish community since the creation of the Empire, their rising
standard of living, their steady influx into the free professions,
commerce and banking, but also the press, the arts and the
theatre, aroused mounting resentment on a widening social scale.
Charges about the growing stranglehold which Jews were allegedly exerting over Germany's economic and cultural life were
raised in public meetings, newspapers, pamphlets and in the
Reichstag and Diets. The destructive (zersetzend) Jewish spirit
was depicted as a threat to the moral fibre of the nation. This line
of argument, most resolutely advanced by advocates of racial
antisemitism, the Völkischen,[28] fused with the traditional forms
of religious and social anti-Jewish prejudice prevalent among the
Junkers, the officer corps, bureaucracy, but also among many
German Catholics. Thus the eighties saw a proliferation of antisemitic organisations, prevented from forming a strong and unified bloc only by their internecine squabbles, whose agitation left
its murky imprint on the German scene. Among other effects,
antisemitism encouraged the Conservative Party (Deutschkonservativen) and the government, notably Bismarck, to exploit the

issue in the political sphere by using it as a weapon against the left parliamentary opposition.[29] But it had its most disastrous effect on those segments of the population that in the past had been indifferent, if not immune, to this particular affliction, notably the propertied and educated middle class, once the bastion of liberalism to which the Jews owed whatever progress their struggle for full emancipation had made during the century. As liberalism yielded to national chauvinism, and as the teachings of Treitschke and like-minded mandarins put their stamp upon the *Weltanschauung* of a new generation, antisemitism made inroads into the universities, the training grounds for future officials, judges and army reserve officers.[30] While not a cohesive movement, it was gaining ground in the eighties and nineties, encouraged from above by the intense conservative resurgence in Prussia's bureaucracy and army. The combination of these trends, which manifested themselves to differing degrees in all walks of life and affected the prevailing political and social climate,[31] was exceedingly detrimental to Jewish hopes for attaining the full measure of their civil rights.

During the height of antisemitic agitation, the Jews had focused their attention on defending themselves against calumny and slander. These efforts resulted in 1890 in the founding of the interdenominational *Verein zur Abwehr des Antisemitismus (Abwehrverein)*, and of the *Centralverein deutscher Staatsbürger jüdischen Glaubens* (C.V.) in 1893.[32] Only when the crassest manifestations of antisemitism began to recede after 1896, with the end of the economic depression, the decline of the Stoecker movement and the public disgrace of some of the most notorious antisemitic spokesmen[33] did German Jewry shift the emphasis from a primarily defensive stance to the larger and more fundamental task of securing equitable treatment with non-Jews in the civilian and military sectors of state service. In this endeavour they derived little comfort from the fact that some of their fellow Germans also had justified grievances. Governmental discrimination against Social Democrats, Poles and other national minorities beyond the pale were notorious. But even "respectable" middle-class Germans kept raising charges that the nobility still received preferential treatment in appointments to prestigious posts in administration and army, notably the diplomatic service, the upper bureaucracy, the guards and the General Staff.[34] Catholics in particular complained that the higher echelons of the Prussian and Imperial governments remained closed to them, and that the army expelled Catholic officers, who for religious reasons refused to fight duels, from the corps.[35] Yet despite these justified complaints, on the whole the bourgeoisie had undeniably made impressive progress since 1871 in competing with the nobility for respectable, if not always exalted, positions in public life. In contrast, Jews continued to remain virtually excluded from any public appointments, constitutional guarantees and the important Jewish contributions to Germany's economic and cultural life over the past decades notwithstanding. The method by which they were excluded in Prussia was based on what Rudolf v. Gneist once had termed the tendency in that state to subvert the laws by means of administrative practice.[36] In other words, some justification was always found for not appointing or promoting a person, either in a civilian or military capacity, and during the Wilheminian era Jews became well acquainted with the vast reservoir of official excuses. It was this awareness of being singled out for continued discrimination, at a time when old barriers were rapidly falling for most other middle-class citizens, that moved the Jews around 1900 to assert their slighted civil rights with renewed vigour, and even a touch of defiance.[37]

Symptomatic for this new spirit was the founding of the *Verband der Deutschen Juden* (VDJ) in April 1904.[38] Originally conceived as a strong central organisation that would speak and act on behalf of all German Jews—whether orthodox, liberal, reform, or Zionist—the *Verband* did not get the necessary support from the various Jewish factions to realise its objective. Yet while this setback prevented it from becoming an effective, because unified, force on the German political scene, the VDJ resolved in October 1905 to make the redress of Jewish grievances one of its principal functions. Especially the discriminatory practices of the bureaucracy and army received high priority, involving among others the objective of securing reserve officer status for qualified Jewish applicants.

Given the traditional elitist attitude of Prussia's regular army officer corps, it was generally agreed in Jewish circles not to press for admission to this inner sanctum and to concentrate instead on the reserves.[39] The Prussian reserve officer corps had been created during v. Roon's military reforms of 1860/1 which had substantially increased the size and efficiency of the army.[40] However, prior to the founding of the Empire, and even during the Franco-Prussian War, the reserve officer corps remained small in numbers. Its expansion, and with it its social impact, came only after 1871. As is well known by now, the social prestige of a Prussian reserve officer was quite disproportionate to the actual functional significance of a lieutenant or even a captain. To belong to the corps was an essential preliminary step towards a "respectable" career, notably in state service, but also reassuring proof to the person concerned that he was a *"vornehmer Mann"*, since those who did not fit this category received no commission.[41] Qualified personnel was drawn exclusively from sons of economically well-situated families, preferably industrialists, higher officials, the legal profession, army officers and other "desirable" and politically reliable circles. A candidate was expected to have attended a secondary school for at least six years and to have attained *Obersekundareife*. This made him automatically eligible for only one year (instead of the usual three, or, after 1893, two) of military service for which he volunteered as an *Einjährig-Freiwilliger*. At the end of the year, during which he was under constant observation of his superior officers, a decision on his qualification for reserve officer status was taken. But only volunteers enrolled in an officer training course, to which admission was not automatic, were eligible. If admitted, a candidate had to meet a number of requirements. He had to be promoted at least to the rank of lance-corporal (*Gefreiter*), preferably corporal (*Unteroffizier*) and, after passing a comprehensive examination, be officially designated an officer candidate (*Offiziersaspirant*). If he reached this stage he had to participate in two eight-week courses of tactical exercises, *Übungen* A and B. Only then could his regimental commander recommend him to the local military district commander for election by the district's reserve officer corps. If elected, the candidate still required the final approval of the Military Cabinet which, after closely checking up on his credentials, could then appoint him in the Emperor's name to the rank of reserve lieutenant.[42]

A principal object of this rigid selection process by which candidacy could be terminated at every step of the line was to protect the homogeneity of the corps from elements considered unsuitable by the army on political, social or other grounds. For whether Junkers or bourgeois, regulars or reserves, its members regarded themselves a social elite—*Herren der Welt*, as one of them has put it in his memoirs—imbued with proverbial loyalty to their monarch, a pronounced and often excessive concept of honour, and a fierce *esprit de corps*.[43] Thus careful screening during the year of active service went far to preserve this homogeneity, and candidates who passed every hurdle were ordinarily elected by the district's reserve officers to join them in becoming *Manöveronkels*, as the public liked to refer to them.

As has been shown, Jews had been able to obtain reserve commissions during the wars of unification and the liberal seventies, despite the army's careful selection procedures. Thereafter, for reasons mentioned above, they no longer qualified. But it should be noted that throughout the three decades preceding the First World War, individual officers of all ranks were known to recommend Jewish *Einjährig-Freiwillige* at various stages of the officer training course for the next higher step up the ladder to a reserve officer appointment. In so doing, these officers adhered strictly to the pertinent laws and regulations, thereby comparing favourably with their fellow officers in the reserves. This difference in attitude may be explained by the fact that the reserve officers who had matured during the eighties and nineties were more apt to display their chauvinism, antisemitism and boundless adoration of Kaiser and Reich than the frequently more fair-minded line officers, including the Junkers among them. To this generation of reserve officers, essentially parvenues within the military, the generation of Heinrich Mann's fictitious and yet so real Diederich Hessling, the eternal *Untertan*, Jews were unacceptable as social equals. And if they had needed a handy excuse—as they did not —for excluding Jews from their ranks, they could always point— as they did—to their Emperor's decree of 29th March 1890, where William II had invited bourgeois families to send their sons into the officer corps provided they possessed "love for King and Fatherland, a warm heart for the soldier's calling, and Christian demeanour [*Gesittung*] . . ."[44]

Why, then, did the Jews seize upon the reserve officer issue when there were so many other, weightier areas of discrimination, especially in judiciary appointments, the universities, public schools and, last but not least, recognition of the Jewish religion and its institutions on an equal basis with the two major Christian denominations?[45] The question was, in fact, raised in 1911, during the fourth general meeting of the VDJ, when its chairman, Maximilian Horwitz, commented: "Some of our co-religionists are amazed that we devote so much work to specifically this problem. Even without stretching one's imagination unduly it would seem that it can hardly be considered the pinnacle of all glory to become a lieutenant."[46] Yet the matter was pressed none the less because of its symbolic significance. *Heeresdienst* was *Ehrendienst*. Insistence on the right to serve as reserve officers like everybody else was to Jews a point of honour and personal dignity. Its achievement would have signified their unequivocal acceptance as equals. Conversely, its denial placed a stigma on their standing within society (notably one which put so much stress on honour and soldierly virtues), a point publicly acknowledged already in 1847 by Count Ludwig York during a debate on the civic status of the Jews in the Prussian United Diet.[47] The principle of the matter was clearly stated by the Progressive Reichstag deputy Ludwig Haas. Speaking in 1913 at a meeting of the C.V. in Berlin on "The German Jew in the Army," Haas said: " . . . We are not concerned [with the question] whether X or Y becomes a reserve officer, or not . . . What is at stake is much, much more than any individual [case]. We are concerned about justice [*das Recht*]; . . . the German army must finally acknowledge the constitution (*Bravo!*). We want nothing but our *gutes Recht!*" And, touching upon more fundamental implications, he added: "If the constitution in the long run means nothing, what, then, can endure in the Reich, the state? We are fighting for extremely important rights and principles, and not for the [particular interests of any] individual."[48]

But it was the question of "our right" rather than other, perhaps loftier, considerations which determined the Jewish attitude during the decade before the war. The campaign began spontaneously in 1903 when one *Justizrat* from Breslau wrote a letter of complaint to William II because his son had been denied a reserve commission on account of his creed.[49] Although we do not know the nature of the reply, the complaint had no effect. A year later, in March 1904, the issue was debated for the first time in the Reichstag[50] where it continued to come up as a regular feature whenever the subject of military appropriations was on the agenda. Throughout the period, the charge of discrimination against Jewish *Einjährig-Freiwillige* by the army was nearly always raised first by a member of one of the Progressive *Fraktionen*. This was remarkable in so far as the close ties that in the past had existed between German Jewry and the Progressives had severely deteriorated ever since 1893 when the *Deutsch-Freisinnige Partei* had split into Eugen Richter's *Freisinnige Volkspartei* and Heinrich Rickert's *Freisinnige Vereinigung*. During the following years, the Jews noticed with growing anger and dismay that both Progressive parties repeatedly put up baptised rather than unbaptised Jewish candidates during elections, and on more than one occasion supported antisemitic over Social Democratic candidates in run-off contests. Estrangement grew further in 1907 when both parties supported antisemitic candidates during the Reichstag election of that year, and subsequently joined them in the Bülow Bloc as well.[51] But despite these tensions, individual Progressive deputies in the Reichstag were willing to champion Jewish demands for equity in the matter of reserve officer appointments.[52]

There was no debate on the question in 1906 and 1907. It was resumed in 1908 and remained an annual affair until 1914. When the issue had been raised on 4th February 1908, without evoking a satisfactory reply from the War Minister, the VDJ, now sufficiently well organised to play its part, intervened. Prior to the third reading of the military appropriations bill on 30th March, the *Verband* sent appeals to selected deputies of various political parties, asking for "support to restore lawful conditions in this sphere", i.e., the Jewish reserve officer question, and to put pressure on the military to investigate and redress particular Jewish grievances since brought to the War Minister's attention. The appeal stressed the common interest of all parties in making the army observe the law and to prevent legislative decisions from becoming a mockery.[53] At the same time, the *Verband* provided both War Minister v. Einem and the Progressive deputy Julius Kopsch with a list of specific cases of Jewish *Einjährig-Freiwillige,* allegedly denied reserve commissions because of their creed. On 30th March Kopsch then referred to this list in his address to the Reichstag.[54] This approach became a regular practice. The VDJ, in conjunction with C.V. and *Abwehrverein,* directed specific complaints to the War Minister and simultaneously to one or several Progressive deputies designated by their *Fraktion* to speak on the military appropriations bill. These speakers then introduced the Jewish complaints into the debate. This tactic became a smooth routine after 1909 when the Progressive deputy Georg Gothein became chairman of the *Abwehrverein* and used letters, sent to him in this new capacity, for his sincere, though painfully repetitious speeches in the Reichstag on the Jewish reserve officer issue.[55]

Rather striking was the virtually unchanging nature of the charges that were raised year after year. No Jewish *Einjährig-Freiwilliger* serving in the Prussian army or one of the contingents under the jurisdiction of the War Ministry had received a reserve commission since 1885, although by 1910 an estimated 20,000 to 30,000 had absolved their year of service.[56] The stages at which they were cut off differed from case to case. As they were volunteers and not draftees, the simplest method available to an antisemitic unit commander was to refuse them acceptance into his regiment. Those admitted were often denied enrolment into an officer training course. Of the men lucky enough to take such a course, some either failed to pass the comprehensive examination that concluded it, were not promoted to non-commissioned officer's rank—a prerequisite step up the ladder—or were ruled unqualified for certification as official officer candidates. The small number of Jews who in the various army units survived the screening process up to this stage had undoubtedly proven themselves qualified officer material, at least as far as the training cadres were concerned. Yet there were still additional hurdles. Candidates had to pass the two final Exercises A and B and, if they did, the regimental commander frequently struck their names off the list submitted to the district commander who had to approve all candidates before they could be presented to the army district's reserve officers for election. That these self-styled pillars of Wilhelminian society inevitably turned Jews down has been mentioned. To be sure, a certain number of Jewish candidates were undoubtedly not qualified for commission, as were some non-Jews. But could that have been true of all of them? On some occasions, Jews were discreetly advised during their year of training to be baptised, and of those who complied a substantial number were commissioned.[57] But ordinarily the army refrained from bringing up the question of religion. Rejected Jewish candidates who inquired why they had been turned down, some of them after they had passed all but the final recommendation stage, were either given no explanation, or were told that they had been found "unqualified". There was no effective appeal. The Prussian army's procedure for registering complaints was as cumbersome as it was hazardous, and most rejected candidates thought it wiser to desist. For this reason, nearly all complaints that eventually reached the Reichstag were lodged by the fathers of the individuals concerned, an annoyance which the army accepted with equanimity.[58]

After the charges had been raised from the floor, the War Minister at the ministerial bench either answered or ignored them. His was not an enviable position. Strictly speaking, the Reichstag lacked the right to question him on matters pertaining to the Emperor's jealously guarded *Kommandogewalt* which included personnel policy and thus officer appointments and promotions, but it did have the right of interpellation with regard to administrative matters, including incidents that occurred during military training. By this time, however, the Reichstag had abandoned earlier constraints at observing these distinctions and had got into the habit of interpellating the War Minister on many aspects of military affairs which, at least in the eyes of the monarch, the government and the military command, lay outside its proper jurisdiction. Nevertheless, in most instances the War Minister

did reply, even if reluctantly, and did so to questions about the
Jewish reserve officer problem. To be sure, this was essentially a
personnel matter, thus theoretically the Emperor's preserve,
though in practice personnel policies were handled ever since
1883 by the Military Cabinet, acting for the Emperor, and the
chief of this elusive but powerful institution was not constitutionally bound to render accounts to the Reichstag. But the War
Minister was, and while he could have quite properly refused to
answer questions about any adverse verdicts on Jewish officer
candidates reached by the Military Cabinet—a situation which
thanks to the reserve officer's election practices never arose—he
had to answer all interpellations by the deputies that related to
complaints involving the military training period, as most of them
actually did.[59]

During the period in question, three War Ministers held office:
Generals Karl v. Einem (1903–1909), Josias v. Heeringen (1909–
1913) and Erich v. Falkenhayn (1913–1915). All reacted to the
charges in nearly identical fashion. In 1904, v. Einem simply
ignored them, as he did the subsequent antisemitic exegesis by
Liebermann v. Sonnenberg.[60] When pressed on one particular
aspect, v. Einem replied briefly and evasively, and there the matter rested until 1905.[61] During that year's session, the Progressive
deputy Richard Eickhoff who had spoken on the question in 1904
criticised the War Minister for his silence at the time, whereupon
v. Einem presented the army's official views on the Jewish reserve officer. Jews, he said, were on the whole good soldiers (*sie
haben gut gedient*). He admitted that antisemitic sentiments existed both in the officer corps and among enlisted men, but claimed
that the army made no concessions to prejudices. "If they do not
like a Jewish *Kamerad,* they still must put up with him." And as
to promotion, "the Jewish faith was never a valid criterion for
evaluating" a man's fitness for officer status.[62] From this stereotyped and, to the interpellating deputies, wholly unsatisfactory
reply neither he nor his successors ever deviated in substance.
Nevertheless, over the course of the years even the War Ministry
had to face facts, and v. Einem did. He conceded on 19th March
1909 that on occasion a "young man of the Israelite faith" did not
become a reserve officer solely because he was a Jew. This, he

added—arguing much like Christian Morgenstern's Palmström that *nicht sein kann, was nicht sein darf*—was contrary to "All Highest" decrees, and he cited an imperial ordinance of 10th June 1908 which specifically reminded all superior officers not to "exclude *Einjährig-Freiwillige* and officer candidates from special training, . . . examination, promotion, etc., solely because of their religion or their fathers' professional status".[63] A similar admission was extracted from v. Heeringen on 25th February 1911. The constitutional question, he stated, was not in doubt, citing chapter and verse. But, he added, no Jewish reserve officers had been appointed since 1885 on account of antisemitic sentiments within the army, sentiments of which, he hastened to say, he disapproved.[64] Unfortunately, Heeringen's credibility had been tarnished the previous year when he had said in this connection: "We must not only demand that the individual possesses ability and knowledge and . . . character, but we must demand additional [qualities] from a superior. The entire personality of the man concerned, the way he stands in front of the troops, must inspire respect. (Very true! on the Right) . . . Now far be it from me to claim . . . that this is missing in our Jewish fellow citizens. But, on the other hand, we cannot deny that a different view prevails . . . among the lower classes [*niederen Volk*]."[65] To this, Gothein replied—and repeated it the following year—that v. Heeringen's statement openly invited superior officers to use external appearance as an excuse for eliminating Jews as officer candidates. And did a Jew's unmilitary bearing disappear the minute he converted to Christianity, Gothein asked?[66]

Heeringen's successor, v. Falkenhayn, whose barely concealed contempt for the whole controversy is evident from the debates, stuck to the same ingenuous argument used by his predecessors. The army did not deny promotion to Jews on account of their faith. To do so would be in violation of "All Highest" wishes. But he, too, conceded that since 1885 no Jew had become an army reserve officer, regardless of his qualifications. "That this situation seems [he said "is"] essentially unconstitutional I must, of course, admit. But I deny that it has been the result of any unconstitutional procedures. . . . Gentlemen . . . there is not the smallest doubt that an Israelite can be promoted . . . an officer, provided he fulfils all requirements uniformly established for all reserve officer candidates.''[67] And herein, of course, lay the rub, for those who decided whether these requirements had been met were the candidate's superior officers. It emerged with increasing regularity during this decade of futile debates that the army, from the War Minister on down to the line officers, blatantly prevaricated on this issue. The way in which the specific examples of discriminatory acts presented to the War Minister and the Reichstag were treated showed this quite clearly. The War Minister always promised to review each case, which he did. But instead of appointing an impartial board of inquiry he simply turned for information to the former military superiors of the rejected candidate in question, and as the replies always confirmed the original findings the War Minister could declare himself satisfied that no discrimination on religious grounds had, in fact, taken place.[68] This was, of course, in open contradiction to the repeated admissions by all three War Ministers that antisemitism was operative in the army, a discrepancy they never bothered to explain. They merely contented themselves with refuting charges in connection with individual cases. And as to the handful of candidates who did reach the election stage but were always turned down, the War Ministers assured the Reichstag that they had no authority over these traditional procedures and neither could nor would interfere with them.[69]

Of the various cases brought to the Reichstag's attention, one might serve as an example—the "Case of Arthur Lieber's *Eiertante*" which was debated on 10th, 11th and 22nd May, 1912. Lieber, a Jewish resident of Strasbourg, served as *Einjährig-Freiwilliger* in an Alsatian regiment whose commander recommended him in October 1911 for promotion to reserve officer. But the military district commander, without giving any reasons, refused Lieber permission to present himself for election. Being apparently a stubborn man, Lieber sent a formal complaint to the commanding general who promptly rejected it with the generous comment that he would refrain from punishing Lieber for having submitted an unjustified complaint. Thereupon Lieber's father wrote to the War Minister, v. Heeringen, who upheld the district commander's decision but emphasised in his written reply that

Lieber's rejection had nothing to do with his religion. Gothein, who had presented the case to the Reichstag, challenged v. Heeringen to prove his assertion. The War Minister replied that circumstances now compelled him to reveal the reasons for Lieber's rejection, and to the amazement of the house (judging from the interruptions and subsequent debate) told the deputies that Lieber's father owned a hardware store where the son had been known to sell stoves. Worse yet, Lieber's aunt, his father's sister, had once been in the egg business and was currently running a therapeutic institute for people afflicted with a stutter. Only his family background and not his creed had disqualified Lieber for a reserve commission, v. Heeringen insisted. We need not dwell on the ensuing three-day discussion of the "Case Lieber", except to note that it was not the War Minister's finest hour.[70]

Whereas debate on the issue remained from 1904 through 1910 largely a contest between Progressive deputies and the olympian, thoroughly non-committal War Ministers, with speakers of the several antisemitic *Fraktionen* adding colour to the proceedings, by 1911 deputies from other political parties began to show a growing interest. This coincided outside the Reichstag with increased agitation by the C.V. and VDJ which sponsored public meetings where resolutions protesting the army's discriminatory practices were passed and forwarded to the War Ministry.[71] But the principal forum remained the Reichstag where the periodic debates on the Jewish reserve officer were held in an atmosphere ranging from the grotesque to the Kafkaesque. Great hilarity was not unusual in the house, notably when speakers of an antisemitic *Fraktion* took the floor and regaled their audience with diatribe. The only argument of substance which these speakers ever produced was their insistence that Jews should be excluded on racial rather than on religious grounds,[72] a point of view not shared by the army. But in their own inimitable way the antisemites were more honest and consistent than the military which withheld commissions from unbaptised Jews while granting them readily to converts. On this point the army adhered strictly to a tradition which originated in the early nineteenth century, and it did so despite the fact that among many segments of German society around 1900 racial antisemitism was rapidly displacing anti-Jewish sentiments based on religious prejudice.[73] That its position left the army open to frequent charges of hypocrisy did not disturb either the War Ministers or the officer corps.

Closest in attitude to the antisemites were the two Conservative *Fraktionen* whose speakers employed a barely less offensive style;[74] but they spoke rarely, usually confining themselves to applause whenever the War Minister refuted the argument of a critic. Cautious and reserved was the *Zentrum* although one of its deputies, the South German Adolf Gröber, took a consistently outspoken stand against discrimination, occasionally supported by one of his colleagues.[75] To be sure, the *Zentrum* was in a peculiar situation. On the one hand, Catholics remembered the *Kulturkampf* when many Jews had stood in the liberal camp; but as a religious minority themselves the *Zentrum* deputies were also concerned with combating prejudice, in the army and elsewhere, which forced them into a position of uneasy tolerance *vis-à-vis* their Jewish fellow citizens.[76] Interestingly enough, Matthias Erzberger sat through years of antisemitic tirades without opening his mouth once. But in 1913, when an antisemitic speaker taunted him by saying that Erzberger, too, had been known to have made derogatory remarks about Jews—as he had—the *gute Mond aus Buttenhausen* rose up in support of the Jewish reserve officer.[77] The National Liberals did not join the fray until 1911, when both Hermann Paasche and Arthur Osann, Jr. spoke out on discrimination by the army, as did Ernst Bassermann in 1913.

Finally, there were the Social Democrats. As a working-class party they could have no interest in securing reserve commissions for the sons of bourgeois Jews, for proletarian Jews there were few, and these had doubly no chance for promotion. Nor did the Jewish community, which by 1907 consisted of over 70% of middle-class citizens, primarily engaged in some kind of business enterprise or the free professions, feel strong sympathies for the anti-capitalist SPD—smaller sections of Jewish intellectuals and employees excepted.[78] Nevertheless, Social Democratic speakers did take a stand by including this particular injustice into their own extensive catalogue of grievances with regard to unfair army practices.[79] With one exception, only Gentile SPD

deputies took the floor on this question. This was Eduard Bernstein, always a maverick, who in 1913 spoke in support of a
resolution introduced by his party to make promotion in the army
solely dependent on ability, irrespective of a person's social
standing, religious affiliation or political association. In the course
of the debate he engaged in a bitter exchange with an antisemitic
deputy, Professor Ferdinand Werner, who subsequently scored a
cheap triumph when he suggested the formation of Jewish regiments with Jewish officers. "And when the first Jewish heavy
cavalry regiment charges across the field [against the Russian
cossacks], I shall stand by watching, and shall sing with all my
voice: *Das ist Bernsteins wilde verwegene Jagd* [Continued strong
hilarity. Vivid applause on the Right]."[80] Only one other unbaptised Jew, the Progressive deputy David Waldstein, spoke over
the years on the Jewish reserve officer question, and then likewise only in response to Werner's vituperations.[81] For although
Jewish deputies, notably the Progressives Oskar Cassel and Martin Peltasohn in the Prussian Landtag, did on occasion speak out
against other instances of governmental discrimination, in the
matter of reserve commissions, which fell to the Reichstag's domain, the Jewish organisations preferred to work behind the
scenes, apparently deeming it wiser, literally, to let George
(Gothein) do it.[82]

None of the arguments, presented by speaker after speaker for
a decade, affected the position of the military: the acute shortage
of officers, notably in the medical corps; the presence of Jewish
regular and reserve officers, some in high positions, in the armies
of other European countries; and the Bavarian practice of appointing qualified Jews to reserve officer status.[83] Finally, far-
reaching agreement prevailed from the National Liberals to the
SPD that War Ministry and officer corps deliberately violated
letter and spirit of specific constitutional guarantees while priding
themselves on living in a *Rechtsstaat*. On 19th April 1913 the
Reichstag actually adopted three separate resolutions, moved by
the Budget Committee, the Progressive and Social Democratic
Fraktionen respectively, all designed to curb the army's discriminatory practices. But on 7th January 1914 the Bundesrat rejected
them with the comment that the resolutions were superfluous in

that all army appointments and promotions were based exclusively on ability; a person's religion or politics did not enter into the
process at all as this would be contrary to the army's fundamental
conviction.[84]

Nor did the efforts of the Jewish organisations outside the
Reichstag fare any better. Protest meetings, resolutions, petitions
to the War Minister and, in the spring of 1914, a personal talk
between two leading representatives of the VDJ with v. Falkenhayn were all met with the same familiar assurances that the army
did not discriminate against anybody on account of his creed, and
that was that.[85] All efforts combined merely amounted to an extended exercise in futility. Only after war was declared in 1914
were Jews allowed to fight and die as reserve officers of the
Prussian army and its attached contingents.

The drawn-out struggle over the issue calls for a few concluding
observations. If ever there was a lost cause, this was one of them,
although this fact is more easily perceived in retrospect than it
was by those who fought for their rights sixty odd years ago. The
army's position was based on its concern with the officer corps'
homogeneity which was to be preserved at all costs. In the 1870s,
during the heyday of liberal ascendancy and in the wake of unification and glorious victory, the army apparently had not considered Jews as a threat to its sacred traditions. Thereafter, for
reasons outlined above, it did, and without ever owning up to its
practices prevented them from becoming reserve officers. The
public was expected to believe that among the twenty to thirty
thousand Jewish *Einjährig-Freiwillige* over a period of three decades, not one was qualified for a commission. Yet into this close-
knit, martial brotherhood with its exclusiveness, snooty *Kasino*
(mess) tone, and *Liebesmahle*,[86] Jews wanted to be accepted, and
accepted as equals. Were the Jewish notables and their organisations that initiated and led this campaign aware of the odds they
were facing? Did they realise that Jews, even if they had been
admitted to the reserve officer corps of the 1900s, would have
remained conspicuous outsiders? Though the great majority of
Jews proudly considered themselves completely assimilated, loyal and for the most part intensely patriotic Germans, many of

their fellow citizens preferred to accentuate their differences.
Their mysterious religious cult was suspect, their still rather isolated social milieu alien. For whereas Jews and non-Jews went to
school together, worked and lived side by side, many subtle—and
sometimes not so subtle—barriers kept social relations between
them tenuous and circumscribed, except among artists, certain
intellectual circles, and the very rich.[87] Army officers in particular stereotyped them as shrewd *Koofmichs* and shysters with too
much money and devoid of tact, manners and class—in short, as
socially inferior people.

Returning to our initial question, we may assume that the Jews
were indeed aware of their situation. That they nevertheless persisted in pressing the issue indicates that they accepted the risk of
being made uncomfortable if they intruded where they were not
wanted as the price to be paid for achieving a fundamental objective—the public acknowledgment of their equal rights and standing as citizens, denied to them for so long.

And yet, despite their recognition of the odds, a good deal of
self-deception on their part seems to have clouded this particular
campaign. Perhaps the fact that the Jews did receive some support in the Reichstag, not only from the Progressives, the *Juden-
schutztruppe*, but also from other political parties, restored some
of their sorely abused faith in the essential fairmindedness of
Germany's educated middle class, including the predominantly
bourgeois reserve officer corps. Even as astute an observer as the
Progressive Reichstag deputy Ludwig Haas told his listeners in
1913 that the reserve officers were bound to admit Jews to their
corps, if only the army command would relinquish its discriminatory practices during the military training phase and would cease
to exert pressure on the reserve officer elections.[88] After all, it
had worked prior to 1885, why not now? Such arguments ignored
the transformation of Germany's educated middle class during
the preceding twenty-five years, when an entire generation of
Germans had absorbed generous doses of antisemitism at the
Gymnasium and the university. Unlike their still rather liberal
fathers, these men were not inclined to share any of their social
privileges with Jews, least of all the epaulettes of a reserve
officer.

And what were the prospects in Wilhelminian Germany of compelling the army to change its devious but unyielding attitude? Under a regime which did not yield one inch of ground to the growing pressure from various segments of German society for electoral reforms in Prussia; under which several million workers remained cut off from the mainstream of national life; under which blatant misconduct on the part of Prussian army officers during the Zabern incident was publicly countenanced by Crown Prince and Chancellor—under such a regime the Prussian *maison militaire* was hardly likely to make concessions to Jews in the matter of reserve commissions. To be sure, this meant in effect that constitutional guarantees were nimbly side-stepped; but then, neither Emperor nor army put much stock in legal niceties, especially when the citizens affected were regarded—with apologies to Rudyard Kipling—as "lesser breeds", although "*within* the law".

NOTES

* This is an expanded version of a paper delivered at the 86th Annual Meeting of the American Historical Association. The author would like to express his sincere appreciation to Kathleen M. Pearle for her able and valuable assistance during the research stage of this article.

¹ This right was based on Articles 4 and 12 of the Prussian Constitution of 5th December 1848, subsequently incorporated with a slightly altered wording into the revised Constitution of 31st January 1850; and the Law of 3rd July 1869 which, as Article 191b, was adopted into the Constitution of the North German Confederation and was subsequently incorporated into the Constitution of the German Empire. Ernst Rudolf Huber, ed., *Dokumente zur Deutschen Verfassungsgeschichte*, I, Stuttgart 1961, pp. 386, 402; and II, Stuttgart 1964, p. 248 and n. 18.

² The principal grievances pertained to employment in the administrative and legal branches of the governments, Reich and *Länder*; the primary and secondary school systems; the universities and, of course, the officer corps. For details see Ernest Hamburger, *Juden im öffentlichen Leben Deutschlands. Regierungsmitglieder, Beamte und Parlamentarier in der monarchischen Zeit 1848–1918*, Tübingen 1968 (Schriftenreihe wissenschaftlicher Abhandlungen des Leo Baeck Instituts 19), pp. 32–66 and *passim*.

³ Of a total of 607,862 Jews residing in 1905 in the German Empire, 409,301 lived in Prussia. By 1910, their number in Prussia had risen to 415,926. Jakob Segall, *Die beruflichen und sozialen Verhältnisse der Juden in Deutschland*, Berlin 1912, pp. 1, 4, and Heinrich Silbergleit, *Die Bevölkerungs-und Berufsverhältnisse der Juden im Deutschen Reich*, I: *Freistaat Preussen*, Berlin 1930, p. 19.

⁴ A useful introduction to the history of officer appointments and promotions in the armies of the German states from the seventeenth to the twentieth century are the essays and documents in *Untersuchungen zur Geschichte des Offizierkorps. Anciennität und Beförderung nach Leistung. Beiträge zur Militär-und Kriegsgeschichte*, ed. Militärgeschichtliches Forschungsamt, IV, Stuttgart 1962. Although the essays deal with the various officer corps as a whole, the discussions are equally applicable to the reserve officer corps. For the specific constitutional stipulations governing the German Emperor's functions *vis-à-vis* the Prussian army and the contingents of the other German states, see Huber, *Dokumente*, II, pp. 237–239, 261–267, 273–276, 301–304. According to Article 66 of the Constitutions of 16th April 1867 and 16th April 1871, all except the highest ranking officers in the various army contingents were subject to appointment by their respective princes, "except where special arrangements determine otherwise" (*ibid.*, pp. 238, 303). In practice, however, the constitutional stipulations were soon superseded by the military agreements (*Militärkonventionen*) which Prussia concluded with all non-Prussian German states between 1867 and 1871. As a result of these agreements, the sovereign rights (*Hoheitsrechte*) relating to the military contingents of these states which had been constitutionally granted to their rulers

—including the right to appoint and promote all but the highest ranking officers— were now transferred to the Emperor, thereby creating for all practical purposes a unified German army over which the King of Prussia, as German Emperor, exercised unrestricted control (*Kommandogewalt*). Only Bavaria was exempt from the Emperor's *Kommandogewalt* in peacetime, leaving the Bavarian King and his military forces unlimited leeway with regard to personnel policies and other internal functions. This arrangement worked to the benefit of the Jews who, if found "qualified", could become reserve officers in the Bavarian army. (See, however, below, n. 83, for some additional comments on this particular matter.) In addition to Bavaria, the Kings of Württemberg and Saxony retained their privilege of nominating all but their top officers, though in their case the German Emperor merely delegated this function to them while retaining his *Kommandogewalt* over their contingents in peace time as well as in war time. And since their army contingents, in contrast to that of Bavaria, remained in every other respect closely tied to the Prussian army, Württemberg and Saxony adhered strictly to the Prussian personnel policies with regard to officer appointments and promotions, very much to the detriment of Jews who aspired to reserve commissions in the military forces of these two kingdoms. On the complex military relations in the German Empire see, above all, Ernst Rudolf Huber, *Heer und Staat in der deutschen Geschichte*, Hamburg 1938, specifically pp. 247–251. For additional information on various aspects of this problem consult the following accounts: Gordon Craig, *The Politics of the Prussian Army 1640–1945*, New York and Oxford 1956, pp. 217–232 and *passim*; Johannes Ziekursch, *Politische Geschichte des Neuen Deutschen Kaiserreiches, I: Die Reichsgründung*, Frankfurt/Main 1932, pp. 221, 347; Otto Graf zu Stolberg-Wernigerode, *Die unentschiedene Generation. Deutschlands konservative Führungsschichten am Vorabend des Ersten Weltkrieges*, Munich and Vienna 1968, p. 109; Hans Black, 'Die Grundzüge der Beförderungsordnungen', *Untersuchungen zur Geschichte des Offizierkorps*, p. 136; and Jürgen Schmädeke, *Militärische Kommandogewalt und parlamentarische Demokratie. Zum Problem der Verantwortlichkeit des Reichswehrministers in der Weimarer Republik*, Heft 398 of *Historische Studien*, Lübeck and Hamburg 1966, p. 14. On the less than clear-cut state of German military administration see, besides Huber, *Heer and Staat*, *passim*, also Rudolf Morsey, *Die Oberste Reichsverwaltung unter Bismarck 1867–1890* Münster, Westfalen 1957, pp. 226–241; and Gerhard Ritter, *Staatskunst und Kriegshandwerk. Das Problem des "Militarismus" in Deutschland, II: Die Hauptmächte Europas und das wilhelminische Reich (1890–1914)*, Munich 1960, pp. 151–154, and *passim*.

[5] Text in Huber, *Dokumente*, I, pp. 45–47. On its significance see Hamburger, *op. cit.*, pp. 9–10.

[6] Horst Fischer, *Judentum, Staat und Heer in Preussen im frühen 19. Jahrhundert. Zur Geschichte der staatlichen Judenpolitik*, Tübingen 1968 (Schriftenreihe wissenschaftlicher Abhandlungen des Leo Baeck Instituts 20), pp. 25–28; Manfred Messerschmidt's review of Fischer's study, in *Militärgeschichtliche Mitteilungen*, 1/70, pp. 151–152.

[7] Fischer, *op. cit.*, pp. 24, 27–28.

[8] *Ibid.*, pp. 41–44.

[9] *Ibid.*, pp. 53–62, 203.

[10] *Ibid.*, pp. 127–130, 203; Hamburger, *op. cit.*, pp. 15, 69–70; Jacob Toury, *Die politischen Orientierungen der Juden in Deutschland. Von Jena bis Weimar*, Tübingen 1966 (Schriftenreihe wissenschaftlicher Abhandlungen des Leo Baeck Instituts 15), p. 3, n. 12.

[11] See above, n. 1.

[12] Wanda Kampmann, *Deutsche und Juden. Studien zur Geschichte des deutschen Judentums*, Heidelberg 1963, pp. 212–215; Hamburger, *op. cit.*, pp. 24–26; Toury, *Die politischen Orientierungen . . .* , pp. 99–102, incl. n. 11. None of the authors mentions officer commissions specifically, but it is clearly implied that these were equally affected. For a rather grim account of the period of reaction and its antisemitism see Eleonore Sterling, *Er ist wie du. Aus der Frühgeschichte des Antisemitismus in Deutschland (1815–1850)*, Munich 1956, pp. 150–164.

[13] 'Die Juden als Soldaten', *Im deutschen Reich*, VII, No. 1 (January 1901), pp. 3–4, 14; No. 4 (April 1901), pp. 208–210; Julius Kopsch, *Die Juden im deutschen Heer*, Berlin 1910, p. 9; *Allgemeine Zeitung des Judentums*, vol. 71, No. 30 (26th July 1907), p. 352 (hereafter *AZdJ*). It was estimated that approximately 100 Jews were commissioned during the Franco-Prussian War, 60 of them in the Prussian army. Like all statistical data involving Jewish officers, these are, unfortunately, mere approximations because no complete records were kept and not all Jews revealed their religion. See also *Verhandlungen des Reichstags. Stenographische Berichte*, vol. 259, 32nd Session (10th February 1910), p. 1104 (Gothein, who stated that 120 Jewish reserve officers participated in the war of 1870/71); and vol. 264, 136th Session (27th February 1911), p. 4986 (Gröber); ref. hereafter: *Reichstag. Sten. Ber.*

[14] See above, n. 1.

[15] Hamburger, *op. cit.*, p. 38; Max J. Loewenthal, *Das jüdische Bekenntnis als Hinderungsgrund bei der Beförderung zum preussischen Reserveoffizier*, Berlin 1911, pp. 5–8 and *passim*; Max J. Loewenthal, *Jüdische Reserveoffiziere*, Berlin 1914, pp. 5–9 and *passim; Reichstag. Sten. Ber.*, vol. 235, 228th Sess. (19th March 1909), p. 7622 (v. Einem); Martin Kitchen, *The German Officer Corps 1890–1914*, Oxford 1968, p. 39, gives 1878 as the actual cut-off date, but during the ten years of debate on the issue in the *Reichstag* the later date was usually given. Here again the absence of reliable statistical data, coupled with the emotionalism which intruded upon all discussions on the subject, handicap the historian. It should be added that during this period Jewish reserve officers appointed prior to the 1880s still served in the Prussian and other German armies, as well as a number of army (regular) officials with equivalent officer's rank, such as paymasters and veterinarians. The number of these officials dropped between 1895 and 1907 from 38 to 16. Hans Martin Klinkenberg, 'Zwischen Liberalismus und Nationalismus. Im zweiten Kaiserreich (1870–1918)', in *Monumenta Judaica. 2000 Jahre Geschichte und Kultur der Juden am Rhein*. Handbuch, Cologne 1964, pp. 375–376.

[16] See in this connection the excellent and stimulating contributions of Helmut Böhme, Hans Boldt and Michael Stürmer, in Michael Stürmer (ed.), *Das kaiser-*

liche Deutschland. Politik und Gesellschaft 1870–1918, Düsseldorf 1970; and Hans-Ulrich Wehler, *Bismarck und der Imperialismus*, Cologne and Berlin 1969, esp. pp. 105–108, 122, 434–474.

[17] Basic is Eckart Kehr, *Der Primat der Innenpolitik. Gesammelte Aufsätze zur preussisch-deutschen Sozialgeschichte im 19. und 20. Jahrhundert* (ed.), Hans-Ulrich Wehler, Berlin 1965, pp. 53–86. See also Theodor Eschenburg, *Das Kaiserreich am Scheidewege. Bassermann, Bülow und der Block. Nach unveröffentlichten Papieren aus dem Nachlass Ernst Bassermanns*, introduction by Gustav Stresemann, Berlin 1929, p. 31; Morsey, *op. cit.*, p. 263, incl. n. 3; Fritz Hartung, *Deutsche Verfassungsgeschichte. Vom 15. Jahrhundert bis zur Gegenwart*, 6th ed., Stuttgart 1950, p. 301. For the period after 1890 see John C. G. Röhl, 'Higher Civil Servants in Germany, 1890–1900', *Journal of Contemporary History*, vol. 2, No. 3 (1967), pp. 101–121. Much less critical Stolberg-Wernigerode, *op. cit.*, pp. 250–274.

[18] Franz Carl Endres, 'Soziologische Struktur und ihr entsprechende Ideologien des deutschen Offizierkorps vor dem Weltkriege,' *Archiv für Sozialwissenschaft und Sozialpolitik*, vol. 58 (1927), p. 303; Stolberg-Wernigerode, *op. cit.*, pp. 307–310.

[19] Quoted by Craig, *op. cit.*, p. 236. See also the excellent discussion by Manfred Messerschmidt, 'Die Armee in Staat und Gesellschaft—die Bismarckzeit', Stürmer (ed.), *Das kaiserliche Deutschland*, esp. pp. 108–112.

[20] Messerschmidt, *loc. cit.*, p. 103.

[21] Craig, *op. cit.*, pp. 232–238; Kitchen, *op. cit.*, pp. 22–36; Karl Demeter, *Das Deutsche Offizierkorps in Gesellschaft und Staat 1650–1945*, 4th ed., Frankfurt/Main 1965, pp. 19–22 and *passim*. See also the expert's report (*Gutachten*) by Reichsarchivrat Erich O. Volkmann, 'Soziale Heeresmisstände als Mitursache des deutschen Zusammenbruches von 1918', *Die Ursachen des Deutschen Zusammenbruches im Jahre 1918. Das Werk des Untersuchungsausschusses der Verfassunggebenden Deutschen Nationalversammlung und des Deutschen Reichstages 1919–1928. Verhandlungen, Gutachen, Urkunden*, 4. Reihe, 2. Abteilung: *Der Innere Zusammenbruch*, vol. 11, part 2, Berlin 1929, pp. 11–29. Despite its obvious apologetic tenor the report is a devastating indictment of the pre-war officer corps' social exclusiveness and educational backwardness.

[22] Ernst Rudolf Huber, *Deutsche Verfassungsgeschichte seit 1789*. Band IV: *Struktur und Krisen des Kaiserreichs*, Stuttgart–Berlin–Köln–Mainz, p. 531, Huber, *Heer und Staat*, pp. 330–331; Rudolf Schmidt-Bückeburg, *Das Militärkabinett der preussischen Könige und deutschen Kaiser. Seine geschichtliche Entwicklung und staatsrechtliche Stellung 1787–1918*, Berlin 1933, pp. 130–151; Craig, *op. cit.*, pp. 225–232; Ritter, *op. cit.*, II, pp. 150–151; Morsey, *op. cit.*, pp. 236–239; Kehr, *op. cit.*, pp. 78–79, incl. n. 48.

[23] Craig, *op. cit.*, p. 234; Kitchen, *op. cit.*, p. 9, n. 1; pp. 26, 84 and *passim*. See also the chapter on Waldersee in Walter Görlitz, *Der Deutsche Generalstab. Geschichte und Gestalt 1657–1945*, Frankfurt/Main n.d., esp. pp. 140–143; and 'Paul Bronsart v. Schellendorf', *Neue Deutsche Biographie*, II, Berlin 1955, p. 637.

[24] Toury, *Die politischen Orientierungen . . .* , pp. 174 ff., 229–245 and *passim*. A

table showing which Jews were Social Democratic *Reichstag* deputies between 1884 and 1918 is in Hamburger, *op. cit.,* p. 406.

[25] As the literature on German antisemitism has become voluminous, I shall restrict myself to listing only three of the best-known studies which deal with the topic on a broad scale. Some of their general findings have since been supplemented and revised, and much additional research is in progress. Paul W. Massing, *Rehearsal for Destruction. A Study of Political Anti-Semitism in Imperial Germany,* reprint, New York 1967; Peter G. J. Pulzer, *The Rise of Anti-Semitism in Germany and Austria,* New York, London, Sidney 1964; and the penetrating comparative study by Hannah Arendt, *The Origins of Totalitarianism,* Cleveland and New York 1962, esp. Part I. For Paul de Lagarde and Julius Langbehn, two intellectual fathers of modern antisemitism, see Fritz Stern, *The Politics of Cultural Despair. A Study of the Rise of the Germanic Ideology,* Berkeley and Los Angeles 1961.

[26] Two recent studies have treated this particular aspect of German antisemitism thoroughly, searchingly, and convincingly: Hans Rosenberg, *Grosse Depression und Bismarckzeit. Wirtschaftsablauf, Gesellschaft und Politik in Mitteleuropa,* Berlin 1967, pp. 88–117; and Hans-Jürgen Puhle, *Agrarische Interessenpolitik und preussischer Konservatismus im wilhelminischen Reich (1893–1914). Ein Beitrag zur Analyse des Nationalismus in Deutschland am Beispiel des Bundes der Landwirte und der Deutsch-Konservativen Partei,* Hanover 1966/7, pp. 111–140, 298–302. See also Wehler, *Bismarck und der Imperialismus,* pp. 470–474; Adolf Leschnitzer, *Saul und David. Die Problematik der deutsch-jüdischen Lebensgemeinschaft,* Heidelberg 1954, pp. 90–91; and Kampmann, *op. cit.,* pp. 229–232.

[27] Andreas Dorpalen, *Heinrich von Treitschke,* New Haven 1957, pp. 240–247; Kampmann, *op. cit.,* pp. 265–279; Walter Boehlich (ed.), *Der Berliner Antisemitismusstreit,* Frankfurt/Main 1965.

[28] On the *Völkischen* see esp. George L. Mosse, *The Crisis of German Ideology. Intellectual Origins of the Third Reich,* New York 1964, Parts I and II; and Uwe Lohalm, *Völkischer Radikalismus. Die Geschichte des Deutschvölkischen Schutz- und Trutz-Bundes 1919–1923,* Hamburger Beiträge zur Zeitgeschichte Bd. VI, Hamburg 1970, pp. 27–46, where the author traces the pre-war antecedents of the movement.

[29] See in this connection Stanley Zucker, 'Ludwig Bamberger and the Rise of Anti-Semitism in Germany, 1848–1893', *Central European History,* III, No. 4 (December 1970), pp. 332–352; and Dirk Stegmann, *Die Erben Bismarcks. Parteien und Verbände in der Spätphase des Wilhelminischen Deutschlands. Sammlungspolitik 1897–1918,* Cologne and Berlin 1970, pp. 22–24 (on the *Deutschkonservativen*).

[30] Fritz K. Ringer, *The Decline of the German Mandarins. The German Academic Community 1890–1933,* Cambridge, Mass. 1969, pp. 135–139; Kampmann, *op. cit.,* pp. 270–274.

[31] Toury, *Die politischen Orientierungen . . . ,* p. 175, n. 38.

[32] Klinkenberg, *op. cit.,* pp. 322–327.

³³ Initially at least, the decline of the so-called *Radauantisemitismus* generated optimistic notes in the Jewish press. See, for example, *Im deutschen Reich*, VII, No. 1 (January 1901), pp. 23–26, and *AZdJ*, vol. 68, No. 36 (2nd September 1904), p. 422. Yet before long, traditional complaints about antisemitism re-emerged: "Antisemitism in Germany is strong, stronger than in most other civilized states [*Kulturstaaten*]. Equal rights for Jews as laid down by the constitution do not, in reality, exist." *Ibid.*, vol. 71, No. 15 (12th April 1907), pp. 169–170. Similar statements recurred throughout the decade, occasionally interspersed by new notes of optimism whenever an antisemitic agitator was convicted in court for slander, as happened periodically. Few Jews realised at the time that while the vulgar street antisemitism did indeed die down, it reappeared in a somewhat camouflaged but also better organised form among the *Bund der Landwirte*, the *Alldeutschen* and other conservative and/or nationalist pressure groups. See esp. Puhle and Lohalm, cited above, and also Werner Jochmann, 'Die Ausbreitung des Antisemitismus', in *Deutsches Judentum in Krieg und Revolution 1916–1923*. Ein Sammelband herausgegeben von Werner E. Mosse unter Mitwirkung von Arnold Paucker, Tübingen 1971 (Schriftenreihe wissenschaftlicher Abhandlungen des Leo Baeck Instituts 25), pp. 409–510.

³⁴ The *Reichstag* debates between 1904 and 1914 contain numerous complaints of this nature; they were regularly raised whenever the military budget was on the agenda.

³⁵ Klaus Epstein, *Matthias Erzberger and the Dilemma of German Democracy*, Princeton 1959, pp. 69–70.

³⁶ Hamburger, *op. cit.*, p. 32. *Reichstag. Sten. Ber.*, vol. 259, 32nd Sess. (10th Feb. 1910), p. 1104 (Gothein). However, Article 14 of the Prussian Constitution did include some restrictions pertaining to appointments involving supervision of religious affairs. Without so specifying, the Article implied that only Christians could be appointed to positions in the Prussian Ministry of Culture and Religion, for instance. Huber, *op. cit.*, I, p. 402.

³⁷ Such an assertive tone, expressive of mounting Jewish discontent, began to emerge in the Jewish press, e.g., *Im deutschen Reich*, VII, No. 3 (March 1901), pp. 121–126, 162–163; No. 4 (April 1901), pp. 212–222; *AZdJ*, vol. 68, No. 53 (30th December 1904), p. 625, to give but a few examples. It was conceivably in part the reflection of a more widespread trend among Germans at the time to speak out on issues of concern with diminishing restraint, possibly as a result of the repeated defeats which the government had suffered during the late 1890s in trying to pass repressive legislation threatening not merely the SPD. Though this phenomenon should not be exaggerated, a change of tone was noticeable in German public life, both in parliament and the press. This aspect of the period warrants further investigation. See, however, Ernst Deuerlein, *Der Reichstag. Aufsätze, Protokolle und Darstellungen zur Geschichte der parlamentarischen Vertretung des deutschen Volkes 1871–1933*, Bonn 1963, pp. 67–69; and Heinrich Heffter, *Die Deutsche Selbstverwaltung im 19. Jahrhundert. Geschichte der Ideen und Institutionen*, Stuttgart 1950, pp. 759–766.

³⁸ For this and the following brief sketch of the VDJ, see Marjorie Lamberti,

'The Attempt to Form a Jewish Bloc: Jewish Notables and Politics in Wilhelmian Germany', *Central European History*, III, No. 1/2 (March/June 1970), pp. 73–93; Walter Breslauer, 'Der Verband der Deutschen Juden (1904–1922),' *Bulletin des Leo Baeck Instituts*, 7 (1964), No. 28, pp. 345–379; and Jacob Toury, 'Organizational Problems of German Jewry. Steps towards the Establishment of a Central Organization (1893–1920)', in *LBI Year Book XIII* (1968), pp. 57–90.

[39] Breslauer, *loc. cit.*, p. 365.

[40] Craig, *op. cit.*, pp. 136–179 treats the reforms and the constitutional struggle they engendered, as does Gerhard Ritter, *Staatskunst und Kriegshandwerk. Das Problem des "Militarismus" in Deutschland*, I: *Die altpreussische Tradition (1740–1890)*, 2nd ed., Munich 1959, pp. 159–206. Ritter also discusses the reserves (which displaced all but one contingent of the traditional *Landwehr*) in *Staatskunst und Kriegshandwerk*, II, pp. 128–131. See also Alfred Vagts, *A History of Militarism*, rev. ed., New York 1959, pp. 189–195.

[41] Ritter, *op. cit.*, II, p. 129; Endres, *loc. cit.*, pp. 293, 302–303 and *passim*; Kehr, *op. cit.*, pp. 53–63. See also H. Fick, *Der deutsche Militarismus der Vorkriegszeit. Ein Beitrag zur Soziologie des Militarismus*, Potsdam 1932, esp. pp. 45–46, 59–68.

[42] Loewenthal, *Das jüdische Bekenntnis* . . . , pp. 26–36; Ernst v. Eisenhart-Rothe and Franz Schauwecker (eds.), *So war die alte Armee*, Berlin n.d. (ca. 1935), p. 194. See also *AZdJ*, vol. 75, No. 6 (10th February 1911), pp. 63–64, and *Reichstag. Sten. Ber.*, vol. 294, 250th Sess. (6th May 1914), p. 8515 (v. Falkenhayn).

[43] Gustav Hillard (pseud. for Gustav Steinbömer), *Herren und Narren der Welt*, Munich 1954, esp. pp. 135–164; Demeter, *op. cit.*, pp. 116–153 and *passim*; Kitchen, *op. cit.*, pp. 49–63, 115–123; Craig, *op. cit.*, pp. 232–238; Rainer Wohlfeil, 'Die Beförderungsgrundsätze', *Untersuchungen zur Geschichte des Offizierkorps*, p. 26.

[44] Quoted in Demeter, *op. cit.*, p. 22, and Militärgeschichtliches Forschungsamt (ed.), *Offiziere im Bild von Dokumenten aus drei Jahrhunderten. Beiträge zur Militär-und Kriegsgeschichte*, VI, introduction by Manfred Messerschmidt, Stuttgart 1964, p. 82; English translation in Craig, *op. cit.*, p. 235. For the attitude of the reserve officer corps, including their antisemitic tendencies, Kitchen, *op. cit.*, pp. 37–48; Kehr, *op. cit.*, pp. 53–63, esp. pp. 61–63; Endres, *loc. cit.*, 302–304; Ritter, *op. cit.*, II, pp. 128–131; Harry Pross (ed.), *Die Zerstörung der deutschen Politik. Dokumente 1871–1933*, Frankfurt/Main 1959, pp. 33–34; Demeter, *op. cit.*, pp. 217–220. Demeter cites, and accepts as valid, the claim of a German general that the pre-war army was neither philosemitic nor antisemitic (p. 220); this is a rather charitable assessment.

[45] A revealing editorial on this situation, entitled 'Unsere Lage', appeared in *AZdJ*, vol. 69, No. 1 (6th January 1905), pp. 1–2, culminating in the complaint that Jews were still being treated as "third-class citizens" when it came to holding public office. See also above, n. 33.

[46] Breslauer, *loc. cit.*, p. 364.

[47] *Reichstag. Sten. Ber.*, vol. 294, 252nd Sess. (8th May 1914), p. 8566 (Gothein,

who erroneously referred to "Yorck v. Wartenburg"). Reference to this debate also in Hamburger, *op. cit.*, p. 18, and Fischer, *op. cit.*, p. 187. On the problem as such, Leschnitzer, *op. cit.*, pp. 63–65. One German general wrote after the war: "Die Uniform und das Patent als Offizier war [sic] im alten Staat ein Passepartout für das ganze Leben." G. v. Gleich, Generalmajor z.D., *Die alte Armee und ihre Verirrungen. Eine kritische Studie,* 2nd ed., Leipzig 1919, p. 42. This little pamphlet, despite its title, is essentially an apologia of the Prussian/German officer corps.

⁴⁸ Ludwig Haas, *Der deutsche Jude in der Armee,* Berlin 1913, pp. 17, 18. In this address at a meeting of the C.V. organisation in Berlin, Haas spoke both as a Jew and a patriotic German liberal, a position rather representative of German Jewry at the time.

⁴⁹ Ludwig Geiger, *Die deutschen Juden und der Krieg,* Berlin n.d. (1915), p. 64.

⁵⁰ Loewenthal, *Das jüdische Bekenntnis . . . ,* p. 13. *Reichstag. Sten. Ber.,* vol. 198, 50th Sess. (5th March 1904), pp. 1577–1579 (Eickhoff); 51st Sess. (7th March 1904), p. 1614 (Eickhoff).

⁵¹ Toury, *Die politischen Orientierungen . . . ,* pp. 177–212; Lamberti, *loc. cit.,* pp. 79–82, 87–88. On the Progressives see, above all, Huber, *Deutsche Verfassungsgeschichte,* IV, pp. 75–91; Dieter Fricke, *et al.* (eds.), *Die bürgerlichen Parteien in Deutschland. Handbuch der Geschichte der bürgerlichen Parteien und anderer bürgerlicher Interessenorganisationen vom Vormärz bis zum Jahre 1945,* two volumes, Leipzig 1968 and 1970, I, pp. 333–363, 798–806, and II, pp. 69–89; and Thomas Nipperdey, *Die Organisation der deutschen Parteien vor 1918. Beiträge zur Geschichte des Parlamentarismus und der politischen Parteien,* vol. 18, Düsseldorf 1961, pp. 176–240, esp. pp. 201, 234, n. 4. See also Ludwig Bergsträsser, *Geschichte der politischen Parteien in Deutschland,* 8th and 9th rev. ed., Munich 1955, pp. 118–214, *passim,* and Heffter, pp. 747–751 and ff., *passim.* Despite the growing disenchantment, a majority of German Jews seems to have continued to support the Progressives during elections throughout the pre-war period, although this support fluctuated somewhat. According to Toury, *Die politischen Orientierungen . . . ,* p. 192, n. 111, the various Progressive factions received together an estimated 65%–67% of the Jewish vote between 1879 and 1892. During the following decade and a half, this support may have dropped to some extent, with a growing number of Jewish voters either abstaining from elections altogether (*ibid.,* p. 211), or supporting the Social Democrats (*ibid.,* p. 224). Yet after 1907, many Jewish voters seem to have reverted to their traditional policy of supporting the Progressives, a trend which lasted throughout the remaining pre-war period, including the election of 1912 (see *ibid.,* pp. 226–229), although it was accompanied by a simultaneous, albeit not equally strong, support of the Social Democrats by especially the younger generation of German Jews (*ibid.,* p. 224; Toury estimates that 12%–14% of the Jewish voters supported the SPD in 1903, and while implying, on p. 228, that this support may have been somewhat stronger in 1912, he gives no figures for this particular Reichstag election; see also the very similar estimates of Jewish support for SPD and Progressives respectively in Hamburger, *op. cit.,* pp. 147, 162–163).

[52] In 1904 and 1905, the Progressive deputies who spoke on the issue apparently did so without prior consultation with Jewish organisations; this is implied in Loewenthal, *Das jüdische Bekenntnis . . . ,* pp. 13–17. In April 1905, thus after that year's debate on the military budget in the Reichstag, a notice in the Jewish press announced that the recently founded *Verband der Deutschen Juden* would henceforth concern itself with this and related matters. *AZdJ,* vol. 69, No. 14 (7th April 1905), Beilage, p. 1.

[53] Loewenthal, *Das jüdische Bekenntnis . . . ,* pp. 17–18.

[54] *Ibid.,* p. 19; *Reichstag. Sten. Ber.,* vol. 232, 94th Sess. (30th March 1908), pp. 4430, 4431.

[55] Loewenthal, *Das jüdische Bekenntnis . . . ,* pp. 18–26; Loewenthal, *Jüdische Reserveoffiziere,* p. 6, and, for a list of sample cases, pp. 14–18; Geiger, *op. cit.,* p. 63; Breslauer, *loc. cit.,* pp. 360, 364; *Nachlass* Gothein, Bundesarchiv Koblenz, Folder 13, No. 26, 27. Georg Gothein was, on his father's side, of Jewish descent, but this fact does not seem to have been generally known at the time. Other Progressive deputies who spoke frequently on this issue were Julius Kopsch, Ernst Müller-Meiningen, and Otto Mugdan (on Mugdan see below, n. 81).

[56] Kopsch, *op. cit.,* p. 10, gives the figures as 25–30,000; Gothein, in the *Reichstag,* mentioned 20–25,000. *Reichstag. Sten. Ber.,* vol. 259, 32nd Sess. (10th February 1910), p. 1105.

[57] Kopsch, *op. cit.,* p. 10, estimates from 1,200 to 1,500 baptised *Einjährig-Freiwillige,* of whom approximately 300 received commissions. Loewenthal, *Das jüdische Bekenntnis . . . ,* p. 37, claims that in 1911 approximately 30 Christian sons of Jewish parents served as reserve officers in the Prussian army. See also Loewenthal, *Jüdische Reserveoffiziere,* p. 7, which gives the figure as 26; and *AZdJ,* vol. 73, No. 21 (21st May 1909), p. 244, which gives the following figures: 25–30,000 total since 1880, among them 1,200–1,500 baptised, of whom approximately 300 were commissioned.

[58] E.g., Loewenthal, *Das jüdische Bekenntnis . . . ,* pp. 21, 35, and *Reichstag. Sten. Ber.,* vol. 285, 59th Sess. (10th May 1912), p. 1856 (Gothein).

[59] On the complex and constitutionally by no means clear-cut problem regarding relations between War Minister and *Reichstag* see Huber, *Heer und Staat,* pp. 321–324, and by the same author, *Deutsche Verfassungsgeschichte,* IV, pp. 515–528, in particular pp. 527–528. See also Craig, *op. cit.,* 223–224, 228–232; Ritter, *op. cit.,* II, p. 152, who points out that the War Minister was also Prussian plenipotentiary to the *Bundesrat* and chairman of the Committee for Military Affairs in that body; and Schmädeke, *op. cit.,* p. 14. On the Military Cabinet, basic is still Rudolf Schmidt-Bückeburg, *Das Militärkabinett der preussischen Könige und deutschen Kaiser. Seine geschichtliche Entwicklung und staatsrechtliche Stellung 1787–1918,* Berlin 1933, notably pp. 130–240, as well as Huber's two works, *Heer und Staat,* pp. 329–335, and *Deutsche Verfassungsgeschichte,* IV, pp. 530–532. Schmidt-Bückeburg's account is written from a liberal point of view and thus conflicts in interpretation with Huber's *Heer und Staat;* however, Huber's subsequently written *Deutsche Verfassungsgeschichte* is very close to Schmidt-Bückeburg's point of view.

[60] Max Hugo Liebermann von Sonnenberg was from 1890 until his death in 1911

deputy for the antisemitic Deutschsoziale Partei and a prominent *völkisch* agitator. Fricke, *op. cit.*, I, pp. 754–756; but cf. Max Schwarz, *MdR, Biographisches Handbuch der Reichstage*, Hanover 1965, p. 388, who lists him, incorrectly, with the Deutschsoziale Wirtschaftliche Vereinigung; see also Lohalm, *op. cit.*, pp. 58–59, 67–68, and Hellmut v. Gerlach, *Erinnerungen eines Junkers*, Berlin n.d. [1924], pp. 110–112.

[61] *Reichstag. Sten. Ber.*, vol. 198, 50th Sess. (5th March 1904), pp. 1577–1579; 51st Sess. (7th March 1904), pp. 1603–1605, 1614.

[62] *Ibid.*, vol. 203, 170th Sess. (22nd March 1905), pp. 5501–5505; 171st Sess. (23rd March 1905), pp. 5550–5552 (only the exchanges between Eickhoff and v. Einem are cited here).

[63] *Ibid.*, vol. 235, 228th Sess. (19th March 1909), p. 7622.

[64] *Ibid.*, vol. 264, 135th Sess. (25th February 1911), pp. 4967–4968.

[65] *Ibid.*, vol. 259, 32nd Sess. (10th February 1910), p. 1105.

[66] *Ibid.*, vol. 259, 32nd Sess. (10th February 1910), p. 1106; vol. 264, 135th Sess. (25th February 1911), p. 4961. The question whether conversion to Christianity wrought miracles concerning a candidate's Jewish appearance and military qualification as reserve officer was repeatedly brought up, throughout the decade of debates, by various speakers in the Reichstag and by the Jewish press.

[67] *Reichstag. Sten. Ber.*, vol. 294, 252nd Sess. (8th May 1914), p. 8580. Falkenhayn subsequently changed his wording in the stenographic record of the proceedings from "that the situation *is* essentially unconstitutional . . ." to "*seems* unconstitutional" (*ist* to *scheint*), as he admitted to the Progressive deputy Ernst Müller-Meiningen; *Mitteilungen aus dem Verein zur Abwehr des Antisemitismus*, XXIV, No. 10 (20th May 1914), p. 83; Breslauer, *loc. cit.*, pp. 264–265. (Author's italics.)

[68] Loewenthal, *Das jüdische Bekenntnis . . .* , pp. 8–9 (letter of v. Heeringen to the VDJ, dated 12th April 1910). It reflected the War Ministry's official attitude regarding individual cases presented for review.

[69] *Reichstag. Sten. Ber.*, vol. 230, 94th Sess. (4th February 1908), p. 2880 (General Sixt v. Armin, then acting as deputy to War Minister v. Einem). See also the revealing meeting between v. Heeringen and the Budget Committee of the *Reichstag* on 9th April 1913, summarised in Loewenthal, *Jüdische Reserveoffiziere*, pp. 118–125, and Count Westarp's comments on the issue of Jewish reserve officers: "For tactical reasons we therefore stressed in the *Reichstag* the independence [*Freiheit*] of the officer elections, where the War Minister also drew the line, as well as the fact that especially the reserve officers corps would not countenance the election of a Jew." Graf [Kuno v.] Westarp, *Konservative Politik im letzten Jahrzehnt des Kaiserreiches*, I: *Von 1908 bis 1914*, Berlin 1935, p. 299.

Interestingly enough, neither v. Einem in his memoirs nor v. Falkenhayn's biographer mentions the Jewish reserve officer question, although both books discuss relations with the *Reichstag* during their respective terms of office as War Minister. Generaloberst von Einem, *Erinnerungen eines Soldaten 1853–1933*, 6th ed., Leipzig 1933, pp. 64–82; H. von Zwehl, *Erich von Falkenhayn. Eine biographische Studie*, Berlin 1926, pp. 34–50.

[70] When Gothein first introduced the case in the *Reichstag* (*Sten. Ber.*, vol. 285,

59th Sess. [10th May 1912], pp. 1855–1856), he said that L. "has served with the 152nd—I believe Saxon—Regiment." The 152nd Regiment was the Deutsch-Ordens Infanterieregiment, then stationed in East Prussia. Since Lieber addressed his complaints to the local reserve district officer, Colonel Schultze-Klosterfelde (not Schultz-Klosterfelde, as given in the Sten. Record), the 152nd could not have been the unit which Gothein referred to. In all probability it was the 132nd, 1st Unter-Elsässische Infanterieregiment, stationed in Strasbourg, which was part of the 31st Division, whose 61st Brigade, to which the 132nd Inf. Regt. belonged, was commanded by Generalmajor Dernen (not Dern, as given in the Sten. Record). See *Kürschners Staats-, Hof- und Kommunal-Handbuch des Reichs und der Einzelstaaten*, Wilhelm Gier (ed.), Munich [1911], pp. 510, 523, 542. For the debates see *Reichstag. Sten. Ber.*, vol. 285, 59th Sess. (10th May 1912), pp. 1855–1856, 1860, 1868–1869; 60th Sess. (11th May 1912), pp. 1875, 1885, 1901–1904; 69th Sess. (22nd May 1912), pp. 2258–2260, 2262.

71 *AZdJ*, vol. 74, No. 46 (18th Nov. 1910), Beilage, pp. 1–2; No. 47 (25th November 1910), pp. 556–558; No. 48 (2nd December 1910), pp. 568–569; *ibid.*, vol. 75, No. 18 (5th May 1911), Beilage, p. 3; No. 19 (12th May 1911), pp. 217–218; *ibid.*, vol. 77, No. 17 (25th April 1913), p. 194 (speech of Progressive deputy Bruno Ablass in Prussian *Landtag* on Jewish reserve officer); Geiger, *op. cit.*, p. 64; and the petition sent to War Minister v. Heeringen by the VDJ on 24th January 1910, reprinted in Loewenthal, *Das jüdische Bekenntnis . . .* , pp. 5–8. See also the addresses to the C.V. by Kopsch (1910) and Haas (1913), already cited. Kopsch was not a Jew, and neither was Ablass.

72 See, for example, *Reichstag. Sten. Ber.*, vol. 198, 51st Sess. (7th March 1904), p. 1603 (Liebermann v. Sonnenberg); *ibid.*, vol. 203, 171st Sess. (23rd March 1905), p. 5546 (Otto Böckler, *Deutschsoziale Partei*); *ibid.*, vol. 230, 134th Sess. (30th March 1908), p. 4446 (Friedrich Bindewald, *Deutsche Reformpartei*); *ibid.*, vol. 264, 135th Sess. (25th February 1911), pp. 4973–4979, esp. p. 4974 (Friedrich Raab, *Deutschsoziale Partei*); *ibid.*, vol. 290, 166th Sess. (20th June 1913), pp. 5649–5650 (Ferdinand Werner, *Deutschsoziale Partei*).

73 For a challenging recent contribution to the complex interrelationship between religious and racial antisemitism, which often overlapped and interacted, Uriel Tal, *Religious and Anti-Religious Roots of Modern Anti-Semitism*, Leo Baeck Memorial Lecture 14, New York 1971. On the army's traditional attitude in this respect see Fischer, *op. cit., passim*.

74 *Reichstag. Sten. Ber.*, vol. 264, 136th Sess. (27th February 1911), pp. 5006–5007 (Ulrich v. Oertzen, *Deutsche Reichspartei); ibid.*, vol. 289, 133rd Sess. (7th April 1913), pp. 4534–4535 (Eduard v. Liebert, *Deutsche Reichspartei*); and *ibid.*, vol. 290, 164th Sess. (18th June 1913), pp. 5591–5592 (Albrecht v. Graefe, *Deutschkonservative Partei*).

75 On Gröber, see Epstein, *op. cit.*, pp. 39–41.

76 *Ibid.*, p. 69.

77 *Ibid.*, p. 402; Kurt Tucholsky, *Gesammelte Werke*, I, Hamburg 1960, p. 441 ("Erzberger"); *Reichstag. Sten. Ber.*, vol. 290, 166th Sess. (20th June 1913), p. 5655.

[78] See the statistical tables in Segall, *op. cit.*, p. 30, and Klinkenberg, *loc. cit.*, pp. 371–372; see also above, n. 51.

[79] The two principal Social Democratic deputies who from 1911 on participated in the debates on the issue were Georg Schöpflin and Heinrich Schulz, both very capable and effective speakers. Short sketches of their lives in Franz Osteroth, *Biographisches Lexikon des Sozialismus*, I: *Verstorbene Persönlichkeiten*, Hanover 1960, pp. 270, 277–279. Prior to 1911, the only Social Democratic deputy who spoke on this matter in the *Reichstag* was Georg Ledebour, in March 1905.

[80] *Reichstag. Sten. Ber.*, vol. 290, 165th Sess. (19th June 1913), pp. 5637–5640; 160th Sess. (20th June 1913), pp. 5648–5652, 5656–5658. Strictly speaking, Bernstein had not been authorised to touch on the issue at all. The SPD deputy assigned to speak for the party during the debate on the military budget, which included discussion on the Jewish reserve officer, had been Georg Schöpflin. Bernstein's assignment had been "freedom of speech" (*Sicherung der Gesinnungsfreiheit*). See the notes on the SPD *Fraktionssitzung* of 11th June 1913, in Erich Matthias and Eberhard Pikart (eds.), *Die Reichstagsfraktion der deutschen Sozialdemokratie 1898–1918*, vol. 3/I of *Quellen zur Geschichte des Parlamentarismus und der politischen Parteien*, Erste Reihe, Düsseldorf 1966, p. 298.

[81] Like Bernstein, Waldstein spoke on 20th June 1913. In 1908 and 1910, the baptised Progressive deputy Dr. Otto Mugdan, a physician, had also participated in the debate. For personal data on Waldstein and Mugdan see Hamburger, *op. cit.*, pp. 364–367.

[82] Jews, by and large, were traditionally reluctant to speak in parliament on Jewish concerns (*in eigener Sache*), the few Jewish deputies of middle-class parties because they considered themselves primarily Germans who happened to be Jewish, those in the ranks of the SPD (most of whom listed themselves officially as having no religious affiliation) because they saw themselves first and foremost as Socialists and were generally disinclined to support Jewish causes. See Toury, *Die politischen Orientierungen . . .*, pp. 150–151, 231 and *passim*; a more fundamental treatment in Hamburger, *op. cit.*, pp. 410–413.

[83] Despite the fact that Bavaria was the only German state which before 1914 permitted Jews, including Jews from Prussia and other North German states, to become reserve officers in the Bavarian army, antisemitism was by no means negligible in the Bavarian officer corps. See Hermann Rumschöttel, 'Bildung und Herkunft der bayerischen Offiziere 1866 bis 1914. Zur Geschichte von Mentalität und Ideologie des bayerischen Offizierkorps', *Militärgeschichtliche Mitteilungen*, 2/70, pp. 95–96 and Documents 10 and 11, pp. 127–129; see also *AZdJ*, vol. 74, No. 32 (12th August 1910), p. 375. For figures, aside from those listed in Document 11 (Rumschöttel article), see Kitchen, *op. cit.*, p. 46, and *K.C. Blätter*, IV, No. 2 (1st November 1913), pp. 32–33. The number of Jewish reserve officers in the Bavarian army during the first decade of the twentieth century ranged between 50 and 100.

[84] *Reichstag. Sten. Ber.*, vol. 289, 144th Sess. (19th April 1913), pp. 4929–4931. The first resolution (IIa, No. 900) had been moved by the Budget Committee. It asked the Reich Chancellor to submit to the Reichstag an annual statistical report

on the promotion of *Einjährig-Freiwillige* to reserve officer status, listing their religious affiliations. The second (No. 417), was a Progressive motion which demanded that personal ability should be the only criterion for army promotions. The third (No. 425), moved by the SPD, asked the Reich Chancellor to enjoin the army not to discriminate against anybody because of his creed or political conviction. See also Loewenthal, *Jüdische Reserveoffiziere,* pp. 11–12, 135. For the reaction to the Bundesrat's reply to the Reichstag see *Reichstag. Sten. Ber.,* vol. 294, 249th Sess. (5th May 1914), p. 8468; 250th Sess. (6th May 1914), pp. 8513–8514; 252nd Sess. (8th May 1914), pp. 8564–8565; and *ibid.,* vol. 295, 252nd Sess. (8th May 1914), pp. 8591–8592.

[85] Breslauer, *loc. cit.,* pp. 364–365; *Deutsche Israelitische Zeitung,* XXXI, No. 14/15 (9th April 1914), p. 16; on petitions and protest meetings see above, n. 71.

[86] On *Liebesmahle* see Hillard, *op. cit.,* pp. 140–146.

[87] I am aware that this general statement must be qualified by the additional comments that Jewish-Gentile social relations were complex; that they differed widely in nature and degree; that Jews living in villages and small towns faced different problems in this connection from those encountered by the great majority of German Jews dwelling in the big cities; and, finally, that compared to the situation in 1850, or even 1871, much quiet progress has been made in this respect on the part of many individual Jews. I intend to treat this particular aspect in greater depth in a future publication now in progress. For a brief sketch of the Jewish community in Berlin see Gerhard Masur, *Imperial Berlin,* New York and London 1970, pp. 109–118 and *passim.*

[88] Haas, *op. cit.,* p. 9.

5

Higher Civil Servants in Germany, 1890–1900

JOHN C. G. RÖHL

In the last two or three decades of the nineteenth century, the scope of governmental activity began to increase at an unprecedented rate in the advanced countries of Europe and North America. As it did so, as governments came to intervene more and more in the day-to-day lives of individuals, demands for a thorough reform of recruitment methods to the higher branches of the civil service grew more insistent. In Britain, France, and the United States, patronage had to make way for recruitment by competition, for it was intolerable that the affairs of a modern industrialized society should be in the hands of men who might not be able to read or write.[1] In Germany the problem was the very reverse. Ever since the days of Frederick William I, Prussia had recruited talented commoners to the bureaucracy. Frederick the Great had set up a Commission to test aspirants to public office, and candidates were expected to have a university education and to pass two or even three examinations. The late-eighteenth-century Prussian law code, *Allgemeines Landrecht,* laid down that 'no-one must receive a post who is not sufficiently qualified and has not given proof of his ability. Whoever has achieved office through bribery or other impermissible means must be dismissed forthwith'. 'Public offices are open to all who have the talent thereto', read clause 4 of the Prussian Constitution of 1850, 'provided they fulfil the conditions laid down by the law'. By the time Bismarck united Germany and transferred the Prussian tradition to the Reich administration, candidates had to study jurisprudence for three years at university, undergo a four-year training period in the law courts, and pass two stiff civil service examinations before qualifying for the higher grade of the civil service. The problem in Germany was not insufficient education, but an excess of education, or rather of education of the wrong kind.

For the character of German society was rapidly changing. When the Reich was founded, two-thirds of its population lived and worked in the countryside; by 1914 two-thirds lived in the towns. The peasants who went to work in the factories became politically conscious, joined the trade unions, and voted for the Social-Democratic Party, which by 1890 had become the largest single party; in 1912 it received no less than one-third of the votes cast. Other sections of the community were also organizing with a view to participating in politics. The Conservatives adopted 'demagogy' at a conference in 1892. The Agrarian League, founded in 1893, soon had a membership of some 200,000. The Navy League, founded by Krupp in 1898, had a million members by 1906. There were nearly 5000 ex-servicemen's clubs in 1889 with a combined membership of over 400,000. Nine years later there were 19,626 such clubs with a membership of 1,613,962.[2] At the same time the bureaucracy was playing an ever greater part in the life of every citizen. The amount of money spent by the Reich Office of the Interior jumped from eight million marks in 1890 to 108 million in 1914. The length of railway owned and administered by the Prussian State rose from under 5000 kilometres in 1878 to over 25,000 in 1890, and over 37,000 in 1910. It was only natural that people should question whether a bureaucracy composed almost entirely of lawyers was really in keeping with contemporary needs.

The first breach in the old system of recruitment came, after mounting public pressure, in 1879. By a law of that year, implemented in Prussia in 1883, those graduates in jurisprudence who aspired to a post in the higher civil service had to spend only two (instead of four) years practising at a law court; the rest of the four-year probationary period was to be spent gaining practical experience in one of the provincial administrative bodies *(Ober-präsident, Regierungspräsident,* or *Landrat).* Candidates could then sit the second civil service examination and, if successful, enter one of the Reich or Prussian central departments on a provisional basis until a permanent post fell vacant.[3] This reform did little to satisfy the critics inside or outside the executive. Bismarck, who once remarked that a dozen civil servants should be shot every three years to keep the others on their toes, talked shortly before his dismissal of further reforms to turn the bureaucrats into 'educated Europeans'.[4] In 1895 Johannes Miquel, the dynamic Prussian Finance Minister who had earlier been a banker and brilliant parliamentarian, complained of 'hair-raising gaps' in the education of most civil servants. He proposed reducing the training period in the law courts to one year, and raising that in the provincial administration to three. He also demanded that at university candidates should be required to study the social sciences, economics, and administrative law in addition to theoretical law. Miquel was opposed by Chancellor Hohenlohe, who denied that a legal education encouraged narrow-mindedness and pointed to himself and his colleagues as living proof of his view. He went so far as to claim that the pre-1879 system was ideal, as it ensured greater mobility between the bureaucracy and the entire legal profession, and thus enabled the civil service to recruit its members from a wider range.[5] A committee set up under the under-secretary in the Prussian Ministry of the Interior recommended only minor changes to the existing system. At university, there should be compulsory lectures on administrative law, economics, and fiscal policy, and students should be given the chance to attend seminars on practical problems in the vacations. In line with Miquel's proposals, the committee recommended the reduction of the period spent in the law courts to one year. The remaining three years were to be spent in the provincial administration, including at least three months with an urban council. Another report, completed in 1900, proposed more radical changes. The university course should be extended from six to seven semesters, only three of which would be concerned with jurisprudence and the rest with more practical subjects. In addition, a Civil Service Academy should be set up at which all aspirants to the higher bureaucracy would have to spend at least one year. To broaden the outlook of civil servants already in office, lectures and seminars should be arranged on economics and other subjects. Finally, the report strongly recommended greater flexibility in recruitment, and above all the appointment of able men from the universities, from agriculture, and from industry.[6] The Bill introduced in 1902, which eventually passed into law in 1906, was more in line with the recommendations of the first committee than with those of the second. The university course was left at three years, though some knowledge of economics and political science now became a requirement. The training period, too, was left at its former length of four years, but the time spent at a law court was now reduced to one year (and in some cases only nine months), while that in the administration was extended to three years. This system survived until 1920, when further piecemeal changes were made.

The civil servants who administered the most dynamic society in Europe were thus trained lawyers with little or no practical experience of the world. As Herman Finer put it:

> The training of future officials and their selection had in process of time ceased to keep pace with the demands of the modern State. Law had become divorced from its origin and its purpose, and a narrow and pedantic formalism had invaded a field in which pre-eminently the truth of real life is essential.[7]

Young men entering the administrative branch of the German civil service were already approaching thirty years of age—five or six years older than their British counterparts. The general narrowness of vision which the system produced was further encouraged by the fact that about a quarter of the men appointed to public office had taken a doctorate in jurisprudence.[8] In the technical departments especially there was a desperate need for men 'who were not exhausted after many years of legal studies and out of touch with practical needs'.[9] Yet the number of those appointed to the central Prussian and Reich departments without a training in law was insignificant. Dr Hugo Thiel of the Prussian Ministry of Agriculture had begun life as a farmer, had taken a doctorate of philology at Bonn university, and had then become a lecturer in Agriculture and National Economy at the Darmstadt and Munich Polytechnics. In 1879, at the age of 40, he became a *Vortragender Rat* at the Ministry. Professor Post, a chemist at Göttingen university until 1891, became increasingly interested in questions of public health and was called into the Prussian Ministry of Trade by the progressive Minister, Freiherr von Berlepsch. There was considerable resistance within the bureaucracy itself to such outside appointments, as Hohenlohe discovered when he tried to appoint a Bavarian university professor to the secretariat of the Prussian Ministry of State.

> *Whoever has not been a Prussian* Landrat, *Prussian* Regierungsrat, *etc., for the required number of years cannot enter this sanctuary ... If the Reich Chancellor and even His Majesty fail in the attempt to appoint an able and decent man to the Prussian bureaucracy, then I must concede defeat and record with dismay that the bureaucracy is more powerful than the Kaiser and the Chancellor.* [10]

Rules for entry into the consular and diplomatic services were less rigid. The 1867 Law on Federal Consulates laid down that apart from the normal civil service examinations there should be another method of entry designed 'to attract good men from other professions into the consular service'. A special examination could be taken by men who had not qualified in the usual way. An official handbook published in 1896 pointed out that in the consular service 'practical experience is more important than in any other branch of the Reich service', since its function was 'to encourage trade, commerce and shipping abroad'. It advised aspirants to learn Turkish, Arabic, and other oriental languages in addition to the European languages which were an entrance requirement. In the final examination, jurisprudence carried little weight. Candidates had to demonstrate their knowledge of history 'with special reference to Germany', and of the geography of 'the main countries and peoples of the earth, their forms of government, population, produce, trade, industry, financial position and colonies'. A good grounding in economics, with a knowledge of the development of the discipline since Adam Smith, was also essential.[11] Similarly, a degree in jurisprudence was not a requirement for entry into the diplomatic corps. A memorandum of 1908 on recruitment to the Foreign Office said only that 'a sound education' was necessary; those who did not have a degree would be required to spend five instead of four years on probation, and to attend lectures in history, economics, international law, finance, and commerce. In the final examination there were papers in English and French, and some of the essays written in the examination room had to be written in these two languages. The oral examination in history and geography was likewise conducted in French and English. The main requirement, however, was 'the possession of qualities essential in diplomacy', and the Chancellor was entirely free to decide what these qualities were, and who did or did not possess them.[12]

Noble birth was almost essential for service in the embassies: the only ambassadors of bourgeois origin were those in Peru, Venezuela, Colombia, and Siam. In 1914, the German foreign service consisted of eight Princes, 29 Counts, 20 Barons, 54 untitled nobles, and only 11 commoners.[13] Alexander von Hohenlohe, who was noted for his liberal opinions, justified the predominance of the aristocracy in the diplomatic corps on the grounds that noblemen were acquainted with the outside world to a greater degree than commoners. It was certainly true that young aristocrats who aspired to serve in the diplomatic corps were often more widely-travelled than their middle-class rivals. Most of them, furthermore, had foreign wives: in 1891 only one of Germany's ambassadors—Prince Reuss in Vienna—was married to a German, and the proportion among the younger diplomats was similar.[14] Those commoners who entered the service were mainly the sons of great industrialists or rich traders, many of whom had in fact acquired a title through their wealth and influence. Membership of one of the 'feudal' student corps—especially the *Borussen* in Bonn, the *Saxo-Borussen* in Heidelberg, and the *Sachsen* in Göttingen—was as important a precondition of entry into the diplomatic service as having a commission in one of the Guards regiments. The consular service, on the other hand, was wholly middle class, though even here it was useful to have studied at the right university, joined the right student corps, and to have a sizable income.[15]

The stiffness of the entrance requirements for all departments other than the Foreign Office might lead one to suppose that talent was the only criterion. This was far from being the case. In contrast to the British system, the Prussian (and therefore also the Imperial) system of recruitment was not *open* competition. The Government made extensive use of its right to refuse to appoint qualified candidates for political or other reasons. Conservatives might have liked to recall Hegel's words that the Prussian system guaranteed 'to every citizen the chance of joining the class of civil servants', but in practice more than half of those citizens were excluded for reasons which had nothing to do with their ability.

Only with regard to regional origin was an attempt made to achieve a kind of proportional representation in public appointments. An elaborate system operated to ensure that each of the larger states in the Reich received a number of places in the Imperial bureaucracy in keeping with its size. Hohenlohe once insisted on the appointment of a Saxon to a vacancy in the Reich Treasury because 'the number of Saxons in the higher Reich civil service is disproportionately small'.[16] Caprivi refused to appoint a Hanoverian as Secretary of the Reich Justice Office as there were already two Hanoverians on the committee drafting the *Bürgerliches Gesetzbuch*.[17] When Huber left the Reich Office of the Interior in 1895, care was taken to put another Württemberger in his place. Similarly, when Berchem, a Bavarian, was dismissed as under-secretary of the Foreign Office, another Bavarian, Rotenhan, replaced him. In the Reichsgericht, the Supreme Court in Leipzig, all posts were allocated on a quota basis, and when Prussia tried to secure for herself one of the four posts reserved for Württemberg, the non-Prussian states prevented the change in the Bundesrat.[18]

Nothing reveals more clearly the fragility of the Second Reich than this constant preoccupation with the rights of the states. It was perhaps understandable that most Bavarians should have 'displayed some estrangement' when Count Berchem decided to enter the Foreign Office in 1871. That such resentment should still have been smouldering a quarter of a century later was most disconcerting, and gave rise to strong fears that the Reich would disintegrate if put to the test.[19] Yet Marschall von Bieberstein could at first turn down the Foreign Secretaryship in 1890 because he feared that the Prussian civil servants in Berlin would be offended by the appointment of a young non-Prussian.[20] And Buchenberger, the Baden Finance Minister, refused to become Secretary of the Reich Treasury on the grounds that he detested the Prussian landowners and would in turn be disliked as a South German with a middle-class name.[21] Those non-Prussians who were appointed were carefully vetted for signs of particularism. Chancellor Caprivi had to be assured, when considering a Bavarian for the Justice Office in 1892, that the man in question

> is politically gut deutsch, *stands firmly in support of Kaiser and Reich and is free of all particularist leanings. Indeed, if he has such leanings at all they are more of the black-and-white [i.e. Prussian] than the blue-and-white [Bavarian] variety. For during his nearly 20 years of service in Berlin he has grown close to Prussia.* [22]

Such screening did little to remove the mutual hostility between Prussians and non-Prussians in Berlin. When the South German Prince Hohenlohe was made Chancellor in 1894, a South German baroness living in Berlin predicted an outcry among the Prussians:

> *A Bavarian Catholic as Chancellor and Prussian Minister-President, a Protestant Bavarian (Rotenhan) in the Foreign Office, a Badener as Secretary of the latter, and a Württemberger as Statthalter [of Alsace-Lorraine]—that will cause a pretty outburst among the dyed-in-the-wool Prussians.*[23]

After four years in office, Hohenlohe was still struck by the vast gulf between him and 'the Prussian Excellencies'.

> *South German liberalism is helpless against the junkers. They are too numerous, too powerful, and have the throne and the army on their side . . . My task here is to keep Prussia attached to the Reich. For all these gentlemen despise the Reich and would sooner be rid of it today than tomorrow.* [24]

In sharp contrast to the desire of the Government to allocate a fair share of the Reich posts to non-Prussian citizens was its attitude towards Catholics and Jews. Almost one-third of Germany's population was Catholic, yet Catholics were virtually excluded from holding high office either in the Reich or in the Prussian bureaucracy. One Catholic publicist, collecting statistics on the 'parity' question in 1899, established 'that the proportion of Catholics employed in public office falls as the importance of the post increases, so that hardly any Catholics are to be found in the highest positions'.[25] Another calculated (not entirely accurately) that out of a total of 90 Chancellors, Reich Secretaries, and Prussian Ministers to hold office in the period 1888–1914, only seven were Catholics.[26] Of the men appointed in the 1890s, the Chancellor Hohenlohe, the Secretaries of Justice Hanauer and Nieberding, and the Prussian Minister of Justice Schönstedt were Catholic, but Hohenlohe had stood on the Liberal side in the *Kulturkampf* and Schönstedt had married a Protestant and allowed his children to be brought up in the Lutheran faith.

In the body of the bureaucracy the situation was if anything worse. At the end of the decade, there were four Directors, 25 *Vortragende Räte* and 20 *Hilfsarbeiter* in the Foreign Office; of these, two *Vortragende Räte* and three *Hilfsarbeiter* were members of the Roman Church. In the other Reich Offices I could discover only two Catholics—Seckendorff of the Justice Office and Wackerzapp of the Railway Office—though there may have been one or two others. In recommending Seckendorff as head of the Ministry of State secretariat in 1899, Hohenlohe wrote of his 'unconditional reliability', and added: 'The fact that he is a Catholic does not affect this judgment, as he is a declared opponent of the Centre [Catholic] party.' In the Prussian bureaucracy the most notorious department was the Ministry of the Interior, where the only Catholic was a messenger boy. One Minister, Hammerstein, was so anxious to appoint members of his student corps *Vandalia* that people spoke of the invasion of Berlin by the Vandals. In the Finance Ministry there was only one Catholic, Vagedes, 'of whose loyalty and reliability there are no doubts whatever'.[27] In the Ministry of Ecclesiastical Affairs and Education, in whose activities the Catholics were more than usually interested, there were two Catholic civil servants, Ludwig Renvers and Adolph Förster. The latter, whose '*staatstreue Gesin-*

nung is beyond question', would have been made a Director in 1899 if he had been a Protestant. In 1902, when his promotion became inescapable, an elaborate reshuffle was executed to avoid putting him in charge of the schools department.[28] The only Ministry in which some degree of religious parity was achieved was Agriculture, where the under-secretary and four of the *Vortragende Räte* were Catholics. There was some talk in the early 1890s of appointing a member of the Centre party as Minister of Agriculture, but the idea was shelved. In 1911, Klemens von Schorlemer-Lieser, one of the very few Catholic *Oberpräsidenten*, was made Minister of Agriculture.

If Catholics were the least educated sector of the German population, the most educated were the Jews. For every 100,000 males of each denomination in Prussia, 33 Catholics, 58 Protestants, and 519 Jews became university students.[29] Though they made up less than one per cent of the population, Jews should have had far more than that percentage of public offices if recruitment had been based on the merit system alone, and if the Law of 1869 which guaranteed that appointments would be made irrespective of religious denomination had not been a dead letter. In practice it was almost as difficult for an unbaptised Jew to enter the higher civil service as to become an army officer. Bülow appointed the last of the German Rothschilds to a minor diplomatic post after he had failed to enter the army, and incurred the hostility of the otherwise liberal Holstein for so doing.[30] When the banker Bernhard Dernburg was appointed head of the Colonial Office, Holstein strongly advised Bülow against appointing 'more non-professional civil servants, especially Semites', because it would undermine public confidence in the bureaucracy. In 1908 Holstein noted with satisfaction that 'Dernburg has remained the only wedge'.[31] Baptised Jews could enter both the army and the higher bureaucracy, including the Foreign Office. As Alexander Hohenlohe observed in his Memoirs (p. 328):

> *If the father or grandfather had allowed himself to be baptised . . . and if the son had refurbished the tarnished glory of some noble family with his inherited wealth by marrying one of the daughters, then people were prepared to disregard his race so long as this was not all-too-obvious in his facial features.*

Nevertheless, even the Christian of Jewish origin was seldom allowed to forget that origin. Dr Paul Kayser, the tutor of Bismarck's children and Director of the Colonial Department of the Foreign Office, came under vicious attack from anti-semites like Ahlwardt. In 1891 he wrote to an uncle with some bitterness: 'I take all this trouble only to get insulted and to prepare a comfortable place for my Aryan successor'.[32] Heinrich Friedberg, the brilliant Minister of Justice of the later Bismarck era, was depressed after the accession of Wilhelm II because 'he knows that the Kaiser does not protect Semites'.[33] Dr Karl Julius von Bitter, once a civil servant in the Ministry of the Interior and then *Regierungspräsident* in Silesia, was turned down as Minister of the Interior in 1895 because of 'his still somewhat Semitic tendencies'. Most Ministers and the Kaiser were prepared to accept him in 1896 as Minister of Trade, but Hohenlohe prevented his appointment because he was 'an ambitious Jew (*ein jüdischer Streber*)'.[34] Even men whose Jewish ancestry was remote were regarded with some suspicion. Schelling, the arch-conservative Justice Minister, was referred to by Holstein as a '*Semitenmischling*'. Count Berchem, a Catholic whose mother was Jewish, was said by Holstein to be 'inclined to flaunt his Catholic tendencies so as to obscure the fact of his Jewish blood'.[35] Philipp Eulenburg once suggested that it would be to Prussia's advantage if Berchem became Barvarian Prime Minister, as his Jewish blood would make him totally unacceptable in Court circles in Vienna. In 1892, when Hanauer (another Bavarian Catholic) was being considered for the Reich Justice Office, an ex-Secretary of that Office assured the Chancellor that Hanauer was not a Jew. 'His external appearance and name admittedly indicate a Jewish origin. However, that must lie a long way back, for the family is said to be a well-known Catholic one and Hanauer's wife is of noble birth'.[36]

Social-Democrats and even the sons of known Social-Democrats were excluded from the bureaucracy automatically. In view of the long training period and the expensive education necessary for entry into the higher civil service, there was in any case little opportunity for factory workers and others without private means to become contenders for a place. In 1889, when Wilhelm II suggested lowering the entrance requirements for high schools, Hohenlohe protested that that would lead to the creation of an 'educated proletariat'.[37] Most of the internal memoranda on entrance to the civil service stressed that throughout the four-year probationary period there must be neither payment of any kind (not even expenses) nor a promise of eventual appointment. To embark on a public career without adequate financial support was foolhardy. Kirschner, the head of the Bundesrat secretariat (a post in the middle grade), got as far as the *Referendar* stage before being forced by lack of means to abandon the attempt to enter the higher grade.[38] The civil servant's salary was not commensurate with his social obligations. A *Vortragender Rat* generally earned under 10,000 marks, a Director 15,000, and a State Secretary 24,000. The Chancellor himself received only 54,000 marks, which was less than half the amount earned by a top ambassador.

If capable men were nonetheless attracted to a career in the bureaucracy, this was because of the prestige which holding high office conferred. After the army officer no-one was more respected in Wilhelmine Germany than the higher civil servant. To the educated middle classes a career in the bureaucracy could bring rank, decorations, perhaps ennoblement, and in exceptional cases political power. Social advancement for one's family was another important motive for joining the civil service. Upward social mobility was naturally greatest where, as in the case of the Wilmowski family, both father and son held high office in the bureaucracy. The family, which had moved from Silesia to Brandenburg in the seventeenth century, was relatively undistinguished (there was only one estate) until Karl von Wilmowski became head of the Civil Cabinet in 1870. On retiring in 1888 he received the title of Freiherr for himself and his heirs. His son Kurt served in the Franco-Prussian war, passed the second civil service examination in 1876, and, after some years in the provincial administration, became a *Vortragender Rat* in the Ministry of Agriculture. In 1894, on Bennigsen's suggestion, he had become head of Hohenlohe's Reich Chancellery. Soon after the Chancellor's retirement he was made *Oberpräsident* first of Schleswig-

Holstein and then of his native province of Prussian Saxony. He ended his career as leader of the Conservatives in the Prussian House of Lords, and his son Tilo married Barbara Krupp herself.[39]

There were, of course, some who were not satisfied with prestige. Ludwig Raschdau, a member of the Foreign Office, married a rich Jewish widow some twenty years his senior. 'My salary', he explained afterwards, 'enabled me to live comfortably enough, and I was even able to save a little. But with my marriage my financial position became what most people would term brilliant . . . I was now able to develop my naturally independent character to the full. From now on I really was a completely free man.'[40] Others jumped from the bureaucracy into industry and back again. Karl Jacobi became under-secretary in the Ministry of Trade in 1879. Two years later he gave up that post to become chairman of the Prussian Land Credit Bank. In 1886 he returned to the Ministry of Trade. A few months later Bismarck made him Secretary of the Treasury. After a further two years he left the bureaucracy for good, returned to the Land Credit Bank, and also joined the board of the Disconto-Gesellschaft and the Norddeutsche Bank. Similarly, General Budde, head of the railways department of the General Staff, left this post to become a director of a big armaments firm and several other concerns because this would 'guarantee him an income of 150,000 marks'.[41] He returned to the public service two years later as Minister of Public Works.

Stock exchange speculation was frowned upon but not disallowed. Freiherr von Broich, born on a large estate near Aachen, became first a *Landrat* and then a *Hilfsarbeiter* in the secretariat of the Prussian Ministry of State. He inherited 600,000 marks and began to found a series of companies designed to rescue 'civil servants, officers, and landowners from the clutches of usurers'. When the first such venture ran into difficulties, Broich unsuccessfully asked for backing from the Society of German Aristocrats (*Deutsche Adelsgenossenschaft*) and the Ministry of the Interior. He invested his entire wealth in the Pioneer Company, which had similar aims, and was by 1897 in debt to the tune of 32,000 marks. Hohenlohe repaid some of this debt from the funds at the Crown's disposal. By this time, Broich's superiors were showing signs of unease. When he asked for permission to join the board of the newly founded German Land Bank—one of the Ministers described it as 'a capitalist undertaking masquerading as an enterprise beneficial to the whole community'—the Government refused on principle. In 1898, Broich asked Brefeld, the Minister of Public Works, to help him out of his difficulties by recommending him to the Bleichröder Bank. The Minister refused to do this but did write a letter expressing complete faith in Broich and the Pioneer Company. Broich thereupon resigned from the civil service to devote himself to speculation. In 1900 the Ministers discovered that he was using Brefeld's letter to borrow huge sums of money from disreputable moneylenders, and promising to use his influence with the Government to secure honours for them in return. Some of the Ministers wanted to institute legal proceedings, but the majority felt that this would create too much of a scandal. Brefeld's letter was retrieved, and Broich was forced to retire from the Pioneer Company by its board of directors.[42]

The landowning aristocracy showed little interest in a career in the central bureaucracy. Apart from the diplomatic service, they were mainly attracted to the Prussian provincial administration. Qualifications for entry into this branch of the bureaucracy were very much lower: candidates had to reside in the locality for at least one year, and to have spent four years either as a *Referendar* or as an elected official. The discrepancy between the salary and the obligations which went with a post in the field was far greater than in Berlin. A *Landrat* would receive about 6,000 marks a year, but would be expected to entertain some 200 guests and to pay the salary of a dozen or so assistants. It was in any case Government policy to appoint the highest possible number of conservative aristocrats to these posts.[43] In 1891, 62 per cent of the *Landräte* were of noble birth. Of the appointments made in the years 1888–1891, 62 per cent of the *Oberpräsidenten*, 73 per cent of the *Regierungspräsidenten*, and 83 per cent of the Police Directors were noble.[44] Twenty years later the situation had not changed. All but one of the 12 *Oberpräsidenten* were aristocratic, as were 23 of the 37 *Regierungspräsidenten* and 268 of the 481

Landräte. Entirely different was the position of the nobility in the Berlin offices. Of the 126 *Vortragende Räte* and Directors who worked in the Reich Offices (excluding the Foreign Office) in the period 1867–90, only 14 were noble.[45] Of the 86 higher civil servants in the same Offices in February 1895, no more than twelve were of noble birth, and the percentage of nobles working in the Prussian Ministries was less than 13.[46] A considerable gulf separated the officials in Berlin from those in the provinces. 'How is it possible for us to pursue liberal policies?' one statesman was heard to ask. 'We find ourselves in an iron net of conservative administrators'.[47] The Bavarian ambassador reported in 1903 that a Chancellor who wished to work with a Liberal majority in the Reichstag would have to begin by re-staffing the entire Prussian provincial administration, since the *Landräte* and *Regierungspräsidenten* would refuse to carry out a policy to which they were opposed.[48]

Unless they were members of the Bundesrat (this included the Ministers and State Secretaries, and the under-secretaries of certain departments), all civil servants had a constitutional right to seek election to parliament, and in the early years of the Reich many of them did so. In the first Reichstag there were 35 civil servants in the National Liberal party alone, and in the second no fewer than 51. From the end of the 1870s, the number of parliamentary civil servants began to fall. There were 17 in the 1890 Reichstag, 12 in the 1893 Reichstag, 7 in the 1898 Reichstag, and only one in the 1903 Reichstag. The number sitting in the Prussian House of Deputies was higher until 1899. Virtually all these parliamentary civil servants were members of the Prussian provincial administration. No more than two central civil servants sat in the Reichstag at any one time. Brauchitsch and Bitter, both of the Prussian Ministry of the Interior, were Reichstag members in the late 1880s. In the 1890 Reichstag, the only central civil servant was Freiherr von Gamp, a *Vortragender Rat* of the Ministry of Trade. He was joined in 1893 by Bernstorff of Ecclesiastical Affairs; both were members of the Free Conservative party.

With the growth of mass politics in the 1890s, the presence of civil servants in the parliaments became an embarrassment to the

Government. Many civil servants had been disciplined during the
Prussian constitutional conflict of the 1860s, and Bismarck had
had to issue a stern warning in 1882 to the effect that civil servants in and out of parliament must toe the official line, but it was
in the post-Bismarck decade that the question caused the greatest
trouble. In October 1891 Caprivi failed to persuade the Prussian
Ministers that public servants should be made to give up their
parliamentary seats before accepting a position in the *central*
departments. He did instruct the State Secretaries to tell future
recruits to the Reich Offices that they were being appointed on
condition that 'they renounce the right to accept a seat in any
parliament for as long as they remain in one of the central offices'.[49] In December 1893, during a Reichstag debate on a trade
treaty, von Colmar, the *Regierungspräsident* of Lüneburg, voted
against the Government, and Gamp of the Ministry of Trade
shouted insulting remarks throughout the Chancellor's speech.
Caprivi complained afterwards that Gamp was becoming 'the
leader of the opposition to the trade treaties in the Free Conservative party'. He demanded Gamp's dismissal, but Gamp remained at his post until October 1895, and took up a seat in the
Prussian House in addition to that in the Reichstag. A wealthy
industrialist who had bought a *Rittergut* and a noble title, Gamp
refused to accept a pension on retirement and instead set up a
'Bismarck Fund' for the benefit of needy civil servants. With
Gamp's retirement the problem caused by the central civil servant in parliament was at an end.[50]

The opposition of the provincial officials was more widespread
and more difficult to deal with. Count Stolberg, the *Oberpräsident*
of East Prussia, was dismissed in 1895 for coming out in support
of the Agrarian League during an election campaign. In the following year the *Regierungspräsident* of Frankfurt-on-the-Oder
was one of the signatories of a petition demanding the abolition of
the civil marriage ceremony. At last the Prussian Ministers decided to issue a decree forbidding all public servants to criticise the
Government. One Minister who had come under attack in the
House of Deputies maintained that unless such behaviour were
stopped, 'civil servants would actually become the leaders of the
opposition'. The Ministers were coming round to the view that

provincial officials must be discouraged from accepting seats in the parliaments. Shortly before the 1898 elections, they decided 'that *Oberpräsidenten* and *Regierungspräsidenten* should on principle refuse to seek election to the Reichstag and the Landtag'. One State Secretary complained that Tiedemann, the *Regierungspräsident* of Bromberg who also sat in the Prussian Lower House, hardly did any work at all. He resided in Berlin throughout the parliamentary session and then spent several weeks on holiday before going to his office for a brief two months. The long-awaited showdown came in August 1899, when the Government's Canal Bill fell because some 26 of the 37 provincial civil servants who were members of the Prussian House of Deputies voted against it. Miquel now admitted that the provincial officials 'have for a long time been putting the interests of their localities before the general welfare of the State, and have for the most part furthered the aims of the Agrarians'. He estimated that almost seven-eighths of the *Landräte* were opposed to the Government's policy. On the Kaiser's orders, those officials who had voted against the Canal Bill were dismissed from their posts; all civil servants were told to leave the Agrarian League. A considerable number of the 'rebels' of 1899 were reinstated within a year, and some were even appointed to the central departments, but in each case reinstatement was conditional on relinquishing his seat in parliament.[51] Henceforth all civil servants were strongly discouraged from seeking election.

The exclusion of officials from parliament was an unavoidable consequence of the advent of mass politics, yet in the long run it made the Government less capable of dealing with that very trend. For a long time it had been the common practice for ambitious officials to stand for election early in their career in order to gain parliamentary experience. A large number of the Ministers and State Secretaries of Bismarck's day had been eminent members of parliament. Bismarck himself had of course made his mark as a parliamentarian, as had Prince Hohenlohe, and even Bethmann Hollweg, the first Chancellor with a civil service background, had had a brief spell in the 1890 Reichstag as a Free Conservative deputy. In Bismarck's last Cabinet, there were some, like Gossler and Lucius, who had been President and Vice-President of the Reichstag before receiving appointment to the Government. Bismarck's son Herbert was a member of the Reichstag from 1884 until his appointment as Foreign Secretary, and then again from 1893 until his death. Maltzahn, the head of the Treasury, owned six large estates in Pomerania. After a brief period as *Landrat* he retired to devote himself to farming and politics: he sat as a Conservative in the Reichstag from 1871 till his appointment in 1888. Of the men prominent in the 1890s, a large number had gained some parliamentary experience. Johannes Miquel had been leader of the National Liberals before his appointment as Finance Minister in 1890. Theodor von Möller, the new Minister of Trade in 1901, was not only a National Liberal deputy in both Berlin parliaments but also a leading member of the Central Association of German Industrialists. General Podbielski, who became Postmaster-General in 1897 and Minister of Agriculture in 1901, was a great landowner with extensive commercial interests and a vociferous Conservative Reichstag member up to his appointment.

Several other men had gained their experience while holding office in the provincial administration. It was partly for this reason that increasingly it was the provincial civil servants rather than the central bureaucrats who rose to become Ministers. The practice of appointing men from the provinces to ministerial office was virtually unknown before 1871. In the period 1871–90, only four *Oberpräsidenten* became Prussian Ministers. Yet in the 1890s alone, half of all ministerial appointments went to *Oberpräsidenten* or *Regierungspräsidenten*. Diplomats, army officers, and some parliamentary leaders were also appointed, but the number of central civil servants was small by comparison. Robert Bosse became under-secretary in the Reich Office of the Interior, then Secretary of the Reich Justice Office, and finally Prussian Minister for Ecclesiastical Affairs; Ludwig Brefeld was promoted from under-secretary in the Ministry of Public Works to Minister of Trade. In the Reich the only men to rise from the central bureaucracy were the three Secretaries of Justice Bosse, Hanauer, and Nieberding. After the turn of the century, when both central and provincial officials were excluded from parliament, the reservoir of civil servants with parliamentary experience began to shrink rapidly, and this undoubtedly aggravated the growing constitutional crisis in the Empire.

In 1890 Holstein could still boast that since the German Government was composed entirely of civil servants, 'it is more comfortable for the monarch and more efficient technically than a parliamentary Cabinet. It is one of the Chancellor's greatest achievements to have isolated the Cabinet from parliamentary majorities and made it independent of them'.[52] Before the century's end men like Holstein had come close to appreciating the serious defects in the Bismarckian constitution. The 'comfortable' Ministers lost the power struggle with the Court in the years 1894–97 because, being loyal servants of the Crown, they could not countenance whole-hearted resistance to the monarch. On the other hand, in an effort to keep abreast of the times, Ministers were being recruited not from the 'technically efficient' bureaucrats in the central departments, but from the aristocrats and landowners of the provincial administration whose educational qualifications often left much to be desired and whose 'isolation from parliamentary majorities' was purely notional. Because of its artificiality and fragility, the Second Reich was incapable of organic growth. Its civil service, though highly trained, had to be recruited from that diminishing section of the population which was regarded as *staatserhaltend* [state-sustaining—ed.]; Catholics and Jews, Radicals and Socialists were almost wholly excluded. The myth had to be upheld that Germany was governed not by politicians but by professional civil servants who stood above party, yet increasingly after Bismarck's dismissal *political* skill came to be recognized as essential at the ministerial level. The number of men in Germany who were both civil servants and able politicians was exceedingly small, and declined still further after the exclusion of civil servants from parliament at the turn of the century. 'It is frightening to see', wrote Alexander Hohenlohe when a Ministry fell vacant in 1899, 'how few suitable people there are for such a post'.[53]

NOTES

[1] About one-quarter of the candidates failed to pass the simple spelling and arithmetic tests instituted by the Order in Council of 1855 in Great Britain. See W. A. Robson, ed., *The Civil Service in Britain and France* (London, 1956), 35.

[2] Deutsches Zentralarchiv (DZA) Merseburg, Rep. 89H, XXI, Deutsches Reich, 1.

[3] According to the 1907 census, over one million people could claim the title of *Beamte* (official), but this figure included officers, teachers, and postal and railway workers. Civil servants in the narrower sense, but including judges and public prosecutors, numbered 390,000. See O. Hintze, 'Der Beamtenstand', in *Soziologie und Geschichte* (Göttingen, 1964), 68. The number of higher civil servants in the central offices in Berlin (i.e. those with the rank of *Vortragender Rat* and above), was tiny by comparison: about 200 in the Prussian Ministries and 120 in the Reich Offices in the 1890s. It is primarily with these three or four hundred men that this essay is concerned.

[4] Rudolf Morsey, *Die oberste Reichsverwaltung unter Bismarck 1867–1890* (Münster, 1957), 251.

[5] DZA Merseburg, Ministry of State meeting, 29 June 1895.

[6] Committee Reports of 31 July 1898, and 3 September 1900. DZA Potsdam, Reichskanzlei, Nr. 1903.

[7] H. Finer, *The Theory and Practice of Modern Government* (London, 1946), 1261.

[8] In the Reich Offices in Bismarck's time, 5 of the 23 State Secretaries and 26 of the 167 *Vortragende Räte* had the Dr. jur. degree (Morsey, *op. cit.*, 250). Of the 113 *Vortragende Räte* in the Reich service in 1895, 30 possessed the degree. Nearly half of those in the Reich Justice Office, a third of those in the Foreign and Interior Offices, and a quarter of those in the Treasury and the Navy and Railway Offices were doctors of law. On the other hand, contemporary accounts agree that drunkenness and indolence were more prevalent among law students than in any other faculty. See e.g. Gustav Schmoller, 'Zur Frage der Einrichtung des akademischen Studiums, hauptsächlich der Juristen' (1886), reprinted in *Zwanzig Jahre Deutscher Politik* (Munich, 1920), 191ff.

[9] *Die Zukunft des preussischen Staatseisenbahn und Staatsbauwesens und ihrer höheren Beamten, von Einem Freunde Derselben* (Leipzig, 1892), 17.

[10] Fürst Chlodwig zu Hohenlohe-Schillingsfürst, *Denkwürdigkeiten der Reichskanzlerzeit* (Stuttgart, 1931), 290.

[11] B. W. v. König, *Handbuch des Deutschen Konsularwesens* (Berlin, 1896), 45ff.

[12] DZA Potsdam, Reichskanzlei, Nr. 1903. Memorandum of 8 May 1908.

[13] Morsey, *op. cit.*, 246.

[14] Brauer's Report No. 71, 13 November 1891. Badisches Generallandesarchiv (GLA) Karlsruhe, 49/8. The Kaiser had the right to dismiss anyone from the

service if he married a foreign woman. Under Bismarck this right was never invoked, but in 1891 Wilhelm II dismissed Freiherr von Mentzingen, Secretary of Legation in Brussels, for marrying the Belgian Countess Liedkerke. Not until 1895 did the monarch rescind his order, so enabling Mentzingen to be sent to Buenos Aires. For a similar incident, see G. W. F. Hallgarten, *Imperialismus vor 1914* (Munich, 1951), I, 414.

[15] Morsey, *op. cit.*, 246. The diplomat Kiderlen-Wächter received a letter from a member of his student corps in 1895 asking whether, to enter the consular service, one university was better than another, whether a large private income or a doctorate were necessary, and whether 'entering the career is difficult without connections'. Curt Weinert to Kiderlen, 28 March 1895. DZA Merseburg, Kiderlen Papers. The diplomat's reply has unfortunately not been preserved.

[16] DZA Merseburg, Rep. 89H, VII Deutsches Reich 1, vol. I.

[17] Oelschläger to Caprivi, 29 March 1892. DZA Potsdam, Reichskanzlei, Nr. 1616.

[18] Jagemann's Report No. 133, 30 November 1895. GLA Karlsruhe, 49/14; Brauer's Report No. 3, 16 June 1890, ibid., 49/7; Jagemann's Report No. 144, 30 September 1897, ibid., 49/16.

[19] Berchem to Caprivi, 10 March 1894. DZA Potsdam, Reichskanzlei, Nr. 1443. For the way in which this fear affected policy in the 1890s, see my book *Germany without Bismarck* (London, 1967).

[20] J. C. G. Röhl, 'Friedrich von Holstein', *The Historical Journal*, IX, III, 384.

[21] E. v. Jagemann, 75 *Jahre des Erlebens und Erfahrens* (Heidelberg, 1925), 146.

[22] Oelschläger to Caprivi, 29 March 1892. DZA Potsdam, Reichskanzlei, Nr. 1616.

[23] *Das Tagebuch der Baronin Spitzemberg*, ed. R. Vierhaus (Göttingen, 1960), 327.

[24] Hohenlohe, *Denkwürdigkeiten der Reichskanzlerzeit*, 474.

[25] Julius Bachem, *Erinnerungen eines alten Publizisten und Politikers* (Cologne, 1913), 38. See also J. Bachem, *Die Parität in Preussen* (Cologne, 1899).

[26] Karl Bachem, *Vorgeschichte, Geschichte und Politik der deutschen Zentrumspartei*, 9 vols., vol. IX (Cologne, 1932), 67f. Bachem asserts that Brefeld was a Catholic, which he was not, and omits Maybach and Hanauer from his list.

[27] DZA Merseburg, Rep. 89H, II Preussen 1, Vol. iii; VII Preussen 1, Vols. x and xi.

[28] Ibid., Rep. 89H, IX Gen. 1, Vols. vi, vii, viii.

[29] P. G. J. Pulzer, *The Rise of Political Anti-Semitism in Germany and Austria* (London, 1964), 12.

[30] Count Zedlitz-Trützschler, *Zwölf Jahre am Deutschen Kaiserhof* (Berlin, 1924), 187f.

[31] *The Holstein Papers*, ed. Norman Rich and M. H. Fisher (Cambridge, 1955–63), iv, 525ff.

[32] Walter Frank, 'Der Geheime Rat Paul Kayser', *Historische Zeitschrift*, vol. 168, 326.

[33] C. von Hohenlohe-Schillingsfürst, *Denkwürdigkeiten* (Stuttgart, 1907), II, 440.

[34] The Diary of Robert Bosse, 5 December 1895. Bundesarchiv Koblenz; Marschall's Diary, 27 May 1896. Politisches Archiv, Bonn.

[35] Holstein to Eulenburg, 23 March 1892. Bundesarchiv Koblenz, Eulenburg Papers, 18, 207ff; *Holstein Papers*, I, 150.

[36] Eulenburg to Holstein, 9 February 1892. Bundesarchiv Koblenz, Eulenburg Papers, 17, 65ff; Oelschläger to Caprivi, 29 March 1892, DZA Potsdam, Reichskanzlei, Nr. 1616.

[37] Hohenlohe, *Denkwürdigkeiten* II, 449.

[38] DZA Merseburg, Ministry of State meeting, 12 December 1895.

[39] Wilmowski's personal file. Bundesarchiv Koblenz, R 43/I 3627; Lysbeth W. Muncy, *The Junker in the Prussian Administration under William II, 1888–1914* (Providence, Rhode Island, 1944), 97; Hallgarten, *op. cit.*, I, 422, n.

[40] L. Raschdau, *Unter Bismarck und Caprivi* (Berlin, 1939), 87. In the Weimar Republic, Conservatives maintained that the Imperial bureaucracy had been free from all involvement in business. Some historians still uphold this view today. See e.g. A. v. Tirpitz, *Erinnerungen* (Leipzig, 1919), 33f.; Karl Erich Born, *Staat und Sozialpolitik seit Bismarcks Sturz* (Wiesbaden, 1957), *passim*.

[41] Rassow and Born, *Akten zur staatlichen Sozialpolitik in Deutschland* (Wiesbaden, 1959), 134.

[42] DZA Merseburg, Rep. 89H, II Preussen 1, vol. III. Also Ministry of State meetings, 26 January 1897, 16 April 1898, 28 April 1900.

[43] This policy began with the appointment of Puttkamer as Minister of the Interior in 1881. On hearing that Bismarck might be appointing a Liberal to this post, Kleist-Retzow wrote: 'Please, don't do that. The Ministry of the Interior must have an Old Prussian who is respected as a Conservative and who will favour the aristocracy'. Kleist-Retzow to Bismarck, 28 February 1881, DZA Potsdam, Reichskanzlei, Nr. 1457. See Helmut Böhme, *Deutschlands Weg zur Grossmacht* (Cologne, 1966), 567; Eckart Kehr, 'Das soziale System der Reaktion in Preussen unter dem Ministerium Puttkamer', reprinted in Kehr, *Der Primat der Innenpolitik*, ed. H.-U. Wehler (Berlin, 1965), 64ff.

[44] Herrfurth to Lucanus, 20 June 1891. DZA Potsdam, Reichskanzlei, Nr. 1445. Böhme, *op. cit.*, 582, n.

[45] Fritz Hartung, 'Studien zur Geschichte der preussischen Verwaltung', in *Staatsbildende Kräfte der Neuzeit* (Berlin, 1961), 326, 336; P. Molt, *Der Reichstag vor der improvisierten Revolution* (Cologne, 1963), 143; Morsey, *op. cit.*, 246.

[46] Seven of the twelve were in the Reich Office of the Interior and three in the small Reich Justice Office. The Navy and Post Offices had none. The most aristocratic Prussian department was the Interior, which controlled the provincial administration. There about one third of the higher officials were noble. The Finance, Public Works, and Justice Ministries were almost wholly middle-class.

[47] Molt, *op. cit.*, 142.

[48] Rassow and Born, *op. cit.*, 146.

[49] DZA Merseburg, Ministry of State meeting, 16 October 1891; Caprivi to Secretaries, 31 October 1891. Based on Goering's memorandum of 20 October 1891, DZA Potsdam, Reichskanzlei, Nr. 1423. The Reich Justice Office warned

the Chancellor that the prohibition was unconstitutional. Bosse Diary, 29 October 1891, Bundesarchiv Koblenz.

[50] DZA Merseburg, Ministry of State meetings, 18 Dec. 1893, 26 May 1894.

[51] DZA Merseburg, Ministry of State meetings, 25 March 1896, 2 April 1898, 20, 21, 28, 31 August, 21 September 1899, 28 February 1900.

[52] Memorandum of 10 February 1890. Bundesarchiv Koblenz, Eulenburg Papers, 8, 122f.

[53] Hohenlohe, *Denkwürdigkeiten der Reichskanzlerzeit*, 524.

Part III

Foreign Policy: Domestic Origins and Consequences

It was of both practical and symbolic significance that in 1866 the Austrians' defeat at Königgrätz and the liberals' defeat in the Prussian elections occurred on the same day. From the very beginning, therefore, the German Empire's domestic and foreign political developments were inexorably intertwined. The three essays that follow all consider different facets of this relationship.

In his examination of Bismarck's political strategy, Otto Pflanze (Professor of History at the University of Minnesota) suggests both the reasons for Bismarck's triumphs during the period of national unification and the unfortunate legacies he bequeathed to the new nation. Since this essay first appeared in the Review of Politics *(vol. 20, 1958), Pflanze has expanded his analyses of Bismarck's* Realpolitik *in his* Bismarck and the Development of Germany *(Princeton, N.J., 1963).*

Hans-Ulrich Wehler's article considers Germany's sudden move for colonies in 1884. His objective, however, is not simply to explain a set of events that have always puzzled historians but to see Bismarck's imperialism in terms of the economic, social, and political structure of the Empire. Wehler's essay was first published in Past and Present *(no. 48, 1970); he is Professor of Modern History at the University of Bielefeld.*

The final article in this section deals with Germany's role in the outbreak of World War I, a subject that has aroused a furious historiographical debate since it was reopened by Fritz Fischer's Griff nach der Weltmacht *in 1961. Mommsen's study analyzes the domestic background for German foreign policy on the eve of the First World War, critically assesses some of the most important recent work on German politics, and provides illuminating insights into the governmental system in operation at the end of the Imperial period. For all of these reasons, his article is a fitting selection with which to conclude this volume. The article first appeared in* Central European History *(vol. 6, 1973). Wolfgang J. Mommsen is Professor of Modern History at the University of Düsseldorf.*

6

Bismarck's *Realpolitik*
OTTO PFLANZE

From the time of Metternich to that of Hitler and Stalin no other figure cast so large a shadow as Bismarck on the pages of European and world history.[1] He began his career in 1862 as the hated minister of a faltering monarchy and of a state which for decades had accepted a secondary position in both Germany and Europe. And yet the political virtuosity of this Pomeranian Junker made him the decisive influence in German political life and the arbiter of European diplomacy for nearly a quarter of a century.

His accomplishments unquestionably buttressed and perpetuated the European order of his day beyond its time. He unified Germany and made her a power of the first rank without serious upset to the European equilibrium and, thereafter, steered Europe through a series of crises which might easily have ended in wars of catastrophic size. Within Germany he succeeded in completing the frustration and perversion of the liberal movement and its political parties. The institutions which he created for the German Reich and the new synthesis which he produced in the German popular mind[2] delayed the development of political democracy until its unnatural birth in 1918 in the wake of military defeat. He, of course, suffered some serious reverses, as in his attempts to crush the Center and Socialist Parties. To a remarkable degree, nevertheless, he managed to impose his will upon his contem-

poraries in both domestic and foreign affairs. Although some of
the uses to which he put his talents may be criticized, it can
hardly be denied that he was one of the most successful strate-
gists and tacticians in the history of politics.

Few students of his career have failed to be intrigued by the
problem of explaining how he accomplished what he did. It is not
enough merely to assert that he was a genius. Although the final
secret of his success certainly lay in the sheer facility of his
intellect to judge the implications and possibilities of each political situation more clearly and quickly than his contemporaries, it
may also have been due to the accuracy of his general impression
of the nature of politics and the effectiveness of his political
method. These latter subjects provide a valid field for research
and analysis, which may help us understand this extraordinary
man and even improve our comprehension of the political process itself.

I

The politics of realism, or *Realpolitik*,[3] has a twofold character.
On the one hand, it implies a particular conception of the realities
of political life, and, on the other, techniques of achieving positive results in view of these realities. Machiavelli was long misun-
derstood because those who read him dissociated the former
from the latter. They judged him on the basis of the political
methods which he recommended to the Prince, but ignored his
views about the conditions which seemed to make such tactics
necessary: namely, the depravity of Renaissance man, the disuni-
ty and weakness of Italy under the city-state system, and the
desirability of creating order out of chaos.

Like Machiavelli, Bismarck concluded that the essence of politics is power. This was his great originality in mid-nineteenth-
century Germany. At the time of his first appearance in politics
Prussian conservatives were preoccupied with the theory of the
Ständestaat, and German liberals with that of the *Rechtsstaat*.
What interested Bismarck, however, was not so much the ideal
but the actual. To his coldly realistic eye that which existed was
neither the patrimonial state nor the state of laws, but the power-
state (*Machtstaat*). To be sure there were others with a similar
conception, particularly Hegel, Ranke, and Treitschke. Nev-

ertheless, Bismarck's view differed from theirs. In the tradition of German Idealism all three saw the state as a moral personality.

To Hegel the state was but the supreme manifestation of that great motive force, the *Weltgeist*. He described it variously as "the embodiment of concrete freedom,"[4] "the actually existing, realized moral life," "the Divine Idea as it exists on earth."[5] The personification and deification of the state led logically to the ennoblement of its power. Ranke had this to say: "No state ever existed without a spiritual foundation and a spiritual meaning. In power itself lies a spiritual essence, and original genius, with a life of its own, fulfilling its more or less unique function and forming its own sphere of influence."[6] In Treitschke this tendency to glorify power reached its climax. "The essence of the state," he wrote, "is, first of all, power; second, power; and third, power."[7] To uphold its power is "the highest moral duty" of the state.[8] "States must be conceived as the great collective personalities of history, thoroughly capable of bearing responsibility and blame."[9] "We must always maintain the principle that the state is itself an ethical force and a high moral good."[10]

Bismarck's intellect, however, was far too sober to think of the state in these terms. For him it was primarily a device for governing and its power but a means to concrete, practical ends. Perhaps he derived this viewpoint from the Frederician tradition and that of the Prussian "bureaucratic state," but it was also confirmed by his own experience. In 1848 he observed that control over a loyal army was the margin by which the Prussian monarchy, and the Junker aristocracy, escaped revolutionary reform. Fourteen years later he became Minister-President because of his willingness to force through the plan of William I and Roon for the further consolidation of that control against the opposition in parliament. While appreciating the value of checks and balances in government, he always left open the possibility of upsetting the balance in the crown's favor. In his calculations the final resort of the monarchy in any struggle with parliament was a military *coup d'état* against the constitution.[11] Although he defended himself against the charge of believing that "power takes precedence over law (*Macht geht vor Recht*),"[12] this was essentially his position.

In foreign affairs he also concluded that the final arbiter be-

tween states was not a legal instrument, such as the treaties of
1815 or the German Confederation, but the possession of superi-
or force. After 1851 he was in strong disagreement with the foreign policy of Frederick William IV and his romantic advisers,
particularly Leopold von Gerlach: that of cooperation between
the "legitimate dynasties" of central and eastern Europe against
"the European revolution." Describing himself as a "natural
scientist" with the sole aim of seeing things as they actually are,
he maintained that the only true guide to foreign policy is the
interest of state.[13] "In politics," he argued, "no one does anything for another, unless he also finds it in his own interest to do
so."[14] Since this is natural to the conduct of states, he concluded
that it is, like all things in nature, part of the divine plan. That
 being the case, the pursuit of the reason of state is for the statesman a matter of moral duty. The rational determination of legitimate interests, the careful assessment of the risks involved in
their fulfillment, and the measuring of the power available to that
end are a responsibility imposed upon him by the deity.[15]

II

The establishment of this viewpoint, based largely on Bismarck's
letters to Gerlach in the fifties, does not, however, exhaust the
subject of Bismarck's *Realpolitik* as is often assumed.[16] Just as
important are the statements he made forty years later on the
general nature of politics and its tactics which have received far
less attention.[17]

After his dismissal from office in 1890 Bismarck sought to build
up popular pressure against the policies of his successors in the
Wilhelmstrasse. But the results were disappointing, and he seems
to have concluded that something was fundamentally amiss. The
Germans, he once remarked, had "never outgrown the political
nursery."[18] Hence the many journalists, historians, and delega-
tions of students, teachers and the like who visited him in Friedrichsruh often found him in a didactic mood. Reflecting on what
he had learned through nearly five decades of political activity, he
sought to educate the public in the realities of political life as he
had come to understand them.

Speaking extemporaneously to a group of teachers, he stated

one of his basic conclusions. "It is a principle of creation and of the whole of nature that life consists of strife. Among the plants —as a forester I experience this in my cultures—through the insects to the birds, from birds of prey up to man himself: strife is everywhere. Without struggle there can be no life and, if we wish to continue living, we must also be reconciled to further struggles."[19] On other occasions he elaborated upon this theme insofar as its application to human society is concerned. The struggling forces he had in mind were states, nations, social classes, political parties, economic and sectional interests, and even feuding individuals. The conflict of opposed forces was for him the condition of human progress and hence an intentional part of "the divine plan."[20]

The struggle for survival, however, is not the only hazard that besets the statesman. In Bismarck's view mankind is being swept along by an all-powerful "time stream" before whose compulsion the individual is relatively helpless. To a visiting delegation of students he remarked: "Man can neither create nor direct the stream of time. He can only travel upon it and steer with more or less skill and experience; he can suffer shipwreck and go aground, and he can also arrive in safe harbors."[21] This was one of Bismarck's favorite expressions[22] and a common figure of speech in the romantic thought of his day. We find him using it as early as 1852 when he was on the threshold of his career. He wrote: "The stream of time goes its way just as it ought and, if I plunge my hand into it, I do so because I believe it my duty, not because I intend in this way to change its course."[23]

The strength of the evolutionary current in human affairs seemed to Bismarck so overwhelming that he concluded: "One cannot possibly make history." This seems to have been another favorite observation.[24] To a delegation from the University of Jena he added: "One can always learn from it how one should lead the political life of a great people in accordance with their development and their historical destiny."[25] Like every other seemingly undeniable phenomenon of human experience, the course of historical evolution or "time stream" seemed to Bismarck of divine direction. On one occasion he declared it his duty as a statesman to listen for the step of God resounding through events and to have the presence of mind and decision to spring forward and seize the hem of the divine cloak.[26]

The unending clash of contradictory forces and the all-powerful influence of the "time stream" make the tasks of the statesman forever inconclusive and beset his course with incalculable uncertainties. Bismarck gave his most extensive explanation of this view to Hermann Hofmann, editor of the *Hamburger Nachrichten*, who visited Friedrichsruh on the average of once a month in the nineties and whose journal voiced the ex-Chancellor's attacks on the Caprivi government.[27]

> *My entire life was spent gambling for high stakes with other people's money. I could never foresee with certainty whether my plans would succeed. . . . Politics is a thankless job, chiefly because everything depends on chance and conjecture. One has to reckon with a series of probabilities and improbabilities and base one's plans upon this reckoning. . . . As long as he lives the statesman is always unprepared. In the attainment of that for which he strives he is too dependent on the participation of others, a fluctuating and incalculable factor. . . . Even after the greatest success he cannot say with certainty, 'Now it is achieved; I am done with it,' and look back with complacency at what has been accomplished. . . . To be sure, one can bring individual matters to a conclusion, but even then there is no way of knowing what the consequences will be.*

He came to the conclusion that "in politics there are no such things as complete certainty and definitive results. . . . Everything goes continually uphill, downhill."

Since this is the nature of political life, Bismarck concluded that its phenomena could not be systematized. To a Bavarian journalist, Anton Memminger, he stated: "There is no exact science of politics, just as there is none for political economy. Only professors are able to package the sum of the changing needs of cultural man into scientific laws."[28] Later in the conversation he returned to this theme: "Already many have spoken of my political principles. The professors and their imitators in the newspapers constantly decry the fact that I have not revealed a set of principles by which I directed my policies. . . . Politics is neither arithmetic nor mathematics. To be sure, one has to reckon with given and unknown factors, but there are no rules and formulas with which to sum up the results in advance."[29]

This nasty word "professor" was always one of the most vituperative in the Bismarck vocabulary. Whom did he have in mind? Adam Smith, Malthus, Ricardo, Sismondi, Say, and Bastiat were the names he mentioned to Memminger. The "scientific laws" to which he then referred were such as *laissez-faire*, the "iron law of wages," and the Malthusian theory of population. The economic doctrines of liberalism, he argued, were formulated in the interest of industrial capitalism by "English clergymen," "Jewish bankers," and "French merchants and jurists." "The whole political economy given us by the academicians and the press is a political economy for commerce and not for agriculture as well." It ignores "the actual relationships and overriding circumstances," and "speaks only of one-sided, private interests where general interests are primarily at stake."[30]

What Bismarck objected to, however, was not merely the partiality of the economic doctrines of Manchesterism, but the whole rationalistic belief in the existence of natural laws in society equivalent to those in the structure of the universe. The natural world he knew as the owner of fields and forests was the disorderly one of growing things and not that of algebraic equations and physical laws. In the popular biology of social Darwinism he found a better parallel between science and society. His views reflected the revolt of the nineteenth century against the seventeenth and eighteenth centuries, the period of biological discovery against that of astronomy and physics, the age of romanticism against that of rationalism, and, last but hardly least, the outlook of the conservative against that of the liberal.

III

But what of the techniques of statecraft? Were there no principles which the statesman could follow in coping with the uncertainties of political life, no rules of navigation for those adrift amid the shifting currents and treacherous eddies of the time stream?

Here again Bismarck gave a discouraging answer. "Politics is less a science than an art," he often observed. "It is not a subject which can be taught. One must have the talent for it. Even the best advice is of no avail if improperly carried out."[31] "Politics is not in itself an exact and logical science, but the capacity to choose in each fleeting moment of the situation that which is least harmful or most opportune."[32] "Because they have as yet scarcely outgrown the political nursery, the Germans cannot accustom themselves to regard political affairs as a study of the possible."[33]

If the study of the past could yield no science of politics, Bismarck was far from thinking that it had no value for the statesman. "For me," he told Memminger, "history existed primarily to be learned from. Even if the events do not repeat themselves, at least circumstances and characters do. By observing and studying them one can stimulate and educate one's own mind. I have learned from the mistakes of my predecessors in the art of statesmanship and have built up my 'theory,' although one ought not to speak of such in the narrow sense of the word."[34]

What was this "theory" which was not a theory? One reads further with considerable anticipation. Bismarck said that from the mistakes of Napoleon I he learned to exercise "wise moderation after the greatest successes." From those of Napoleon III he learned not to "confuse slyness with falsehood. I played my cards face up. In contrast to this supposed slyness I spoke the stark truth. That they often didn't believe me and then afterward felt very surprised and disillusioned is not my fault."[35]

Deceptive frankness and moderation in victory were certainly important weapons in Bismarck's tactical armory. The astonishing openness with which he sometimes spoke of his aims gave the appearance of veracity to the untruths and distortions with which he misled his opponents on other occasions. In 1866 his insistence on a quick peace without annexations and indemnities from either Bavaria or Austria eased the voluntary inclusion of southern Germany in the Reich in 1871 and the signing of the Dual Alliance between Germany and Austria in 1879. Although the seizure of Alsace-Lorraine was a costly departure from this rule, Bismarck's conduct after the victory against France was generally moderate. The widespread fear of an imperialistic German nationalism that might endanger the whole of Europe did not materialize until long after his career was over.

Nevertheless, it is doubtful that Bismarck depended very much on historical precedent as a guide to political action. While he may indeed have learned from the fate of the first Bonaparte, Napoleon III was after all not an historical figure, but a contemporary opponent on the chessboard of European politics. Although well versed in recent European history, Bismarck used its facts primarily as a reservoir of argument to support decisions made on other grounds. His knowledge of political tactics stemmed more from his own personal experience and intuition than from historical example.[36]

Although illuminating, these bits of advice are obviously but a partial answer to the problem of Bismarck's tactical genius and must be supplemented with fragments from other speeches and conversations.[37]

> More than anything else politics demands the capacity to recognize intuitively in each new situation where the correct path lies. The statesman must see things coming ahead of time and be prepared for them. . . . An indispensable prerequisite is patience. He must be able to wait until the right moment has come and must precipitate nothing, no matter how great the temptation.

> From childhood I have been a hunter and fisher. In both cases waiting for the right moment has been the rule which I have applied to politics. I have often had to stand for long periods in the hunting blind and let myself be covered and stung by insects before the moment came to shoot.

> Correct evaluation of the opponent is also indispensable to success. This means the exercise of caution. In chess one should never base a move on the positive assumption that the other player will in turn make a certain move. For it may be that this won't happen, and then the game is easily lost. One must always reckon with the possibility that the opponent will at the last moment make another move than that expected and act accordingly. In other words, one must always have two irons in the fire.

These hints are also very helpful, and yet the sum of Bismarck's comments on the technique of politics is rather disappointing. Patience and careful timing, the intuitive recognition of the correct path, and the accurate evaluation of one's opponents were certainly typical of Bismarck and aid in explaining his political virtuosity. But they represent qualities of individual judgment and personality rather than demonstrable methods of political procedure.

One cannot escape the feeling that the aging Chancellor knew more than he told. This is particularly true of that final phrase: "always have two irons in the fire." From the record of his conversation with the historian, Heinrich Friedjung, comes a similar statement: "Many paths led to my goal. I had to try all of them one after the other, the most dangerous at the end. It was not my way to be single-minded in political action."[38] In neither case does the record show that Bismarck elucidated or illustrated these statements. They bring to mind, however, what a Bavarian contemporary once said of him: "In major domestic and foreign affairs and questions Prince Bismarck likes to provide himself with an alternative in order to be able to decide the same in one of two opposed directions."[39]

IV

The full meaning of these remarks only becomes clear after surveying most of Bismarck's career. They are the clues to a general technique of political strategy employed again and again by the wizard of the Wilhelmstrasse in the attempt to maximize his chances of success in the hazardous game of politics. Reduced to its most essential element, his method was that of constantly providing for alternative courses of political action. These courses were twofold in character; sometimes they consisted of alternative solutions to a particular political problem; often they were alternative possibilities of alliance with opposed political forces. With a knowledge of this general pattern of strategy it is possible to follow the thread of Bismarck's policy and conduct through one complicated political situation after another.

Consider the policy he formulated and finally carried out with regard to Austria and the German Confederation. While Prussian delegate to the Confederate Diet in Frankfurt after 1851 he became convinced that the Confederation was but an instrument of Austrian imperialism in Germany. In his messages to Berlin he argued that it was a "noose" which prohibited Prussia from achieving her due position in German and European politics.[40] By no means did he assume, however, that the *only* way in which Berlin could free herself from this restraint was the path he ultimately took, namely, war and the unification of *Kleindeutschland*. On the contrary, this was but the last and "most dangerous" of the "many paths" he explored. While still in Frankfurt he had proposed that the dual powers come to an agreement which would in effect have divided Germany into two spheres along the river Main.[41] Long after he had ceased to believe that the Austrians would agree to it, he continued to hold this alternative open. Even in May, 1866, while steering what appeared to be a collision course against the Hapsburg monarchy, he repeated the offer once more when Gablenz made his last minute attempt to stave off the conflict.[42] To the very end the plan lay in reserve, to be brought up and pressed again if his reluctant royal master could not be induced to set the Prussian troops in motion or if the threat of French intervention should make war against Austria appear too risky.

Amid conflicting forces Bismarck usually sought to occupy the middle ground: that is, the pivot position from which alternative alliances with either of two hostile interests was possible or the fulcrum position from which they could be brought into equilibrium. This technique appears also in the policies he advocated for Prussia in the fifties. Not long after arriving in Frankfurt he began to tell his superiors in Berlin that Prussia must abandon both her traditional alliance with Austria and her traditional hostility toward France. By taking an intermediate position between the two powers, a position from which in time of crisis combination with either was possible, she could exert pressure upon both in her own interest. By such a policy she could lend weight to her warning that the Hofburg must choose between peaceful and warlike solutions to the German question.[43]

By driving a wedge between Austria and Russia in 1854–55 the Crimean war increased the potential gain from such a strategy. For a time it appeared as though Europe might divide into two opposed power blocks, each in search of Prussian support. A Franco-Russian alliance seemed probable, and to this the obvious response was an Anglo-Austrian coalition. Bismarck maintained

that as long as the cleavage between these blocs remained incomplete Prussia should choose neither. By "holding open every
door and every turning" she would be able to exploit each arising
situation to her own advantage.[44] In other words, she must establish for herself that pivotal position in the European balance of
power which would give her maximum freedom of choice between alternative alliances.[45]

These same patterns of strategy—the provision for "many
paths" and the assumption of the middle position between conflicting forces—are also evident in that diplomatic campaign
which Bismarck regarded as his masterpiece, the Schleswig-Holstein question.[46] When the final crisis in this long and complicated
issue arose in 1863–64, Bismarck was almost alone in nourishing
the ambition to annex the Duchies to Prussia. Not one of the
many important interests involved in the controversy desired this
end. The Copenhagen government was attempting to incorporate
the Duchies into Denmark; the British Cabinet desired to maintain the integrity of the Danish monarchy; Austria wanted to
return to the *status quo* before the crisis arose; the lesser German
states wished the creation of a new Confederate state ruled by the
Prince of Augustenburg; the liberal majority in the Prussian parliament[47] and the German liberal-national movement as a whole
desired a similar solution; the Prussian King and Crown Prince
were also sympathetic to the Augustenburg cause. From Napoleon alone, a most unreliable ally, came hints of support for Bismarck's secret aim.[48]

Considering these odds Bismarck analyzed the problem in
terms of its alternative possibilities for Prussia. They were: (1)
annexation, (2) the "real union" of the Duchies in "personal
union" with Denmark under the Danish crown, or (3) their independence under the house of Augustenburg and their inclusion in
the German Confederation. Although the first was what he desired, he was not at all sure that he would emerge from the jungle
of European and German politics at that point. Had it been unattainable, he probably would have accepted the second, since it
certainly would not have ended the problem of the Duchies, but
have left the issue where it might be re-opened at a time more
favorable to Prussian annexation. The third he would have ac-

cepted only under terms tantamount to a Prussian annexation.[49] Moving forward cautiously step by step Bismarck eliminated the second and third alternatives, leaving the first to await the outcome of the war of 1866.

Although the full story of Bismarck's diplomatic maneuvers in the Schleswig-Holstein question is long and complicated, the basic pattern is fairly easy to trace.[50] Favored by the fact that the many interests involved in the controversy were disunited and often in pursuit of conflicting objectives, he assumed that middle position from which he could best take advantage of their mutual antagonisms. By maintaining that his only aim was the moderate one of re-establishing the rights of the Duchies against the misrule of Denmark, he drew the Austrians into an alliance with Prussia, which he then used to dominate the lesser states of the Confederation and frustrate the liberal-national movement. But when the Austrians pressed for a common statement of war aims which would have committed the dual powers to the retention of the sovereignty of the Danish crown over the Duchies, he warned Vienna that the Hohenzollern King was so kindly disposed toward Augustenburg that any attempt to extract such a commitment would cause him to react in the Prince's favor.

When the King, on the other hand, wanted to come out openly for the Prince, Bismarck reversed the argument, pointing out to William that such an act would jeopardize the Austrian alliance and increase the danger of British intervention. This inclination of his monarch was also useful to him in London, where he warned that if his own seemingly moderate policy were not supported by the British they ran the risk that he might be replaced by a minister more willing to carry out the King's desires. Perhaps even more effective in preventing British intervention, however, was the possibility that it would drive Prussia into an alliance with France. In Paris Bismarck nourished the hope of such an alliance with vague promises to Napoleon, spiced, when necessary, with the threat that, should the Emperor grow cold toward Prussia, the latter would consolidate her alliance with Austria and extend it beyond the Danish affair into European questions vital to France.

In short, a disadvantage encountered on one front was converted into advantage on another, each hostile force counterbalanced by its opposite. Out of the resulting equilibrium Bismarck gained the freedom which enabled him to move even closer to the realization of his hidden ambition. When annexation was assured in 1866 he exulted: "I have beaten them all! All!"[51]

V

This technique was by no means limited to foreign policy. On the contrary, one of the best illustrations of its use is to be found in the constitution which Bismarck designed for united Germany. Drafted in late 1866 for the North German Confederation, this document was amended early in the following year by the Constituent Reichstag and again in 1871 on the inclusion of the southern states.[52] It has long been celebrated by historians as a supreme example of Bismarckian realism. By this it is usually meant that he provided a place within the new governmental structure for all the important political forces of the country: the German nation, the various political parties, the Hohenzollern crown, the Prussian government, and the dynasties and governments of the lesser states. But it did more than that. The constitution created the possibility of an equilibrium among these numerous forces, the controlling position of which was that which Bismarck himself occupied.

Through the division of powers and functions the constitution created a balance between the national and state governments. Although its financial powers were extremely limited, the national parliament was granted authority to legislate on a wide range of important subjects. On the other hand, the state governments were invested with the right to execute national laws. Within the national parliament the balance was repeated. Equal legislative power was given to the Bundesrat, whose members were appointed by the state governments, and the Reichstag, whose membership was chosen by universal manhood suffrage. In addition, however, the former was given certain executive functions.

Outside the equilibrium were certain hegemonial powers granted the Prussian crown and state. The Hohenzollern monarch received command over the armed forces and control over foreign policy, including the right to make treaties, declare war, and ne-

gotiate peace. Although given no outright veto over Reich legislation, he possessed the dominant position in the Bundesrat
through his power to appoint the Reich Chancellor and the seven-
teen Prussian members of that body.

In Bismarck's draft of December, 1866, there was no clear
provision for a central executive organ.[53] If this plan had been
carried out, the Chancellor would have been merely the presiding
officer of the Bundesrat.[54] Many of the essential executive functions, such as the preparation of bills to be submitted to the
Reichstag and the supervision over state execution of national
laws, were apparently to have been performed by the Prussian
bureaucracy.

In this system the key post would actually have been that of
Prussian Foreign Minister. Since the Bundesrat was theoretically
but the reformed version of the old Frankfurt Diet of the German
Confederation, he had the power to instruct the Chancellor on the
conduct of his office and to direct the policies and votes of the
Prussian members of that body. This meant that Bismarck, without occupying an office in the national government, would have
had the most decisive influence in the conduct of its affairs. Johannes Ziekursch has pointed out how effectively this pivotal
position might have been exploited.[55]

> As the Reichstag against the Bundesrat, so could Bismarck also play
> the Bundesrat against the Reichstag. Whenever the Reichstag, that is,
> was driven forward by hunger for power, it found no one whom it could
> attack. The Bundesrat voted and drafted its directives in all secrecy; no
> one learned who had voted in the Bundesrat for or against a proposal.
> The members of the Bundesrat acted in accordance with the instruc-
> tions of their governments, whose leaders followed their own ideas and
> the directives of their rulers and had to pay attention to their parlia-
> ments. The Reichstag would have had to attack not the Confederate
> Chancellor, who was not responsible, not a ministry, not one ruler, but
> 19 (apart from the magistrates of the three Hanseatic cities). And by
> skillful procedure the state parliaments, elected by suffrage laws of a
> different type, could be played against the Reichstag. Then the will of
> the people opposed the will of the people.

But Bismarck's draft was altered before it became the German constitution. Early in 1867 the popularly elected Constituent Reichstag amended the document in such a way that the importance of the Chancellor was greatly enhanced. Bismarck now assumed the office himself and it became the nucleus for the development of an executive branch of the national government. As has recently been suggested,[56] it is probable that Bismarck permitted this amendment because it actually fitted in with an ulterior purpose of his own. In the following years by becoming Chancellor and head of the Reich executive he was able to strengthen his dominance over his colleagues in the Prussian cabinet who before 1866 had often opposed his will. Furthermore, the change did not alter the basic structure of the governmental balance he had designed. Although the Reichstag now had a clearer target to attack, the Reich executive was still beyond its control.

Through his multiple posts as Reich Chancellor, Prussian Minister-President, and Prussian Foreign Minister Bismarck had a choice between two executive bodies, those of the Reich and Prussia. As the situation seemed to demand, he could build up the importance of the one at the cost of the other, or use his authority in the one organ to buttress his influence in the other. From this pivotal position he also had the alternative of submitting bills to the national parliament or the Prussian Landtag. Because of Prussia's size and population after the annexations of 1866 the latter body was almost as important as the former. Until the completion of German unity in 1871 he had in certain financial matters yet a third choice, namely the German Zollverein parliament. To none of these chambers, but only to his King and Kaiser, was he politically responsible. By clever choice of the issues he put before them, however, he had the opportunity of influencing their party composition, splitting apart and rendering impotent or amenable those parties hostile to his purposes.

Nevertheless, the construction of a governmental majority, particularly in the Reichstag, continued to be the major internal political problem which Bismarck faced. Because of his feud with the conservatives after 1866, he at first depended primarily upon the National Liberal Party and the Free Conservatives (later the German Reich Party). But after 1874 he became rather uncom-

fortable in this saddle. Through the election in January of that
year the left wing of the NLP, headed by the radical liberal,
Eduard Lasker, gained the controlling position in the chamber. In
1879, however, Bismarck brought about the Party's defeat and
later its cleavage on the tariff issue. This election created in the
Reichstag the sort of situation he knew so well how to exploit.
For a time he had the chance of forming majorities in two alternative directions. The Conservative Party, now completely reorgan-
ized and submissive, could be combined either with the purged
NLP or with the Center Party. When the one grew restive, Bismarck held it in check by combining with the other.[57]

His manipulation of the party structure of the Reichstag was
accompanied by a similar manipulation of the institutional balance of the German government. During his first years as Chancellor, Bismarck's primary worry was not so much the demands
of the liberals in the Reichstag for additional power, as the parti-
cularistic outlook and habits of the state governments, including
the Prussian. If the North German Confederation were to be
viable, he believed it necessary to build up the centralistic side of
the governmental equilibrium in order to counteract these centrifugal elements. This was another reason for his decision to assume
the Chancellorship in 1867. Under the leadership of the able Rudolf von Delbrück the Chancellor's Office proliferated rapidly
into a fully grown executive organ.[58] As a consequence the executive functions of the Bundesrat atrophied, and even the Prussian
cabinet and bureaucracy were put in the shade.[59] Bismarck's
alliance with the NLP made possible a rapid use and even expansion of the legislative authority which the constitution had granted the Reich. In his public speeches and writings Bismarck
summoned forth the moral force of German national sentiment to
weld the new state together. Because he believed the Catholic
minority was unreconciled to German unity under a Protestant
monarchy he unleashed the *Kulturkampf* against the Church and
its political voice, the Center Party.

In the seventies, however, Bismarck's concern over these centrifugal influences waned, while his fear of the Reichstag and its
liberal majority waxed. The state governments and dynasties had
reconciled themselves to their new status much more readily than

he had anticipated.[60] Particularism in general appeared to be on the decline. After the victory of the left-liberals in the election of January, 1874, the crown encountered serious difficulty in securing passage of its vital military bill in the following year.[61] Then, the danger of upset appeared to come from this direction.

After 1875 Bismarck used his position of the fulcrum to reconstruct the balance. In order to depreciate the importance of the Reichstag, he weakened the centralistic organs of the Reich in general. By strengthening the role of the Prussian cabinet and bureaucracy in Reich affairs, he sought to reduce the power and functions of the Reich executive. An attempt to revive the executive functions of the Bundesrat had a similar purpose.[62] By calling into existence a *Volkswirtschaftsrat* he sought to create a new parliamentary organ as an alternative to the Reichstag. Nevertheless, he was dissatisfied with the results, especially when the "Cartel" majority dissolved in the election of 1890. At the time of his dismissal he was busy with a plan for the unilateral revision of the Reichstag electoral law.[63]

VI

Bismarck did succeed in "making history." His own career shows that he was overly pessimistic about the impact of individual personality upon the historical process. This is not to deny the existence of the "time stream" of which he so often spoke. The current of human events is indeed propelled along through time by the push of forces which find expression in popular sympathies, sentiments, loyalties, interests, movements, organizations and institutions. Certainly Bismarck did not create the many forces with which he was compelled to reckon: German nationalism with its vital urge toward unity; the industrial revolution with its impact upon the changing social structure; the many economic and social interests; the ideologies of conservatism, liberalism, and socialism; the political parties representing these interests and ideas; the Prussian monarchy with its authoritarian and militaristic tradition; the European great powers and the German lesser states with their conflicting aims and interests.

But it is true that he helped to mold these forces into new relationships which were to influence the course of German and

European development long after he was gone. Sidney Hook has distinguished between the "eventful" and "event-making" man in history, between the historical figure who by accident of his position fulfills what antecedent events have long been preparing and the "hero in history" who by virtue of "outstanding capacities of intelligence, will, and character" actually helps determine the direction of historical evolution. Bismarck was certainly among the latter.[64]

Bismarck's achievements were largely due to his extraordinary skill in the use of the strategy of alternatives. This technique enabled him to gain and retain the initiative. The knowledge that his quiver held more than one arrow gave him the confidence and sureness that most of his opponents lacked. If one bolt fell short of the mark, another was ready to follow. But the metaphor is inexact, for it was Bismarck's habit not to exhaust but to preserve all alternative possibilities until the time of final decision. By this means he minimized the risk, if at the last moment the route of greatest danger should appear too costly. But the availability of an alternative could also be used to remove obstacles along the way. By candidly revealing his consideration of a course more disadvantageous to his opponents than to himself, he forced them to yield to his own desires. These alternatives were, in fact, seldom bluffs. No matter how drastic, they were usually practical threats which he was ready to carry out if compelled to do so. Often he was able to monopolize the alternative possibilities which the situation afforded and thereby restrict his adversary's sphere of action.

The position of the pivot or fulcrum gave him other unique advantages. From it he had the choice of moving in at least two, often more, directions. By occupying that point in each situation which permitted the greatest freedom, he restricted the maneuverability of his opponents and maximized his own. Through this tactic he was frequently able to isolate his foes and force them to yield without the actual use of violence. But where the tactic failed, the isolation of his antagonist made it possible to employ force with the greatest prospect of success. Often the mechanism of the balance enabled him to frustrate the growth of political forces which might prove inimical. Through the static immobilization of hostile interests he found the liberty to promote his own. His aim was ever to be the final arbiter in whom the necessity as well as the possibility of decision accumulated.

The persistent recurrence of the same general pattern of political conduct throughout Bismarck's career indicates that he did have a basic approach to political strategy. But this raises the question why he failed to leave a fuller description of it to posterity. Certainly there were good reasons for not relating some of the alternative courses he had been willing to consider during his career. Since it became politically expedient after 1866 to identify himself as a German nationalist, he could hardly confess to Friedjung that the division of Germany into dual spheres of influence had been one of the "many paths" he had been willing to consider before that date. Even in our own day it has been difficult for nationalistic historians in Germany to accept this fact.

But it could also be that Bismarck regarded the application of this technique as the "art" which could not be taught. In other words, he may have considered it an intimate and incommunicable part of his own political genius. His physician in the eighties, Dr. Schweninger, has left us an unforgettable account of the "thought experiments" which undermined the patient's health.[65]

> . . . the Prince examined every question and every event from every possible angle . . . with the help of his rich political experience and comprehensive historical knowledge he thought through all possible constellations with all their conceivable consequences, tracing out the details in such a way that not a gap remained, nor for that matter could remain. Through this intensive kind of reflection, to which he was especially addicted at night in bed, his brain developed naturally such a lively phosphorescence that but seldom was there any chance for sleep.

Bismarck may have believed that the knowledge of his technique would be useless baggage for a statesman without this intellectual facility. The man with the "talent" for politics, on the other hand, would not need his instruction.

It may also be, however, that Bismarck's technique was never a conscious formula for political action, but merely the instinctive response of an extreme pragmatist to the difficulties of political life. As we have seen, he found the world of politics a highly

chaotic one of competing, clashing interests in which the statesman is relatively helpless to achieve his will. He is but an eternal
wanderer in the jungle, warily wending his way through its dangers and uncertainties in quest for an exit which can never really
be found. At best he can only hope to have a choice between
routes of greater and lesser danger. Bismarck's strategy of alternatives was his intuitive way of minimizing the risk by creating
the possibility of such a choice. In one equivocal situation after
another it enabled him to seek and find "the possible."

NOTES

[1] The author wishes to express his appreciation to the American Council of Learned Societies for a grant which made possible some of the research for this article. In the preparation of the manuscript he received helpful suggestions from Glenn Tinder.

[2] On the character of this synthesis see the author's "Bismarck and German Nationalism," *American Historical Review*, LX (April, 1955), 555 ff.

[3] This term was coined by the German liberal publicist August Ludwig von Rochau in his *Grundsätze der Realpolitik, angewendet auf die staatlichen Zustände Deutschlands* (Stuttgart, 1853).

[4] Quoted in F. J. C. Hearnshaw, *The Social and Political Ideas of Some Representative Thinkers of the Age of Reaction and Reconstruction 1815–65* (London, 1932), p. 61.

[5] *The Philosophy of History* (New York, 1944), pp. 38–9.

[6] Quoted in T. H. von Laue, *Leopold Ranke, the Formative Years* (Princeton, 1950), p. 86.

[7] *Historische und Politische Aufsätze* (3rd ed., Leipzig, 1867), p. 519.

[8] *Politics* (New York, 1916), I, 94.

[9] *Ibid.*, p. 17.

[10] *Ibid.*, p. 106.

[11] See Egmont Zechlin, *Die Staatsstreichpläne Bismarcks und Wilhelms II* (Stuttgart, 1929).

[12] Landtag debate of January 27, 1863. Herman von Petersdorff and others, eds., *Bismarck: Die Gesammelten Werke* (Berlin, 1924–35), X, 157.

[13] *Ibid.*, I, 40, 70, 104; II, 219 ff.; III, 190; VII, 38; XIV (1), 441.

[14] *Ibid.*, II, 231; XIV (1), 473. Although written in 1857 this judgment was already implicit in one of Bismarck's first letters from Frankfurt (June 29, 1851). *Ibid.*, I, 17.

[15] *Ibid.*, XIV (1), 468, 549; I, 238; III, 148. On the relationship between politics and morality in Bismarck's thinking see O. Vossler, "Bismarck's Ethos," *Historische Zeitschrift*, Vol. 171 (1951), 264 ff.

[16] Hans Mombauer, *Bismarcks Realpolitik als Ausdruck seiner Weltanschauung. Historische Studien*, Vol. 291 (Berlin, 1936).

[17] The only previous attempt to evaluate this material in terms of Bismarck's *Realpolitik* is the inadequate one of the German civil servant, A. v. Brauer, "Bismarcks Staatskunst auf dem Gebiete der auswartigen Politik," in H. von Poschinger, ed., *Neues Bismarck-Jahrbuch* (Vienna, 1911), I, 298–339.

[18] For the context of this remark see [text marked by note 33].

[19] *Werke*, XIII, 555.

[20] *Ibid.*, XIII, 559, 570; IX, 8 ff.

[21] *Ibid.*, XIII, 558.

[22] *Ibid.*, IX, 161; XIV (1), 483, 544; XIV (2), 752, 879; XIII, 304, 456–7.

[23] *Ibid.*, XIV (1), 249.

[24] *Ibid.*, XI, 46; XIII, 304.

[25] *Ibid.*, XIII, 468.

[26] Egmont Zechlin, *Bismarck und die Grundlegung der deutschen Grossmacht* (Stuttgart, 1930), p. 101.

[27] *Werke*, IX, 397 ff.

[28] *Ibid.*, IX, 90.

[29] *Ibid.*, IX, 93, 420.

[30] *Ibid.*, IX, 90.

[31] *Ibid.*, IX, 399; to Hofmann; also XIII, 177.

[32] *Ibid.*, XIII, 468, to a delegation from Jena.

[33] *Ibid.*, IX, 93, to Memminger. See also III, 251, "Die Politik ist eine Wissenschaft der Relativen."

[34] *Ibid.*, IX, 90.

[35] *Ibid.*, IX, 93–4.

[36] Bismarck's use and conception of history has been critically analyzed by Helmuth Wolff, *Geschichtsauffassung und Politik in Bismarcks Bewusstsein* (Munich, 1926).

[37] *Werke:* (1) To Hofmann, IX, 400; (2) to a delegation from Jena, XIII, 468; (3) To Hofmann, IX, 400.

[38] *Ibid.*, IX, 50.

[39] Max. Freiherr Pergler von Perglas, Bavarian envoy in Berlin, quoted in Fritz von Rummel, *Das Ministerium Lutz und seine Gegner 1871–1882* (Munich, 1935), p. 2; also H. von Srbik, *Deutsche Einheit* (Munich, 1935–42), III, 70.

[40] *Werke*, II, 302 ff.; III, 35 ff, 38, 251; XIV (1), 544.

[41] *Ibid.*, XIV (1), 441; A. O. Meyer, *Bismarcks Kampf mit Österreich in Frankfurt* (Berlin, 1927), pp. 549 ff.

[42] See Walter Lipgens, "Bismarcks Österreich-Politik vor 1866," *Die Welt als Geschichte*, X (1950), 240–62; also Otto Becker, "Der Sinn der dualistichen Verständigungsversuche Bismarcks vor dem Kriege 1866," *Historische Zeitschrift*, Vol. 169 (1949), 264–98; Hajo Holborn, "Über die Staatskunst Bismarcks," *Zeitwende*, III (1927), 6 ff.

[43] *Werke*, I, 285–7, 291; XIV (1), 289–91.

[44] *Ibid.*, XIV (1), 473; II, 150, 223.

[45] Egmont Zechlin was the first to give an adequate description of this strategy as Bismarck developed it in the fifties. *Grundlegung der deutschen Grossmacht*, pp. 88 ff.

[46] L. D. Steefel, *The Schleswig-Holstein Question* (Cambridge, 1932), p. 95.

[47] In the early days of the conflict the only deputy who publicly voiced the demand for the Prussian annexation was the leader of the radical minority of the Progressive Party, Waldeck.

[48] Steefel, *Schleswig-Holstein*, pp. 113 ff.

[49] Among German scholars the order of priority which Bismarck gave these alternatives has been disputed. His admirers have found it hard to believe that he had been willing to leave Germans under alien rule rather than accept a solution

disadvantageous to Prussia. See Arnold Oskar Meyer, "Die Zielsetzung in Bismarcks schleswig-holsteinischer Politik von 1855 bis 1864." *Zeitschrift für schleswig-holsteinische Geschichte*, Vol. 53, 103–34. His critics, on the other hand, have been only too glad to affirm it. See Erich Eyck, *Bismarck*, I, 550. Bismarck's own testimony varied according to his political purpose of the moment. In early 1864, while seeking to coerce Augustenburg into making certain important concessions in return for Prussian aid, he gave the second alternative as his preference. Later after concluding his alliance with German nationalism, he reversed himself, insisting that Augustenburg had been his second choice. Meyer, *op. cit.*, 128–30, 105–6. This was also the order he listed in his memoirs. *Werke*, XV, 254. Considering Bismarck's general approach to political strategy, it seems unlikely, however, that he had any rigid order of preference between the second and third alternatives. Everything depended upon the circumstances under which the final decision had to be made.

[50] Although Steefel, Srbik, and Eyck have given good acounts of Bismarck's diplomacy in the Schleswig-Holstein question, it is impossible to comprehend fully the astonishing skill with which he maneuvered his way through and over the many obstacles in his way without reading the two great documentary collections which record the day to day diplomatic transactions in the Wilhelmstrasse. Chr. Friese and others, eds., *Die auswärtige Politik Preussens 1858–71* (Oldenburg, 1933–45), Vol. IV, and H. von Srbik, ed., *Quellen zur deutschen Politik Österreichs 1859–66* (Oldenburg, 1934–8), Vol. III.

[51] *Werke*, VII, 140. The pattern of political strategy evident in Bismarck's diplomacy of the fifties and sixties appears also in that of the seventies and eighties.

[52] Bismarck's draft is printed in Karl Binding, ed., *Deutsche Staatsgrundgesetze in diplomatisch genauem Abdrucke* (Leipzig, 1901), I, 75 ff. In an earlier and incomplete form it is printed in *Werke*, VI, 187 ff. The best source in which to study the development of the constitution is: Otto von Völlendorff, ed., "Deutsche Verfassungen und Verfassungsentwürfe," *Annalen des deutschen Reichs* (1890), pp. 241–401.

[53] It also did not provide for a central judiciary. There was no court to decide questions of constitutional interpretation. Cases of treason were to be handled by the superior court of the Hansa cities (Bremen, Hamburg, Lübeck).

[54] It was originally intended, in fact, for Friedrich Karl von Savigny, the last Prussian delegate to the Frankfurt Diet.

[55] *Politische Geschichte des neuen deutschen Kaiserreiches* (Frankfurt a. M., 1925–30), I, 216–7.

[56] Otto Becker, "Wie Bismarck Kanzler wurde," in Harald Thurau, ed., *Beiträge zur deutschen und nordischen Geschichte, Festschrift für Otto Scheel* (1951), pp. 336 ff.

[57] Hans Herzfeld, *Johannes von Miquel* (Detmold, 1938), I, 450 ff.

[58] See Eberhard von Vietsch, *Die politische Bedeutung des Reichskanzleramts für den inneren Ausbau des Reiches von 1867 bis 1900* (Leipzig, 1936).

[59] Paul Laband, "Die geschichtliche Entwicklung der Reichsverfassung seit der Reichsgründung," *Jahrbuch des öffentlichen Rechts*, I (1907), 22–5.

[60] *Werke*, XV, 448.

[61] Ziekursch, *Politische Geschichte*, II, 294–7.

[62] Hans Goldschmidt, *Das Reich und Preussen im Kampf um die Führung* (Berlin, 1931), pp. 75 ff, 80 ff.

[63] Zechlin, Staatsstreichpläne, pp. 3 ff.

[64] *The Hero in History* (New York, 1943), p. 154.

[65] E. Marcks, K. A. v. Müller, and A. v. Brauer, *Erinnerungen an Bismarck*, pp. 210–12.

7

Bismarck's Imperialism, 1862–1890
HANS-ULRICH WEHLER

I
Introduction

German Imperialism during the Bismarckian era remains a controversial topic.[1] There is disagreement about both its underlying causes and development, and its historical significance. Numerous problems still remain a *terra incognita* for the historian. Above all the question of the continuity of German imperialism from the time of expansion through free trade in the 1850s and 1860s up until Hitler's *Ostland* imperialism still requires close investigation; only the main lines of development can as yet be clearly discerned.

The present state of the debate is in part due to the fact that until a few years ago the most important historical sources—state papers and manuscript collections—were still inaccessible to scholars. Since this is no longer the case, it is possible to make a fresh attempt to analyse these problems, proceeding from surer foundations.[2] This, however, is only one prerequisite, albeit an important one. Very much more to blame for the present state of research into German imperialism has been the lack of an adequate theory.

This is the reason why important inter-relationships and possible explanations have so far been overlooked. The historiography of imperialism urgently needs a critical historical theory before it can provide illuminating analyses and explanations of socio-economic and political

processes. I have tried elsewhere to develop in detail such a
critical historical theory of imperialism, based on that nineteenth-
century phenomenon which was most decisive for world history
—namely industrialization, and its attendant social and political
developments.[3] Such a theory, like any theory in the social
sciences, has to satisfy certain requirements: first, it has to combine a maximum of empirically obtained and verifiable information with as much explanatory power as possible; second, it
should cover a variety of similar phenomena—it must in this case
enable the historian to compare the modern western forms of
imperialism. From this theory of imperialism—which aims to establish a link between the problems of economic growth in industrialized countries and the changes in their social and political
structure—two elements call for discussion here, which are particularly important for the explanatory model.

1. One of the dangerous legends of contemporary develop-
ment-politics is the belief that rapid economic growth promotes
social and political stability, and inhibits radical and irresponsible
policies. Historical experience has shown however that rapid
growth produces extremely acute economic, social and political
problems.[4] Germany is a particularly illuminating case. Here,
after the breakthrough of the industrial revolution 1834/50–1873,
industrialization was necessarily associated with a large number
of profound difficulties in Germany's internal development. More
than half a century ago, Thorstein Veblen stated the basic problem: the absorption of the most advanced technology by a largely
traditional society within a then unprecedentedly short time. And
one of the most important contemporary experts on the problems
of economic growth, Alexander Gerschenkron, had the German
experience particularly in mind, when he propounded his general
theory that the faster and the more abrupt a country's industrial
revolution, the more intractable and complex will be the problems associated with industrialization.[5] After the period from the
onset of the German Industrial Revolution until the second world
economic crisis of 1873, there followed a period of intensive
industrialization, punctuated by lengthy interruptions in the process of economic growth (the three industrial depressions of 1873–
79, 1882–86 and 1890–95, together with the structural crisis of

agriculture from 1876 onwards), and accompanied by social upheavals in which many contemporaries saw the approach of social revolution. In other words, the problems of uneven economic
growth, together with all its effects, were of immense importance
in Bismarck's Germany.[6] It was also as a reaction against this
partly rapid, partly disturbed, in any case uneven growth that the
system of organized capitalism of the large-scale enterprises developed as a means of bringing about stability and the social
control of industrial development. Organized capitalism grew up
in the period before 1896 (that "watershed between two epochs in
the social history of capitalism", as the young Schumpeter called
it),[7] so that one can see the period from 1873 to 1896 as an extremely difficult structural crisis in the development of the modern industrial system. The same period saw the beginnings of the
modern interventionist state, which similarly sought to master the
problems of uneven industrial growth. Both the interventionist
state and organized capitalism saw a pragmatic, anti-cyclical economic policy as an important means of stabilization. Therefore,
both attached decisive importance to the promotion of an export
offensive and to the winning of foreign markets—either through
the methods of informal empire or through direct colonial rule.
This was considered of decisive importance both for economic
prosperity and for domestic social stability—for the same reasons
a sort of law of the increasing importance of foreign trade during
times of economic depression and crisis still seems to be valid
today. The welfare of the country was therefore made dependent
on the successes of informal and formal expansion. Since the
preservation of the traditional social hierarchy was often the
dominant motive behind expansion, one is justified in talking of a
social imperialism. In Germany, there began to develop a broad
ideological consensus of agreement to this effect from the end of
the first depression (1878–9) onwards, and subsequent German
overseas expansionism rested upon this consensus.[8]

2. Bismarck's greater Prussian Imperial State as founded in
1871, was the product of the "revolution from above" in its
military stage. The legitimacy of the young Reich had no generally accepted basis nor was it founded upon a generally accepted
code of basic political convictions, as was to be immediately

demonstrated in the years of crisis after 1873. Bismarck had to cover up the social and political differences in the tension-ridden class society of his new Germany, and to this end he relied on a technique of negative integration. His method was to inflame the conflicts between those groups which were allegedly hostile to the Reich, *Reichsfeinde*, like the Socialists and Catholics, left-wing Liberals and Jews on the one hand, and those groups which were allegedly loyal to the Reich, the *Reichsfreunde*. It was thanks to the permanent conflict between these in- and out-groups that he was able to achieve variously composed majorities for his policies. The Chancellor was thus under constant pressure to provide rallying points for his *Reichspolitik*, and to legitimate his system by periodically producing fresh political successes. Within a typology of contemporary power structures in the second half of the nineteenth century Bismarck's régime can be classified as a Bonapartist dictatorship: a traditional, unstable social and political structure which found itself threatened by strong forces of social and political change, was to be defended and stabilized by diverting attention away from constitutional policy towards economic policy, away from the question of emancipation at home towards compensatory successes abroad; these ends were to be further achieved by undisguised repression as well as by limited concessions. In this way also the neo-absolutist, pseudo-constitutional dictatorship of the Chancellor could be maintained. By guaranteeing the bourgeoisie protection from the workers' demands for political and social emancipation in exchange for its own political abdication, the dictatorial executive gained a noteworthy degree of political independence *vis-à-vis* the component social groups and economic interests. And just as overseas expansion, motivated by domestic and economic consideration, had become an element of the political style of French Bonapartism, so Bismarck too, after a short period of consolidation in foreign affairs, saw the advantages of such expansion as an antidote to recurring economic setbacks and to the permanent direct or latent threat to the whole system and became the "Caesarist statesman".[9]

Early German imperialism can also be viewed as the initial phase of an apparently contemporary phenomenon. Jürgen Habermas has demonstrated recently how, under the present system of state-regulated capitalism, political power is legitimized chiefly by a deliberate policy of state intervention which tries to correct the disfunctions of the economy—in particular disturbances of economic growth—in order to ensure the stability of the economic system. The demand for "legitimation" to which these societies are subject, leads to a situation in which a "substitute programme" replaces the discredited ideology of the liberal-capitalist market economy. Ruling élites are thereby obliged to do two things if they wish to preserve the system and their own vested interests. First, they must ensure that favourable "conditions for stability be maintained for the entire social system and that risks for economic growth be avoided". Second, they must "pursue a policy of avoiding conflict by granting compensations in order to ensure the loyalty of the wage-earning masses". Thus, planned "scientific and technological progress", the main productive force of our times, and a steady rate of economic growth, assume increasingly the function of "legitimizing political power". These problems do not have an exclusively modern significance. Their historical genesis can be traced back to the last third of the nineteenth century. In Germany, as has already been stated, their origins can be clearly traced back to the Bismarckian era. It may be illuminating to view German imperialism during these years— like many other actions of the developing interventionist state— as an attempt on the part of her ruling élites to create improved conditions favourable to the stability of the social and economic system as it stood. They had realized that the traditional and charismatic authority of the government was losing its effectiveness.

In creating better conditions for social and economic stability, they thus hoped to take the heat out of internal disputes about the distribution of the national income and of political power, and at the same time provide new foundations for the rule of an authoritarian leadership and of privileged social groups. Bismarck's Bonapartist and dictatorial régime together with the social forces which supported it, and later on particularly the exponents of *Weltpolitik*, expected that economic and social imperialism would legitimate their authority. Critical observers at the time also recognized this fact quite clearly.[10]

From a consideration of these two theoretical questions—first, the problems of uneven economic growth, and second, the need for an authoritarian system to legitimate itself—there emerges one fundamental point for the following discussion: German imperialism is to be seen primarily as the result of *endogenous* socio-economic and political forces, and not as a reaction to *exogenous* pressure, nor as a means of defending traditional foreign interests. This interpretation is specifically directed against the notions recently put forward by Professor Gallagher, Professor Robinson, Dr. Fieldhouse and others.[11]

II

The Economic Aspect

In view of the long controversy over Bismarck's motives for "entering the arena of *Weltpolitik*", one decisive point must first of all be made and emphasized: in Bismarck's overseas policies there is a remarkable continuity of both the ideas and the methods of free-trade commercial expansionism; he adhered to this particular policy of expansion from 1862 until 1898 because he clearly recognized the financial burdens, the political responsibilities as well as the military risks that were involved in formal colonial rule. He was influenced too by the enormous success of Britain's mid-Victorian Informal Empire, and at the same time he carefully calculated the importance of those interests which could be satisfied by a *laissez-faire* overseas policy. The years 1884–6 did not see a sudden revision of his basic ideas, nor did they see a sudden change of mind, a sudden enthusiasm for colonies. There were however some motives, which, contrary to his previous experience and hopes, induced Bismarck for some time to involve the state in the governance of Protectorates. It is indisputable that he would have preferred to hand these territories over to syndicates of private interest-groups as trading colonies, with some form of loosely formalized Imperial protection. Thereafter too, Bismarck remained convinced that Informal Empire was preferable to colonies under formal state administration. He persisted, moreover, in the belief that economic interests should take the initiative overseas and that the state should merely follow later, without seeing its goal from the very beginning as formal colonial rule. As the colonial publicist, Friedrich Fabri, noted with regret as late as 1889, the "colonial-political programme of the Reich government" was "based on the principle of *laissez-aller*".[12]

It seems hardly possible to dispute this continuity in Bismarck's basic ideas. Only if great prestige value were attached to colonies as the necessary attributes of a world power, or if—contrary to much historical evidence—colonies were considered to be economically more valuable than Informal Empire, could this continuity be denied or overlooked. It is not this continuity of intention which poses the real problems, but rather its relationship to the heterogeneous methods employed in the Protectorate policy of the 1880s.

If however one is convinced by the consistency of Bismarck's statements regarding his basic Imperial conception over three decades—that *laissez-faire* expansion offered the most advantages—then his policy up to 1884 appears quite logical, and shows that he was not just waiting for a favourable opportunity to acquire colonies. Above all, the apparent contradiction between the establishment of Protectorates and his repeated criticism of colonies is then largely resolved. In 1884–6 Bismarck would unquestionably have preferred to avoid the formal acquisition of colonies—on economic and commercial grounds; and for Bismarck, the acquisition of colonies remained a means, rather than an end in itself. The irony of his colonial policy, against which the free-trade Liberals protested so sharply, consists precisely in the fact that he shared for most of the time the misgivings of these critics. He was, therefore, quite sincere when he assured the French Ambassador De Courcel as late as the autumn of 1884, that "the aim of German policy" was only the expansion of unrestricted trade, and not "the territorial expansion of German colonial possessions".[13]

In 1886 Bismarck admitted that "he was as unenthusiastic about overseas colonial policy" as he was about internal colonization, and ten years later, having constantly reiterated his misgivings, he confirmed once again his original wish that "a merchants' government be formed" in the Protectorates:

I certainly hope that we shall still be able to devise in Africa a system

*similar to the one which has made England so strong in the East
Indies. There, the trader is the sole authority.* [14]

When the Hamburg merchant O'Swald maintained that German
overseas policies would be best advanced by

*carefully adapting oneself to the customs of foreign lands and peoples,
. . . by having purely commercial objectives, and by rejecting all political considerations and all suggestions of a possible territorial expansion of power,*

Bismarck agreed emphatically with the principle: "Even the most
powerful nations are well advised to view adaptation as the general rule which should govern trading relations overseas; force
has to be the exception". In 1888 he still believed that "our
colonial programme is subject to this restriction: protection of
German pioneers, yet no formal colonial possessions", and that
such a programme was "practical and right". [15] It could perhaps
be said that Bismarck, with an ambivalence often characteristic
of his policy, was on the one hand pursuing traditional ideas of
expansion through free trade, but on the other anticipating modern conditions: after the end of formal colonial rule, commercial
expansionism by the highly industrialized states has turned out in
the long run to be the more successful system; the economic
dominance of America's Informal Empire is just one illustration
of this.

These developments must be summarized chronologically.
From the beginning of the 1860s onwards, Bismarck pursued an
active, if not always equally intensive overseas policy with an
immediate view to promoting foreign trade in industrial products.
His appointment as Prime Minister of Prussia coincided with the
definitive break-through of the industrial revolution in Germany.
In his free trade policy he was following in the footsteps of his
predecessors, who had already tried to take into account the
requirements of an industrializing economy. In the Far East for
instance, Bismarck pursued an "open-door" policy from 1862 to
1870, and if his intentions had been realized Prussia would probably have acquired a base there by 1870, her own Hong Kong. He
was acquainted with the methods of British and American trade

policy in the Far East and imitated them.[16] But it was not only in the Far East that he refused to acquire colonies; all such projects were systematically turned down in any part of the world. Bismarck held firm to his conviction that the costs of colonial expansion by the state very often outweighed its usefulness, that the "advantages were very largely illusory", and that colonies were a political burden. As he repeated in a memorandum for the Kaiser in 1873, it was for these reasons that he had "consistently pursued a policy of not seeking the acquisition of territory outside Europe", since "such possessions were bound to be for Germany a source of weakness rather than of strength".[17] In his long period of cooperation with the Liberals however, Bismarck continued with his expansionist foreign trade policy and, though he did not consider building a battle fleet, he did use gun-boats and cruisers in support of this policy. Both the "East Asia Station" and the "West Africa Station" were established during his period in office; German warships cruised regularly in the Pacific and were sent to Africa to enforce trade treaties and to support German consuls. His basic attitude during this time—"As long as I am Reichskanzler, we shall not pursue a colonial policy"—was deemed irreversible. The dominant views in London and Washington with regard to the advantages of informal commercial expansion differed little in these years from the views prevailing in the Foreign Office in Berlin.

Bismarck's rejection of a colonial policy was reinforced by a consideration which in London and Washington played hardly any role at all: a colonial empire required in the short or long run considerable sums of money which would have to be granted by parliament and there were few things in which, throughout his period of office, he was less interested, than in increasing the influence of the Reichstag. Thus when a Ruhr industrialist suggested in 1881 that he should acquire Formosa, he rejected this suggestion in the first place with the argument that, "As long as the finances of the Reich have not been consolidated, we cannot consider such expensive undertakings . . . The state cannot administer colonies, directly it can do no more than give support to trading companies". But then he also added: "Colonial administration would be an extension of Parliament's parade-ground".[18]

Another of the Chancellor's arguments—that the state could not initiate a colonial policy "unless there were a national demand" for it—became less plausible as the need for increased exports as a remedy for overproduction, and for those social tensions which arose from economic crises, came to be ever more widely accepted. After 1879 it became more and more difficult to overlook this growing demand for an active policy. Bismarck had reproached many a champion of expansionism for "failing to take into consideration the clashes of real interest which lie at the root of all conflicts".[19] It was however precisely the best-known exponents of the ideological consensus who were demonstrating in many respects an undeniable realism that added persuasive force to their analysis of the conflicts of interest within the economy and society of the liberal-capitalist system. They had a keen eye both for the acute conflicts which dominated an economic system that had to rely on permanent industrial expansion, and for the critical tensions in the social order.

In these views there was a point of contact with Bismarck. He pursued his overseas policy for motives which allow it to be designated as pragmatic expansionism; and he himself belongs in the category of pragmatic expansionists. In contrast to the type of imperialism that was determined by ideas of prestige, of nationalistic self-assertion and of a sense of mission, or by the desire for recognition as a world power, pragmatic expansionism resulted primarily from an assessment of economic and social interests. Its ultimate aims were its "magic triangle": to assure a continuous economic growth and social stability by promoting expansion, which in turn was meant to preserve the social hierarchy and the political power structure. At this point its affinity with social imperialism becomes evident. Pragmatic expansionism reacted to impulses inherent in a socio-economic system which the pragmatic expansionist was inclined to presuppose as "natural". It was guided by considerations of *Realpolitik*, not by utopian dreams, and accommodated itself to those driving forces which were fundamental to the dynamics of the economic system. It is pragmatic expansionism in particular which reveals the indissoluble connection between imperialism and the development of the capitalist system of production. One could choose a dictum of Bismarck—*"fert unda nec regitur"* (the wave carries you on but cannot be ruled)—as the motto of this expansionist *Realpolitik*. Its champions bowed to the pressures of a situation which determined this calculation of their interests. They saw themselves as simply implementing the laws of political economy, while at the same time also trying to counteract or at least to mitigate the effects of industrial development within Germany. Thus they claimed, and for the most part sincerely believed, that their actions had the quality of the historically inevitable. Such a form of pragmatic expansionism corresponded perfectly with certain of Bismarck's basic attitudes concerning *Realpolitik*, attitudes and notions which had grown out of his views about the force of circumstances.[20] His pragmatic expansionism was well attuned to the forces generated by a permanently expanding economy, by its "natural" development as an expansive system. Bismarck had no illusions about the dynamics of economic growth in "the age of material interests"; he had spoken in these terms since 1848, and he came much more fully to terms with the industrial revolution than has been realized by those historians who would like to brand him as an old-fashioned cabinet politician. He recognized that it was clearly a basic tendency of his age that the "driving force" of "economic affairs" was the "principal agent of modern development". Bismarck was far from disagreeing with Hübbe-Schleiden, an expansionist propagandist, in his conviction that "nowadays economic questions are the foundations of politics"; nor was his position far removed from that of Fabri, who called the "intrusion of economic questions as a decisive and prominent factor in the lives of nations" a "basic law of modern world evolution". Bismarck by no means dissociated himself from these bourgeois views on economic determinism; on the contrary he joined their spokesmen in considering economic questions to be "fundamental questions". For some fifteen years he was able to accommodate these economic interests by pursuing a free-trade policy which seemed to satisfy the requirements of the Prussian-German economy. However, while others tended to turn free trade into a dogma, Bismarck chose to resort to protectionist methods when the long period of depression after 1873 and, more important, the agricultural crisis after

1876 made such methods seem necessary. He went back to the eighteenth-century Prussian tradition of "welfare politics" in order to bring a critical situation under control. His policy of a "conservative alliance" (*Sammlung*) between the large landowners and leading industrialists laid the basis for the protectionist system after 1879: the modern German interventionist state began its ascendancy towards the end of the 1870s. Foreign trade was supported, initiatives for its extension were systematically co-ordinated. Bismarck defined his economic policy as a pragmatic adaptation to developments; it was not based on an explicit theory. His pragmatic expansionism was one aspect of the state's early anti-cyclical economic policy.[21]

Why did Bismarck decide in the mid-1880s that it was no longer possible merely to opt for free trade expansion? Why—hesitantly and with many reservations—did he come round to the view that it was necessary to assume formal colonial rule? He saw his own policies as a response to the exigencies of the socio-economic and political system. In Germany, as elsewhere, the new period of depression beginning in 1882 had a catalytic effect on imperialist policies. This change clearly had its antecedents: since 1879 support of the overseas trade offensive had been considered one of the tasks of the interventionist state. But it was not until the shock effects of the second depression were felt after 1882, that state assistance in this sphere was intensified. After the autumn of 1882, when there was the threat of a repetition of the grim experiences of 1873–79 and of a further interruption in economic growth, the traumatic effects of the first depression were deepened. The safeguarding of the home market through protectionist measures, which had for some time been considered the most effective anti-cyclical device, proved to be of little use when the world-wide slump began. A crisis in agriculture coincided with the depression in industry; the agrarian and industrial élites were hard hit.[22] Social tensions became more acute; the "red peril" developed in industrial areas, a feeling that the country was in a state of crisis became more and more widespread; Bismarck's Bonapartist régime and his policy of the "conservative alliance" were faced with a severe test. Confronted with the effects that uneven industrial growth was producing in the economic, social and political spheres, the political leaders in Berlin could not stand idly by—extensive expansion overseas was one of the counter-measures which aimed easing this critical situation. "Industrial development which has resulted in over-production drives Germany to seek the acquisition of colonies"—the opinion of France's representative in Berlin was shared by numerous other observers.

Ever since the second depression of 1882, it had been shown that the liberal-capitalist economy, based as it was on continuous but spasmodic growth, was fundamentally dependent on the extension of the market beyond national boundaries, and this required a kind of assistance that only the power of the state could provide. That assistance became imperative because of the enormity of the problems caused by intensive industrialization: the chronic imbalance between production and consumption, the inherent tendencies towards over-investment, over-capacity and over-production. Furthermore, the importance of the fact that national economic development no longer took place in relative isolation—as had been the case while the British were establishing their unique monopoly in the world markets—can hardly be overestimated; now development was bound up with a bitter economic competition on a world-wide scale between a number of industrial states, each grappling with similar problems of growth. David Landes has singled out this competitive struggle between the western industrial countries as "the most important single factor" in their economic and commercial development from the late 1870s onwards, and as the basic pre-condition of the "New Imperialism." It was futile to hope for success in this struggle unless the state gave energetic backing to the needs of the economy.[23]

During the initial phase of this secular development, at a time when the cyclical crises called more and more urgently for governmental economic policy, Bismarck did initiate strong measures designed to support the export industries. A variety of measures was introduced at the same time: subsidies for steamship lines, the establishment of bank branches overseas, consular support for the export trade, special rates on the railways and canals for export goods, preferential treatment under the tariff of

1879 for the export intensive manufacturing industries. These measures must all be viewed together and in conjunction with the new trade agreements of these same years in order to recognize the way in which the interventionist state pushed its way forward in the sphere of overseas trade. The policy which led to the acquisition of colonies in Africa and in the Pacific was only one of the methods whereby the state promoted foreign trade. There is little doubt that the "open door policy" remained Bismarck's ideal—he was still able to pursue it in China and in the Congo. If England and France had guaranteed free trade in Africa, unrestricted commercial expansion of this sort would have entirely satisfied Bismarck's economic aims—it was his view that, under these circumstances, German interests engaged in overseas competition could have asserted and extended themselves with limited governmental support. But the crucial reasons which induced him from 1883–4 onwards to seek a gradual formalization of Imperial control in Africa and the Pacific were twofold: on the one hand internal pressure resulting from the crises was mounting and had to be reduced; on the other, the end of the free-trade era appeared imminent, and increasing competition together with the use of protectionist methods by other powers made direct state involvement overseas inevitable. In other words, the obvious disadvantages of the state continuing to play a passive rôle were beginning to outweigh the equally obvious disadvantages of increased state activity.[24] In West Africa a complete dependence of Germany on other colonial powers with protective, differential, and even prohibitive tariffs seemed imminent. In South Africa, East Africa and New Guinea, Great Britain and Australia seemed to be on the verge of seizing further territory. It was believed in Berlin that unless the government acted, these rivals with their "preclusive imperialism" would gain ascendancy. There was an unmistakeable fear of being left out in the cold, of arriving too late for the progressive sharing out of the territorial spoils of the non-occidental world. The press constantly repeated that Germany should not stand idly by while "other nations appropriate great tracts of territory and the very rich natural resources that go with them", waiting until "nothing is left for us from this economic conquest of the as yet unexploited parts of the earth". The

government assured the Reichstag that "the expansionist colonial
policies of other powers" compelled Germany to similar action
"unless she wished to be totally excluded from the partition of
the world". The imperialism of the 1880s derived not so much
from irrepressible feelings of strength and vitality, as has often
been claimed, but rather from the incapacity of the industrial
states to deal with the internal problems caused by an explosive
and unstable industrialization. Just as at home leading landowners and industrialists were driven together to form a "cartel of
fear" in the face of economic crises and social revolution, and to
pursue an expansionist policy as a way out of these difficulties, so
were the rival industrial states united in their overseas policies by
their suspicions that they might miss out on something decisive if
they held back. Bülow's often quoted desire for a "place in the
sun" expressed a view which was already gaining ground in the
early 1880s, that the world was to be shared out once and for all,
and that the shares apportioned to the various western states
would, in the long run, have a decisive influence on their welfare
and international standing. Rosebery's aim in 1893 of "pegging
out claims for the future" had been no less keenly felt ten years
previously in the overseas policy of the industrial countries, than
it was later expressed in the concern of social-imperialist theore-
ticians for the future of bourgeois social and economic system.[25]

This feeling of being excluded from the exploitation of undeveloped countries was constantly nurtured by pressure groups
with vested interests. Woermann, Lüderitz and Peters repeatedly
pointed to the strong foreign competition to which they might
succumb. Because it was then difficult to obtain reliable information about what was happening overseas, the state often acted on
the narrow basis of reports from pressure groups. Even an official
of the Foreign Office who favoured colonial expansion considered in 1885 that "too much importance is attached to the wishes
and claims of interested private individuals". But when he criticized a Hamburg merchant, active in trade with Africa, for presenting his personal interests as though they were identical with
"the interests of the fatherland", Bismarck at once reproached
him: "all business affairs are by their very nature selfish", but
what is to the advantage of the Hamburg merchant "is also to the

advantage of the country as a whole and forms a small part of our national interest".[26] Bismarck gradually yielded to the pincer movement from without and within, to the threatening dangers of overseas competition and to the warnings of the interest groups that he should not let chances go begging during the time of the depression. His prophylactic expansionism sought to protect present advantages and potential opportunities from the claims of rival powers in such a way that he eventually had to pay the price of formal colonial rule. In these respects his methods and the motives behind them were unquestionably similar to those of the "preclusive imperialism", then being pursued in London, particularly *vis-à-vis* Germany. It cannot be demonstrated that Bismarck would have assumed formal protectorates in overseas areas without the real or latent threat that rival states would beat him to it. Even during the critical period after 1882, Bismarck was not simply on the lookout for "unowned" territories; he preferred to have the German flag follow the country's trade. Whenever possible, merchants were to take over the administration of the protectorates and exploit them through charter companies and syndicates. The rôle of the state was to remain extremely limited. These intentions came to grief everywhere within the space of a few years—as a result of the weakness and reluctance of the trading interests, great-power rivalries and colonial uprisings. In addition, Bismarck himself failed to hold consistently to his conviction that the German flag was only to follow the trader. An enormous area of the South West African coast was brought under German control before commercial interests had made their presence felt, and expansion into the hinterland was pushed far ahead of them. The same was true of East Africa where the merchants at first did not ask for state protection at all, and also of New Guinea where they were willing to proceed only if such protection was granted. Even in the Cameroons where there were considerable German commercial interests, expansionist policy in the hinterland soon went far beyond the original limits. This contradiction between principle and practice is in the first place explicable by reference to the sense of the necessity of pre-empting rivals. The specific situations in which decisions had to be taken—for example, in the spring of 1884 when Berlin was trying to block British and Cape policies in South West Africa—did not always permit Bismarck to adhere closely to his original intentions.

Above all, overseas expansion remained for Bismarck a question of economic policy, and here too, he did not adhere to any rigid system; the heterogeneity of his techniques and methods corresponded to his policy of pragmatic expansionism. He used both free-trade and protectionist methods, both state subsidies and direct intervention; he both followed the trader and created for him areas in which he could operate. This wide variety of measures of assistance was directed however—as was Bismarck's economic policy in general—towards one permanent objective: that of assuring, securing and increasing economic advantages. Actual trading opportunities were to be defended, future possibilities kept open, and, last but not least, manufacturers were to be reassured of the state's readiness to assist them in overcoming the problems of the economic crisis. Expansion was a part of the anti-cyclical economic policy intended as an antidote to the pessimism of the depression years and as an incentive which would stimulate business. The intention always remained the same: to take pressure off the home market by extending foreign trade, to stimulate an economic revival and thereby to reduce the strain on the social and political system. "Our colonizing efforts are measures designed . . . to help German exports": such was Bismarck's summary of the functional value of the protectorates—they were "nothing more than an additional means of promoting the development . . . of German economic life".[27]

The hope of obtaining trade outlets, initially in the protectorates themselves but subsequently and more decisively in Central Africa, had been a dominant motive from the very start; it was to be the function of Germany's coastal possessions to secure access routes to these central areas. The question of markets was still of over-riding importance in the 1880s, for it stemmed from the serious problems of over-production in all industrial countries. It was not until the 1890s that the quest for raw materials assumed equal importance. Just as the chimera of an East Asian market of supposedly unlimited capacity had for long fascinated businessmen, so, from the 1880s onwards, the illusion of a large Central African market exercised strong attraction.

In many places coastal acquisitions were only considered at all important in so far as they were able to provide controllable routes into Central Africa. When one considers how few of these hopes centred on the African interior were actually fulfilled, the history of European policy in Africa during the 1870s and 1880s can almost be described as the history of an illusion. This illusion, however, was of great importance in determining the actions of contemporaries.[28]

It is not possible to say with certainty which of the three decisive economic considerations in Bismarck's imperialism was given priority at any one time: whether short-term or long-term factors or the need to restore business confidence. Taken together, however, these three considerations were certainly responsible for guiding Bismarck's anti-cyclical and foreign trade policies into the field of formal colonial rule. In recent discussions of imperialism, it has been reaffirmed that "the main cause of capitalist expansion" lay " . . . without doubt in the lack of stability of the economic development". Imperialist policy therefore became "the alternative to the stagnation of economic life as a whole, which would have entailed severe class conflict". Imperialism was intended to flatten the extreme fluctuations of the business cycle; to stabilize the national income, and create "a mechanism whereby the critical problems" caused by the uneven growth of the capitalist economy "could be surmounted".[29] There is no conclusive, empirical way of determining whether state support for foreign trade, state protection for foreign investment or the formal acquisition of colonies did in fact ease the fluctuations of the German economy or lead to the phase of recovery from 1886 onwards. It is on the other hand clear that, of the three important methods by which modern governments seek to control the trade cycle—monetary, financial, and foreign trade policies—the first two were unable to sustain Bismarck's economic policy during the period of extremely uneven economic growth after 1873. Since the *Reichsbank* held to the gold standard, monetary policy could not supplement economic policy; it was not even under the control of the government. Since there

was no central, government-controlled institution, through which
a national financial policy could be made to influence the economy of the whole Reich, budgetary policy could also contribute
little. Thus, according to the then prevalent view, the only remaining sphere within which anti-cyclical economic policies
could operate was that of foreign trade, and Bismarck took this
course: first of all he experimented from 1879 on with measures
for the protection of the home market; then he concentrated increasingly on the promotion of foreign trade by the state, which
was, as subsequent experience has shown, a most promising policy within the framework of organized capitalism. Bismarck's imperialism was also a part of this policy, which, because of the
powerful socio-economic forces behind it, appeared to many contemporaries to bear the hall-mark of historical necessity. "If the
German people as a whole finds that its clothes are too tight-
fitting at home", Bismarck conceded in 1884, then "we are
forced to grant protection to German initiatives" abroad. His
pragmatic expansionism reflected the pressures resulting from
industrial growth.[30]

For a critical theory to be fruitful, it should, especially in an
historical analysis of pragmatic expansionism, be directed only in
the second instance at the leading personalities. Its prime concern
ought to be "the blind, aimless dynamics" of an economic system based on constant expansion, for pragmatic expansionism is
a specific expression of these driving forces and it follows them
"by adapting itself to them". The alternative—that of deliberately embarking upon a restructuring of this system and of rationally
harnessing its dynamic forces—is rarely even discussed by pragmatic expansionists, for it is in the very nature of a policy of
pragmatic expansionism to mistrust all utopian plans for a better
future of the kind essential to such a reconstruction. Even so, the
early German interventionist state did take the first important
steps towards subjecting the process of economic growth to social control. The explosive forces released by uneven economic
growth had widely shown themselves to be too dangerous to be
left any longer to the "invisible hand" of Adam Smith. Henry
Axel Bueck, for three decades chief executive of the "Central
Association of German Industrialists", and from the 1870s one of

the leading champions of the policy of the "conservative alliance", expressed after the turn of the century a view which has since gained ground irresistibly. Twenty years after the basic change of German policy between 1879 and 1885, he was able to say: "It is now generally recognized that economic prosperity is the most important basis of modern civilized states. The main task of national politics (*grosse Politik*) today is to ensure and promote this prosperity under all circumstances".[31]

III

The Domestic Aspect

This revealing statement leads on to our second theme. The early interventionist state was not only compelled by uneven economic growth gradually to extend state interference in its efforts to guarantee material welfare and social stability; it also realized, at a time when old political traditions were crumbling away and the charismatic authority of the Chancellor was more and more coming under attacks, that this wide field of economic policy provided new possibilities whereby governmental authority could be legitimized. Successful imperialist policies promised in the same way to help to legitimize governmental authority, the basis of which was being questioned. Thus Bismarck's expansionist policies were from the outset janus-faced. Not only did he swim with "the tide of his time"; he also endeavoured with all the means at his command so to steer German political development on that tide, that it best met his needs. If from an economic point of view overseas expansion appears primarily as a necessary result of irregular economic growth, from the vantage point of domestic politics the active, guiding, indeed manipulatory rôle played by Bismarck is everywhere apparent, as he used expansion to electoral and parliamentary advantage, and for social-political and party political purposes. On the one hand, his pragmatic expansionism followed the dynamics of the economic system and served as a means of providing an anti-cyclical therapy. On the other, it took over special domestic functions of integrating conflicting forces and of diverting attention from internal problems, thus contributing to the continuation of the Prusso-German "revolution from above". This policy gave Bismarck the chance of exploiting the colonial movement for domestic and electoral ends, of staking out new objectives on the distant horizon and of using the unifying effects of this propaganda to cover up the severe social and political tensions within the Reich; he was thereby able to strengthen his own political position as Bonapartist dictator, and to revive his own dwindling popularity and the battered prestige of the government. In certain respects he carried over into domestic politics the foreign policy of diverting problems towards the geographical periphery; he was also pursuing a policy of social imperialism in that he attempted to force vital domestic conflicts out into the peripheral areas.

The disturbances attendant upon economic growth after 1873 subjected the socio-economic structure of the German Empire to constant strains and helped to drive the bourgeoisie on to the side of order. In the opinion of Jacob Burckhardt, Bismarck became "the pillar and standard-bearer of that mysterious quality, authority". If this eased the way for acceptance of Bismarck's Bonapartist political style, the increasingly acute economic problems intensified the pressure on him to keep the people satisfied with his authoritarian leadership. Thus, after the experience of the first depression from 1873–1879, Bismarck experimented with Bonapartist methods of domestic stabilization. His tentative efforts to establish political representation for economic interest groups on the lines of the Estates of the *ancien régime*, and his corporatist legislation (*Volkswirtschaftsrat*, artisan guilds) were as much influenced by the example of Napoleon III as was his social policy of the 1880s, which, like the anti-Socialist law, was intended as "a prophylactic measure" against social upheavals, completing his policy of taming the working classes: "we are averting a revolution", which "would swallow up far greater sums of money . . . than those measures by which we are trying to avert it". Bismarck's social policy was the internal aspect of a stabilization programme, whose external aspect was imperialism. The fundamental alternative between social imperialism and social reform on the one hand and social revolution on the other was not in the least created by the Bonapartist social insurance laws.[32]

From the end of the 1870s, the tactical social-imperialist component of the programme became increasingly important for Bismarck. This was because of developments which were causally and functionally related to the basic changes which occurred during the period after 1873. After six years of most severe economic depression in Germany, there followed in 1879 the bitter quarrels about the system of protective tariffs, about the new conservative course of the Reich government, about the purge of the liberal bureaucracy conducted by Puttkamer, and about the plans for state monopolies in industry; the same short time-span saw the disintegration of the National Liberal Party and the rise of Social Democracy—in spite of the new emergency law which was approved of by the Liberals and which unmistakeably bore the "mark of brutal class domination" (Schmoller). The satisfaction that the national state had promised its subjects, the hopes of having all citizens live in harmony, enjoy equal rights and participate in the general prosperity—these hopes, which had been nurtured by the national-democratic, egalitarian aspect of nationalist ideology, were all revealed as illusions in the first period of serious economic fluctuations between 1873 and 1879. The harsh reality of the class structure of industrial society broke through to the surface of the new authoritarian state. Since Bismarck kept the political parties "in the ante-chambers of political power" and helped to restrict them to a narrow social basis, they were denied the possibility of representing and integrating a variety of interests. Thus they did not have the strength to unite different social strata, which is the precondition for the working of a political system adequate to the pluralistic social order, which was tending to develop in Germany. On a more general level it can be said that Bismarck's failure to institutionalize the possibility of a parliamentary opposition, such as is required by the constitutional structure of any modern industrial society which seeks to be equal to the demands of constant social change, freed the political and social system of the Reich from legitimate pressures to bring about reform and modernization. This was an important cause of the permanent backwardness of that system, from within which the authoritarian interventionist state emerged more and more clearly after 1879. Bismarck had procured majorities for himself during the first ten years after unification by the technique of negative integration—attacking supposed "enemies of the Reich". But the reaction to the "re-founding" of the Reich on a conservative basis from 1879 onwards was demonstrated most dramatically in the Reichstag elections of 1881, which brought Bismarck his heaviest parliamentary defeat since 1863. The opposition grouped around the large left-liberal block won a majority and the internal crisis of the Bonapartist dictatorship became glaringly apparent.[33]

By this time Bismarck had recognized the potential of overseas policy, both as a long-term integrating factor and as a tactical electoral gambit: the public agitation in favour of colonial expansion and the ideological consensus in favour of social imperialism and an export offensive were becoming unmistakeably more widespread. The Chancellor recognized, as did the leading figures of this consensus, that imperialism could provide a new "vision of hope" (Fabri), "a distant, greater goal" (Hübbe-Schleiden), "a new, additional purpose" (v.d. Brüggen), or that it could at least be held up as a sort of "counter-utopia" in opposition to that of the democratic socialist republic. When these advocates of expansion postulated "common economic interests in an overseas policy" as necessary to the "internal unity of Germany", they showed an awareness of the integrating effects of colonial expansion; again, it was "only through such expansion abroad . . . that the unity of our people . . . [could] be consolidated". It was precisely this effect that Bismarck had in mind in seeing the primary "opportunist side" of his imperialism as "the provision of a new objective for the Germans, one capable of filling them with enthusiasm after the popularity of the government had begun to wane"; he hoped "to steer the Germans towards new paths" abroad, away from the numerous problems at home.[34]

In addition to the economic motives, social imperialism was to divert attention away from the descriptive consequences of uneven economic growth, away from social tensions and away from the emancipatory task of modernizing German constitutional life and of democratizing society. In view of the strength and resilience of traditional forces, the "intensity" with which Germany undertook its imperialistic policies was bound up with the fact *that imperialism stifled discontent about the political structure of the Reich and helped to conceal the latent gulf between the parties and the state; it became, as it were, a substitute area for otherwise inhibited political activity; it was, in addition, able to neutralize class tensions and conflicts. Imperialism was the field within which the adaptation of the bourgeois parties to the reality of the state, its structure and its needs was accomplished.*

From the early 1880s imperialism became an ideological force for integration in a state which lacked stabilizing historical traditions and which was unable to conceal sharp class divisions beneath its authoritarian cloak. "According to the Napoleonic precept that gave birth to it", imperialism was "to dispel domestic problems by means of setting compelling goals for the state abroad"; these problems seemed barely soluble by any other method within the framework of the autocratic pseudo-constitutionalism of the new Reich.[35] When Bismarck recognized the domestic possibilities of imperialism, he did not hesitate to exploit them. The ideological consensus showed him that some of the necessary pre-requisites were fulfilled: the enthusiasm for colonies was sufficiently widespread; its potential appeal, at any rate, was promising enough to act as a rallying point and to make it worthwhile turning to the electorate on this issue; it also gave sufficient scope to illusions and fears for a well-aimed propaganda to be able—with at least the appearance of credibility—to represent the decision to bid for colonies as a decision of fundamental importance; last but by no means least, however, it was able to perform the function of diverting attention from internal problems. The critical state of affairs during the period of depression after 1882 was particularly favourable to the growing emphasis on the domestic-political functions of the enthusiasm for colonies. As early as 1879 Fabri had made the fundamentally important sociological observation that "the mood produced by our economic position" was acting as a stimulus to the expansionist debate, and subsequently other publicists and politicians saw this connection no less clearly: even the left-wing Liberal deputy v. Bunsen had recognized that "the cause of the widespread enthusiasm lay . . . without any doubt in the hope'' that the situation might be relieved by imperialist policies. The growing enthusiasm for empire based as it was on the hope of finding, in the shape of overseas markets and in colonial possessions, a palliative for the continuing misery at home, can thus be understood as a specific crisis ideology designed to channel the emotional tensions, the hysteria and the growing frustration which then, as later, accompanied periods of economic depression, towards a vague external goal. In social-psychological terms, the ''colonial fever'' often worked as a form of escapism from the socio-economic and political problems of the depression and from the far-reaching transformation process that was turning Germany into an industrial society. This is confirmed by the fact that high ''colonial fever'' started to decline when the economic barometer began to rise again after 1886. The parallels with the political anti-semitism of these years—another form of the same escapism—are obvious.[36]

From the spring of 1884 onwards Bismarck began to guide the flood of colonial enthusiasm on to his own electoral mill. Fear of the Socialists had been exploited in previous elections (1877, 1881) as a means of integration; now the ''colonial fever'' was used in the same way. It was used on three different levels: first, against individual Deputies, in particular against the leading representatives of the political opposition like Eugen Richter and Ludwig Bamberger; second, against one or several groups of *''Reichsfeinde''*, particularly against the Progressives; and third, against a foreign power, in this case Great Britain, in much the same way as Catholicism, the Socialist International, and in 1887 France, were designated as opponents of the Reich. In each case the objective was to produce an effect beneficial to the government's policies, putting out in the cold opponents at home and abroad. Electoral propaganda started striking at these three targets from May 1884 onwards. Since the differentiation between domestic friends and foes might not be effective enough, crude nationalistic sentiments were mobilized against Great Britain. For months the government press attacked English policies, and the basis was laid for the subsequently successful propaganda stereotype of ''perfidious Albion''. By emphasizing the tensions in relations with London and playing down the relatively speedy settlement of colonial disputes between the two nations, Bismarck gave renewed proof of his dubious "art of utilizing in domestic affairs the head of steam generated by his foreign policies", and the opposition at home could now be attacked not only for being "hostile to the Reich", but also for being supporters of a foreign power.[37]

In the 1880s and after, anglophobic nationalism was an especially apposite instrument of Bismarck's technique of ruling through diverting the pent-up pressures of internal problems towards foreign territories and towards foreign opponents, because England, the powerful rival with an almost irretrievable lead in world markets, had come to be seen as Germany's most serious competitor in the economic sphere. The rapidly growing economic self-consciousness of the German Reich in the 1870s and after did not view England only as a model to be imitated, but increasingly as the real competitive rival against whom antipathies could quickly be activated. The "hatred of England" which came to the fore during the periods of depression also had to some extent the function of externalizing anti-capitalist sentiment by directing it against the capitalist state *par excellence*. Both anti-semitism and anglophobia gave concrete expression to anti-capitalist resentment. Bismarck, never at a loss for a means of extricating himself from a difficult situation, may have thought that he would be able to keep control of these currents, but the long-term effect of this crude anglophobic nationalism proved to be a severe burden for German policy particularly when the seed of this nationalism came to fruition in the 1890s and thereafter. In the short term however, the electoral tactics paid off: the Progressives were decisively weakened in 1884 and never recovered from this defeat, the parties loyal to the government were clearly strengthened.

Though Bismarck tried to make much domestic political capital out of imperialism, he was far from identifying with noisy nationalist propaganda about Germany's rôle as a "world power". For his own position in international politics, based as it was on Germany's strength in Europe and on his own political genius, the new protectorates were but a *quantité négligeable*. The idea was certainly expressed on occasion that Germany owed it to her status as a great power to procure colonies, as if they were the insignia of a true "world power"—Max Weber's inaugural lecture at Freiburg (1895) was in so far clearly anticipated. Pan-German ideology in the Bismarckian era was also sporadically coupled with demands for colonial expansion: the banker Karl v.d. Heydt, one of the promoters of Peters, considered colonialism—"merely a means of bringing about the world supremacy of Germany, both politically and economically"—as "just one element of Pan-Germanism";[38] in the General German Congress *(Allgemeiner Deutscher Kongress)* of 1886 the supporters of such ideas even set up a short-lived organization, the immediate precursor of the Pan-German League. All these hopes of "world-policy", however, all these abstruse Pan-German ideas, were only incidental to the primary socio-economic reasons for expansion; they had no bearing on the decision-making process in Berlin, either in the 1880s or later.

One aspect of German imperialism before 1890 is the fact that Bismarck's overseas policy in the broad sense—from the promotion of trade and exports to the acquisition of formal empire—was following the expansive tendencies of the German industrial state; this seemed to be necessitated by contemporary circumstances and by the requirements of the socio-economic system. At the same time however, it served to assert the supremacy of the traditional ruling élites and to preserve the hitherto protected social hierarchy and authoritarian power structure. This social and domestic side of imperialism, this primacy of the domestic political constellation, which was in these years under the most severe pressure as the result of the world-wide economic fluctuations, should probably be considered the most important of Bismarck's motives. Here was the juncture, as it were, where the tradition of the Prussian "revolution from above", continued by Bonapartist methods appropriate to the time, was transformed into the social imperialism of an advanced industrial state, open for its part to all the social upheavals and economic fluctuations brought about by advanced capitalism.[39]

Under this head the policies of the "conservative alliance"— the "landowner-industrial condominium directed against the proletariat" (E. Kehr), which had been deliberately pursued since

the middle of the 1870s—the policy of protective tariffs, Puttkamer's handling of the bureaucracy, plans for the establishment of
monopolies, the anti-Socialist law and the social policy: all these
steps, together with the tentative anti-cyclical policy and the first
measures of the interventionist state in the spheres of foreign
trade and imperialism belong to one and the same socio-economic
and, above all, political context, as Bismarck sought by a wide
variety of means not only to curb and restrain the dynamics of the
industrial world, but also to exploit them as a means of preserving
the *status quo* inside Germany. All these efforts show facets of
the same labour of Sisyphus: ensuring and reinforcing the politically and socially threatened position of the ruling classes, as well
as Bismarck's own autocratic position at the peak of the pyramid
of power. He himself was clearly aware of this context. Again
and again he described in his impressive language the defensive
function of these measures for the benefit of the socially conservative, authoritarian state. He remained aware of the fact that the
Kaiserreich of 1871 was a very precarious structure. Above all he
considered that the continued existence of this Reich could be
permanently assured only if the authority of the traditional and
privileged ruling class were preserved, with the assistance of a
compliant conservative bureaucracy and a military machine independent of parliament and run on semi-absolutist lines. He
viewed with profound antipathy the spectre of possible future
parliamentary and democratic rule. Perhaps he secretly felt that
the situation was hopeless; but as long as it was possible, he
thought defence against an inexorable fate worthwhile, regardless of the cost to society as a whole. Holstein, in spite of his
increasing criticism of the Chancellor, admitted that only Bismarck could "accomplish . . . the greatest of all tasks, that of
holding back the revolution".[40]

Bismarck sought to extend the life span of the old authorities
and structures by Bonapartist, and ultimately by social imperialist methods. If one views imperialism as an integral part of this
struggle of Bismarck's to defend his idea of the social order and
his own power position, and if one also views the ultimate basis
of this policy as the "stabilization" of the social order of the
Reich of 1871, then one can understand his statement made to

Ambassador Münster in London that "for internal reasons, the colonial question . . . is one of vital importance for us". It is well known that Bismarck was very reticent in his use of the terms "question of vital importance" and "vital interests". If he did decide to express the matter in those terms, then it was because he ascribed such an important domestic function to imperialist policies that he viewed "the position of the government at home as being dependent on [its] success". In 1886 Herbert v. Bismarck declared on his father's instructions that it had been "this concern for domestic politics" which had "made it essential for us" to embark upon formal colonial expansion, "since all those elements loyal to the Reich have the keenest interest in the success of our colonizing efforts". This shows the same social imperialist link with domestic policy as can be seen in President Grover Cleveland's assessment of American expansionist policy in Latin America, when he said that it was not a question of foreign policy but "the most distinct of home questions" upon the solution of which the "welfare" of the United States depended.[41]

Thus his overseas policy was also a component of Bismarck's policy of preserving the *status quo* in state and society: it held out the prospect of economic advantage, and acted as a sort of tension-conductor. Although the Chancellor was not unfamiliar with the social Darwinism of his time, and recognized that struggle was the essence of politics, he did have a vision of a state of ultimate social and political peace, free of the troubles of permanent conflict, and he did harbour the wish for a sort of armistice like that which appears in the equilibrium models of classical economists or in the harmony of a better world envisaged by social philosophers. And just as the equilibrium model fails to take into account the dynamic nature of the industrial system, and the social philosophers ignore the inherent insolubility of modern social conflict, so Bismarck's vision was enveloped in illusions. In spite of all his predilections for *Realpolitik* he pursued the utopia of a finally ordered and static community which for this reason needed peaceful relations with foreign powers. There is however in the industrial world of continuous social change hardly any other utopia which is more dangerous and more certain to fail than this conservative endeavour to freeze the historically outdated structure of a society and a state. In an age of critical social change and inhibited economic growth, Bismarck sought to pursue a conservative policy, even to the point of exploiting imperialism for the preservation of the internal structure of the Prusso-German state.

In historical perspective the dilemma of his policies and thus also of his social imperialism is to be found in the fact that his vision of a conservative utopia induced him to react to a period of rapid development by repressive and diversionary measures, whereas a truly realistic *Realpolitik*, keeping in step with industrial growth and the process of democratization, should have had as its starting point the political and social process of emancipation, and should indeed have sought to further this process. Like many others after him, Bismarck sought to slow down the irresistible modernization process of the industrial world, and there were present in his Bonapartist system some prerequisites for short-term success: there existed a capable leadership, a strong bureaucratic machine, a relatively clear independence of the rulers from society and from extreme influences from the right and left. Basically, however, the régime's policies faced in the long run an insoluble problem: modernization is impossible without a basic transformation of the social structure and of the power relationships existing within it; and similarly it is impossible without social and political emancipation, if peace at home and abroad is to be preserved. The fatal effects of the government's policy whereby the political control of the pre-industrial ruling classes was preserved during the period of intensive industrialization, finally became definitively clear between 1914 and 1929, when these old structures crumbled. Up till that time these policies had helped to create the foundations which allowed fascism in its most radical form to succeed in Germany (alone among highly industrialized nations): the barriers to the emancipation of broad social strata led to the *révolte des déclassés* of industrialization.[42]

Bismarck's imperialism had far-reaching and grave consequences for German politics. Between 1879 and 1885 the Reich was being set on new foundations. The conservative alliance, protectionism, anti-Socialist measures, overseas expansion—

these were the means whereby the new, conservative, interventionist state was founded, a state hostile to emancipation and prepared to protect itself by social imperialism. Following upon the three hegemonic wars and the ritual at Versailles, Bismarck once again became a "founder", and his overseas policy was cast within the framework of a "founding period". From quite different evaluative standpoints eminent historians have recently reaffirmed the fundamental importance of such "founding periods" when, visibly or invisibly, lines are set which determine the whole course of future developments. They all share, *mutatis mutandis,* the view of Eugen Rosenstock-Huessy that the "climates" which are produced in countries at such times stay with them for long periods.[43] In just such a way the German Reich, during the "founding period" of 1879–1885, set a new direction in opting for state intervention in the social and economic fields. Rather than persist with the less hazardous and more lucrative methods of informal empire, German overseas policy, reacting to the pressure of irregular economic growth, of world-wide competition and of ideas of social imperialism, resorted to formal colonial rule. Until then Bismarck had counted Germany among the "satisfied powers"; he continued to do so in public, and there is no denying that his foreign policy in Europe was conducted on that principle. But the growth of Germany's industrial economy now revealed that the state of national and power-political saturation as Bismarck understood it was being upset by economic forces. After the German-Austrian alliance and the plan for a customs union had made the self-limitation to a *kleindeutsches* Reich seem uncertain, overseas expansion from the 1880s onwards, taken together with modern *Mitteleuropa* plans, meant a new breaking-out from Germany's position in the middle of Europe. As far as it resulted in formal colonial rule overseas it remained an interlude—in the long run informal economic expansion has proved to be safer and more profitable for Germany too—but this interlude was followed after 1914 and 1939 by a move towards open continental and world hegemony. A glance at German policy after Bismarck's dismissal shows the subsequent effects of the change of direction during the "founding period" 1879–1885. As Bismarck sought to defend the authoritarian state with its privileged leadership, while yet seeking to go along with the irresistible development of Germany's industrial economy, the basis of imperial policy remained the "conservative alliance" between big business and the landowning classes, which was one of the inheritances of the depression of 1873–1879. That this "cartel of forces preserving the state" occasionally failed to function, does not disguise its remarkable continuity, as was shown again during the First World War. In this respect too, the effects of the second founding period extended until the decline of Bismarck's Reich.

Miquel explained the programme of his "conservative alliance" in 1897 by saying that "the co-operation of powerful economic groups was a suitable way of bringing the parties closer together". Imperialism should continue to have the purpose of "turning our thoughts abroad", of diverting the "revolutionary element" and of "putting the nation's feelings . . . on a common footing". Thus the social imperialist motive was further pursued, and it later emerged in similar, if modified form with the liberal imperialists of the Wilhelmine Empire, with Friedrich Naumann and Max Weber, with Ernst v. Halle and Ernst Francke and many others: they either held that social policies should help Germany to play a vigorous world rôle by appeasing the working class, or, alternatively, that only a successful world policy would provide the material basis for social policies. This interdependence of social policy and *Weltpolitik* whereby the former was degraded to the point of having only functional value and where class integration was seen merely as a prerequisite of world power was an idea expounded with particular clarity and persistence by Weber and v. Halle. Admiral v. Tirpitz produced a classic statement of social imperialist aims when he said that "in this new and important national task of imperialism and in the economic gain that will result from it, we have a powerful palliative against both educated and uneducated social democrats".[44]

If Wilhelmine *Weltpolitik* stressed the prestige factor more strongly than hitherto, the socio-psychological explanation of it, which emphasizes the growing nationalism, the feeling of overflowing vitality and the wanton urge of self-assertion associated with the economic boom since 1896, does not suffice. To this

must be added the social-historical explanation that the policy of
Weltpolitik had its origins in the internal class divisions and in the
social and political tensions between on the one hand the authoritarian state, the landed nobility and the feudalized bourgeoisie,
and on the other hand, the advancing forces of parliamentarization and democratization and, most important, the social democratic movement towards emancipation. This policy was intended
to heal or at least to cover up the internal divisions by diverting
attention overseas and by achieving prestigious successes or tan-
gible advantage through imperialist policies. Bülow, following in
the footsteps of Miquel, asserted that "only a successful foreign
policy can help, reconcile, conciliate, rally together and unify".
Holstein too was thinking of this motif when, on account of the
hopelessly confused domestic situation, he declared,

> *Kaiser Wilhelm's government needs some tangible success abroad
> which will then have a beneficial effect at home. Such a success can be
> expected either as a result of a European war, a risky policy on a world
> wide scale, or as the result of territorial acquisitions outside Europe.*[45]

IV
Conclusion
Having looked ahead at the Wilhelmine period, the foundations
of which were undoubtedly laid in the Bismarckian era, we may
now summarize the most important aspects of German imperialism under Bismarck.

Political Economy: Bismarck's policy of pragmatic expansionism was one aspect of his policy of giving state support to Germany's foreign trade; it was also part of his experimental anti-
cyclical policy (not then theoretically worked out) whereby the
growing interventionist state risked the transition from informal
empire to formal colonial rule and thereby sought to ensure for
the expanding system of advanced capitalism, particularly during
times of economic hardship, a steady growth rate, commercial
outlets abroad, and an extension of markets beyond national
boundaries. The pressure of forces inherent in the economic system can here be seen clearly at work.

Domestic policy: Imperialism served as a means of integrating
a state torn by class differences, whereby the enthusiasm for

colonies and crude anglophobe nationalism could be manipulated as crisis ideologies for electoral and party political purposes in particular. Using the policy of expansion, the Prusso-German "revolution from above", supplemented by Bonapartist techniques of rule, was continued—under the conditions of advanced industrialization, in the form of social imperialism.

Social Structure: Social imperialism served to defend the traditional social and power structures of the Prusso-German state, and to shield them from the turbulent effects of industrialization as well as from the movements towards parliamentarization and democratization; last but not least, it served to keep the Bonapartist dictator in power. As a diversionary tactic, social imperialism temporarily fulfilled its most important function in slowing down the process of social and political emancipation. From the time of the second founding period of the Reich, the concept of social imperialism remained a blueprint for political action. In this respect it is of fundamental importance to any consideration of the question of continuity in modern German history. "After the fall of Bismarck, there was a growing inclination to neutralize" the inherited "deep discrepancies between the social structure and the political order, which had barely taken into account the changed social situation brought about by the industrial revolution"; this neutralization was "achieved by diverting the pressure of interests towards objectives abroad—in the sense of a social imperialism which helped to conceal the need for the long overdue reforms of the internal structure of Germany". Especially Tirpitz understood Germany's imperialism together with its new instrument of power, the battle fleet, in this sense; he too was aiming for a conservative utopia, but one in which the place of the pre-industrial élite was to be taken by the propertied and educated bourgeoisie. These motive forces continued to propel Germany's policies on war aims and annexations during the First World War, for these policies too demonstrably aimed at postponing further the much delayed internal restructuring of Germany. Once more a successful expansionist and foreign policy was supposed to be a substitute for a modern domestic policy; it was supposed to conceal both the fatal shortcomings of the hegemonic Prussian state and the paralysis of Imperial policy.[46]

Even the débâcle of 1918 did not yet finally destroy the seductive force of this same policy—that of delaying emancipation at home by means of expansion abroad. One last extreme effort was added, not many years later, to the fateful continuity of this policy pursued since the 1870s. In German overseas policies under Bismarck, a form of pragmatic expansionism which was determined by the real or imagined pressures of the industrial system was combined with a form of social imperialism, which served as a model for later rulers, who could justify their political decisions by referring to the legitimizing precedents of the Bismarckian era. It certainly always remains a problematical undertaking to pass judgment on the long-term effects of the thoughts and actions of individuals, and on the degree to which they are responsible for them. But equally undeniable is the dominating influence of successful political actions and the ideological arguments used to justify them, particularly during a founding period and particularly when those actions were initially protected from criticism by the overwhelming authority of a dominant personality—even though the success may later turn out to have been illusory and even disadvantageous. If one then pursues this historically specific line of development—namely, the social imperialist opposition to the emancipation process in German industrial society—then one will be able to trace a line linking Bismarck, Miquel, Bülow and Tirpitz to the extreme social imperialism of the National Socialist variety, which once again sought to block domestic progress by breaking out first towards the *Ostland*, and then overseas, thus diverting attention from the loss of all liberty at home and once again reinforcing the spell of a conservative utopia. "However long and circuitous the path leading from Bismarck to Hitler may have been"—these words of Hans Rothfels can be repeated in this consideration of the continuity of German policy—"the founder of the Reich appears to be the man responsible for a change of policy, responsible at least for legitimizing a policy, the ultimate and fatal consummation of which has, in our own time, become all too obvious".[47]

NOTES

[1] This essay, translated by Norman Porter (Dulwich College), J. Sheehan, and T. W. Mason, summarizes some interpretative results of my researches into German imperialism prior to 1890, published as *Bismarck und der Imperialismus* (Köln, 1969; 2nd edn. 1970). This book also contains a history of the relevant events, which is here left out: pp. 194–407. For a definition of the concept of imperialism, *ibid.*, p. 23.

[2] The book is based, apart from published material, on the unpublished documents of the Prussian and Imperial administrations, some federal German states and the Hanseatic towns, as well as numerous manuscript collections of leading politicians (including the Bismarcks), of important figures in the economy and administration, and of several journalists and makers of public opinion: cf. *ibid.*, pp. 517–66.

[3] Cf., the detailed discussion, *ibid.*, pp. 14–33, as well as the introduction to H.-U. Wehler, ed., *Imperialismus* (Köln, 1970), pp. 11–36.

[4] Cf., M. Olson, "Rapid Growth as a Destabilizing Force", *Jl. Econ. Hist.*, xxiii (1963), pp. 529–52; R. G. Ridker, "Discontent and Economic Growth", *Economic Development and Cultural Change*, xi (1962), pp. 1–15; also, generally, J. C. Davies, "Towards a Theory of Revolution", *Amer. Sociol. Rev.*, xxvii (1962), pp. 1–19; L. Stone, "Theories of Revolution", *World Politics*, xviii (1966), pp. 160–76; C. Johnson, *Revolutionary Change* (Boston, 1966). A very stimulating pioneer study into these aspects of modern German History is H. Rosenberg, *Grosse Depression und Bismarckzeit* (Berlin, 1967).

[5] T. Veblen, *Imperial Germany and the Industrial Revolution* (1915; Ann Arbor, 1966); A. Gerschenkron, *Economic Backwardness in Historical Perspective* (Cambridge, Mass., 1962); *id.*, *Continuity in History* (Cambridge, Mass., 1968); *id.*, "Die Vorbedingungen der europäischen Industrialisierungen im 19. Jahrhundert", in W. Fischer, ed., *Wirtschafts- und sozialgeschichtliche Probleme der frühen Industrialisierung* (Berlin, 1968), pp. 21–8. Generally D. S. Landes, *The Unbound Prometheus. Technological Change and Industrial Development in Western Europe from 1750 to the Present* (Cambridge, 1969). With regard to the country of the first Industrial Revolution cf. in particular T. S. Ashton, *Economic Fluctuations in England, 1700–1800* (Oxford, 1959); A. D. Gayer, W. W. Rostow, and Z. Schwarz, *The Growth and Fluctuation of the British Economy, 1790–1850* (Oxford, 1952), 2 vols; R. C. O. Mathews, *A Study in Trade-Cycle-History. Economic Fluctuations in Great Britain, 1833–42* (Cambridge, 1954); J. R. T. Hughes, *Fluctuations in Trade, Industry and Finance. A Study of British Economic Development 1850–1860* (Oxford, 1960); J. Tinbergen, *Business Cycles in the United Kingdom, 1870–1914* (Amsterdam, 1951); W. W. Rostow, *British Economy of the 19th Century* (London, 1948); *id.*, "Business Cycles, Harvests, and Politics, 1790–1850", *Jl. Econ. Hist.*, i (1941), pp. 206–21. A bibliography of studies on the so-

called "Great Depression" is in Wehler, *Bismarck*, p. 509, and S. B. Saul, *The Myth of the Great Depression, 1873–96* (London, 1969), whose arguments I do not find convincing. The (in my view) most important studies about U.S.A., Russia, France, Italy, Austria, etc. are cited in Wehler, *Bismarck*, pp. 509 f. A general discussion is to be found in H.-U. Wehler, "Theorieprobleme der modernen deutschen Wirtschaftsgeschichte (1800–1945)", in *Festschrift für H. Rosenberg* (Berlin, 1970), pp. 66–107, also printed in *id.*, *Krisenherde des Kaiserreichs, 1871–1918* (Göttingen, 1970).

   6 Cf., B. Semmel, "On the Economics of Imperialism" in B. Hoselitz, ed., *Economics and the Idea of Mankind* (New York, 1965), pp. 192–232; A. G. Meyer, *Leninism*, 3rd edn. (Cambridge, Mass., 1965), pp. 235–73; and T. Kemp, *Theories of Imperialism* (London, 1967). When D. S. Landes "Some Thoughts on the Nature of Economic Imperialism", *Jl. Econ. Hist.*, xxi (1961), pp. 496–512, derives imperialism from "disparities of power", then he is basically linking it to the problems of uneven growth: cf., Wehler ed., *Imperialismus;* a more detailed account of the problems of German economic growth, Wehler, *Bismarck*, pp. 39–111.

   7 J. A. Schumpeter, *The Theory of Economic Development* (New York, 1961), p. 67.

   8 In detail, Wehler, *Bismarck*, pp. 112–93; on social imperialism, pp. 112–20.

   9 Cf., W. Sauer "Das Problem des deutschen Nationalstaats", in *Moderne Deutsche Sozialgeschichte*, ed. H.-U. Wehler, 3rd edn. (Köln, 1970), pp. 407–36; H. Gollwitzer, "Der Cäsarismus Napoleons III. im Widerhall der öffentlichen Meinung Deutschlands", *Historische Zeitschrift*, clxiii (1952), pp. 23–75, particularly pp. 65 ff; E. Engelberg, "Zur Entstehung und historischen Stellung des preussischdeutschen Bonapartismus", in *Festschrift für A. Meusel* (Berlin, 1956), pp. 236–51; F. Borkenau, "Zur Soziologie des Faschismus", *Archiv für Sozialwissenschaft*, lxviii (1933), pp. 527–44. In detail, Wehler, *Bismarck*, pp. 180–93, 454–502. As far as I can see, there is no modern analysis of Bonapartism as a type of rule that is related to particular phases of economic growth—at least in the France of Napoleon III, and in Bismarck's Germany; how would Schwarzenberg, Prim and Disraeli fit in? Unfortunately, there is no such analysis in T. Zeldin, *The Political System of Napoleon III* (London, 1958). The classical analysis can be found in K. Marx, "Der 18. Brumaire", *Marx-Engels-Werke*, viii (Berlin, 1962), pp. 115–207. Cf. however, J. S. Schapiro, *Liberalism and the Challenge of Fascism. Social forces in England and France, 1815–1870* (New York, 1949), pp. 308–31; R. Griepenburg and K. H. Tjaden, "Faschismus und Bonapartismus", *Das Argument*, xxxi (1966), pp. 461–72; O. Bauer *et al.*, *Faschismus und Kapitalismus* (Frankfurt, 1968), pp. 5–18, 19–38.

   10 J. Habermas, *Technik und Wissenschaft als "Ideologie"* (Frankfurt, 1969), pp. 48–103; Habermas is partly following C. Offe, "Politische Herrschaft und Klassenstrukturen", in D. Senghaas ed., *Politikwissenschaft* (Frankfurt, 1969), pp. 155–89. Cf. generally J. K. Galbraith, *The New Industrial State* (New York, 1967); A. Shonfield, *The Changing Balance of Public and Private Power* (London, 1965); A. Löwe, *On Economic Knowledge* (New York, 1965). For contemporary reaction in the 1880s, cf. Wehler, *Bismarck*, p. 479, *et passim*.

[11] R. E. Robinson and D. Gallagher, *Africa and the Victorians. The Official Mind of Imperialism* (London, 1961); "The Partition of Africa", *New Cambridge Modern History*, xi (London, 1963), pp. 593–640; Robinson's introduction to H. Brunschwig, *French Colonialism, 1871–1914* (London, 1966; Fr. Paris, 1960), pp. vii–x; similarly D. K. Fieldhouse, "Imperialism", *Econ. Hist. Rev.*, 2nd ser., xiv (1961–2), pp. 187–209; *id.*, ed., *The Theory of Capitalist Imperialism* (London, 1967), pp. 13–19, 192; A. G. L. Shaw, "A Revision of the Meaning of Imperialism", *Australian Journal of Politics and History*, v (1962), pp. 198–213, also E. M. Winslow, *The Pattern of Imperialism* (New York, 1948); C. J. Lowe, *The Reluctant Imperialists, 1871–1902* (London, 1967), 2 vols; in R. Faber's book *The Vision and the Need. Late Victorian Imperialist Aims* (London, 1966), the "vision" is dealt with, but not the "need". It is known that Gallagher/Robinson, whose impressive achievements in historical research are undisputed, emphatically sought to demonstrate with regard to late-Victorian English policy, that England's ruling élites, in defence of traditional strategic interests (India) or influenced by forces outside Europe (reaction to protonationalist movements in Africa), were forced to extend their formal Empire, but that they were in no way following powerful domestic forces, that imperialism was primarily a political phenomenon. They made claims for the general validity of this theory (*Africa*, p. xi), but immediately destroyed it because of the atypical and special position which England, as the first industrial power, occupied, thanks to having had a monopoly overseas for many years. Nor do they attempt to verify their theory, which, in the case of Germany, the U.S.A., Belgium and so on, would have been impossible. Where can they try to locate traditional interests and proto-nationalistic movements influencing German policy when German Imperialism began? Uncritically they take over A. J. P. Taylor's simplistic theory about German colonial policy (which can easily be falsified), because it suits their purpose. Their model cannot successfully be defended either theoretically or empirically; even British imperialism during those years poses numerous questions which are excluded by their model. Apart from the fact that the description of policy in South Africa undercuts the authors' theories, their theories take no account of the many domestic and foreign interests which everywhere are the basis of certain stereotypes of political language and which condition the political horizon of ruling élites—the self-evident economic importance of India, for instance. In many respects their book is an exercise in belated historicism, with subtle apologetics. The authors set up an artificial "distinction between politics and economics", which, as G. Barraclough, *Introduction to Contemporary History* (London, 1964), pp. 49 ff., immediately objected, "is unreal". It certainly does not correspond to the interdependence of the two factors in industrial countries. For a general criticism cf., D. C. M. Platt, *Finance, Trade and Politics in British Foreign Policy, 1814–1914* (Oxford, 1968); *id.*, "Economic Factors in British Policy During the 'New Imperialism' ", *Past and Present*, no. 39 (1968), pp. 120–38; E. J. Hobsbawm, *Industry and Empire* (London, 1968), pp. 88–127; *id.*, "Die Imperialismusdebatte in der Geschichtsschreibung", *Sozialistische Politik*, i (1969), pp. 16–25; Kemp, *op. cit.*, pp. 134–56; W. J. Mommsen, "Nationale und ökonomische Faktoren im britischen Imperialismus vor 1914", *Hist. Zeitschr.*, ccvi (1968), pp. 618–64. Par-

ticular criticisms: J. Stengers, "L'Imperialisme colonial de la fin du 19e siècle, mythe ou réalité?", *Jl. African Hist.*, iii (1962), pp. 469–91; C. W. Newbury, "Victorians, Republicans, and the Partition of West Africa", *ibid.*, pp. 493–501; G. Shepperson, "Africa, The Victorians and Imperialism", *Revue Belge de Philologie et d'Histoire*, xl (1962), pp. 1228–38; E. Stokes, *Imperialism and the Scramble for Africa* (London, 1963); R. Hyam, "The Partition of Africa", *Hist. Jl.*, iii (1964), pp. 154–69. Unfortunately, no comparable stimulating discussion of the topic has been produced by German historians: cf., only Mommsen, *art. cit.*, pp. 622 ff.; Wehler, *Bismarck*, pp. 25 ff., *passim; id.*, ed., *Imperialismus*.

[12] F. Fabri, *Fünf Jahre deutscher Kolonialpolitik* (Gotha, 1889), p. 26. The expansionist economic policies of the Reich towards Russia and the Balkans as undeveloped areas, are not here considered; cf., H.-U. Wehler, "Bismarcks Imperialismus und Russlandpolitik", in M. Stürmer ed., *Das kaiserliche Deutschland* (Düsseldorf, 1970).

[13] *Documents Diplomatiques Français* (hereafter DDF), 1st ser., v, 14 September 1884, pp. 404 ff. I am arguing here *contra* M. E. Townsend, *Origins of Modern German Colonialism, 1871–85* (New York, 1921); *European Colonial Expansion since 1871* (New York, 1941); "The Impact of Imperial Germany, Commercial and Colonial Policies", *Jl. Econ. Hist.*, Suppl. (1943), pp. 124–34, also in G. N. Nadel and P. Curtis, eds., *Imperialism and Colonialism* (New York, 1964), pp. 130–9.

[14] R. Lucius v. Ballhausen, *Bismarck-Erinnergungen* (Stuttgart, 1921), p. 334 (21 Feb. 1886). *Die Politischen Reden des Fürsten Bismarcks*, ed. H. Kohl, xii (Stuttgart, 1905), p. 320 (1 April 1895).

[15] A note written by Krauel about O'Swald's comments, 9 October 1888, *Reichskolonialamt* (hereafter RKA), vol. 360, pp. 140–9 (marginal note by Bismarck), *Deutsches Zentralarchiv 1*, Postdam (hereafter DZA).

[16] Cf., on policy in China, Wehler, *Bismarck und der Imperialismus*, pp. 195–206, 409 ff.; also H. Stoecker, *Deutschland und China im 19. Jahrhundert* (Berlin, 1958); H. Washausen, *Hamburg und die Kolonialpolitik des deutschen Reiches 1880–90* (Hamburg, 1968); D. Glade, *Bremen und der Ferne Osten* (Bremen, 1966).

[17] Bismarck to Wilhelm I, 2 June 1873, *Reichsamt des Innern*, vol. 5266, pp. 23 ff., DZA.

[18] F. v. Holstein, *Die Geheimen Papiere* (Göttingen, 1957), ii, p. 174; RKA, vol. 7159, pp. 151 ff.—Bismarck's comments upon L. Baare's letter.

[19] H. R. v. Poschinger, ed., *Fürst Bismarck und die Parlamentarier* (Breslau, 1896), iii, p. 106; on the ideological consensus, Wehler, *Bismarck und der Imperialismus*, pp. 112–93.

[20] Cf. the detailed evidence *ibid.*, pp. 430 ff.

[21] H. Hofmann, ed., *Fürst Bismarck, 1890–98* (Stuttgart, 1913), i, p. 106; W. Hübbe-Schleiden, *Überseeische Politik* (Hamburg, 1883), xi, p. 121; F. Fabri, *Deutsch-Ostafrika* (Köln, 1886), p. 8; H. Böhme, *Deutschlands Weg zur Grossmacht* (Köln, 1966), p. 477. In these respects Cleveland, McKinley, Salisbury, Witte, Caprivi, Hohenlohe-Schillingsfürst *et al.* can be considered as pragmatic expansionists.

[22] Cf. in greater detail, Wehler, *Bismarck und der Imperialismus*, chaps. ii and iii.

²³ DDF, v (28 Sept. 1884), 427 ff; Wehler, *Bismarck und der Imperialismus*, pp. 112–93; Landes, *Unbound Prometheus*, p. 240; also *id.* in *Cambridge Economic History of Europe* (London, 1965), vi (1), p. 468.

²⁴ Cf., H. A. Turner, "Bismarck's Imperialist Venture. Anti-British in Origin?", in P. Gifford and W. R. Louis, eds., *Britain and Germany in Africa* (New Haven, 1967), pp. 47–82.

²⁵ *Korrespondent von und für Deutschland*, 3 April 1883, 25 June 1885; Government commissioner v. Kusserow, 2 March 1885, in Stenographische Berichte über die Verhandlungen des deutschen Reichstags (RT) 6:1:3:1501; Wehler, *Bismarck und der Imperialismus*, p. 437 ff; *The Foreign Policy of Lord Rosebery* (London, 1901), Speech to the Royal Colonial Institute, 1 March 1893; cf. R. Koebner and H. D. Schmidt, *Imperialism* (Cambridge, 1965), p. 202; Bülow, RT, 159, 60 (6 December 1897).

²⁶ Krauel to H. v. Bismarck, 20 March 1885, Bismarck Papers, vol. 18, Schloss Friedrichsruh; RKA, vol. 360 1, pp. 140–9, Bismarck's marginal note.

²⁷ Kohl, *Bismarck*, xi, p. 94 (14 March 1885). The heterogeneity can be further seen in the German Charter Companies and also in the legal status of the Protectorates, or the Crown Colonies. Cf. E. R. Huber, *Deutsche Verfassungsgeschichte seit 1789* (Stuttgart, 1969), iv, pp. 604–34; Wehler, *Bismarck und der Imperialismus*, pp. 422–44.

²⁸ For the details, *ibid.*, pp. 446–50.

²⁹ E. Preiser, "Die Imperialismusdebatte", in *Festschrift für F. Lütge* (Stuttgart, 1966), p. 370, cf., p. 366; L. J. Zimmerman, *Geschichte der theoretischen Volkswirtschaftslehre*, 2nd edn. (Köln, 1961), p. 105; *id.*, and F. Grumbach, "Saving, Investment, and Imperialism", *Weltwirtschaftliches Archiv*, lxxi (1953), pp. 1–19; and for another view S. B. Saul, comments, *ibid.*, lxxix (1957), pp. 105–9. Cf. H. Neisser, "Der ökonomische Imperialismus im Lichte moderner Theorie", *Hamburger Jahrbuch für Wirtschafts- und Gesellschaftspolitik*, iv (1959), p. 224; *id.*, *Some International Aspects of the Business Cycle* (Philadelphia, 1936), pp. 161–72; W. Röpke, "Kapitalismus und Imperialismus", *Schweizerische Zeitschrift für Volkswirtschaft und Statistik*, lxx (1934), p. 377. Probably one of the best comments can be found in E. Heimann, *Soziale Theorie der Wirtschaftssysteme* (Tübingen, 1963), *passim*. A conservative position is defended by L. H. Gann and P. Duignan, *Burden of Empire* (New York, 1967); "Reflections on Imperialism and the Scramble for Africa", in Gann and Duignan, eds., *Colonialism in Africa*, i, *The History and Politics of Colonialism, 1870–1914* (Cambridge, 1969), pp. 100–29; *vide* also G. Schulz, "Imperialismus des 19. Jahrhunderts", in his *Das Zeitalter der Gesellschaft* (Munich, 1969), pp. 112–72.

³⁰ *Cf.*, K. W. Hardach, *Die Bedeutung wirtschaftlicher Faktoren bei der Wiedereinführung der Eisen- und Getreidezölle in Deutschland 1879* (Berlin, 1967), pp. 70–2. Bismarck to the Budget Committee of the Reichstag, 23 June 1879, Akten des Reichstags, vol. 2621, p. 186, DZA Potsdam; cf. Kohl, *Bismarck*, x, pp. 167–71; O. v. Bismarck, *Gesammelte Werke*, xii (Berlin, 1935), pp. 471–5.

³¹ Heimann, *op. cit.*, pp. 46, 48, 329; Bueck, Jan. 1906, quoted from H. Kaelble, *Industrielle Interessenpolitik in der Wilhelminischen Gesellschaft. Centralverband deutscher Industrieller, 1895–1914* (Berlin, 1967), p. 149.

[32] Burckhardt to Preen, 26 September 1890, in his *Briefe*, ed. F. Kaphahn (Leipzig, 1935), p. 490. On social policy, Rosenberg, *op. cit.*, pp. 192–227; Wehler, *Bismarck*, pp. 449–64.

[33] G. Schmoller, *Charakterbilder* (Munich, 1913), p. 52; T. Heuss, "Das Bismarckbild im Wandel", in *id.*, ed., O. v. Bismarck, *Gedanken und Erinnerungen* (Berlin, 1951), p. 15; W. Mommsen, ed., *Deutsche Parteiprogramme* (Munich, 1960), p. 791; cf., particularly R. Lepsius, "Parteisystem und Sozialstruktur. Zum Problem der Demokratisierung der deutschen Gesellschaft", in *Festschrift Lütge*, *op. cit.*, pp. 371–93: *id.*, *Extremer Nationalismus* (Stuttgart, 1966); T. Schieder, *Staat und Gesellschaft im Wandel unserer Zeit*, 2nd edn. (Munich, 1970), p. 138; S. M. Lipset, *Political Man* (Garden City, 1963); R. Dahrendorf, "Demokratie und Sozialstruktur in Deutschland", in his *Gesellschaft und Freiheit* (Munich, 1961), pp. 260–99; *id.*, *Gesellschaft und Demokratie in Deutschland* (Munich, 1965).

[34] F. Fabri, *Bedarf Deutschland der Kolonien?* (Gotha, 1879), p. 88; W. Hübbe-Schleiden, *Deutsche Kolonisation* (Hamburg, 1884), p. 8; E. v. d. Brüggen, "Auswanderung, Kolonisation, Zweikindersystem", *Preussische Jahrbücher*, il (1882), p. 311; H. C. Schröder, *Sozialismus und Imperialismus* (Hanover, 1968), i, p. 117; F. Philipp, *Bismarck-Gespräche* (Dresden, 1927), p. 105; M. v. Hagen, "Graf Wolff Metternich über Haldane", *Deutsche Zukunft*, cxi (6 Jan. 1935), p. 5.

[35] T. Nipperdey, "Über einige Grundzüge der deutschen Parteigeschichte", in *Festschrift für H. C. Nipperdey* (Munich, 1965), ii, pp. 832 ff; W. Lipgens, "Bismarck, die öffentliche Meinung und die Annexion von Elass und Lothringen", *Hist. Zeitschr.*, cxcix (1964), p. 97.

[36] Fabri, *Bedarf Deutschland*, p. 3; Bunsen, RT 6:1:1:522 f. (10 Jan. 1885). On anti-semitism, Rosenberg, *op. cit.* pp. 88–117; Wehler, *Bismarck und der Imperialismus*, pp. 470–4; F. Kapp, *Briefe 1843–84*, ed. H.-U. Wehler (Frankfurt, 1969), pp. 39, 129 ff.

[37] H. Oncken, *R. v. Bennigsen* (Stuttgart, 1910), ii, p. 45; Wehler, *Bismarck und der Imperialismus*, pp. 473–83. The best analysis of the Anglo-German competition, Landes, *Prometheus*, *passim*. Cf. P. Bastin, *La Rivalité commerciale anglo-allemande et les Origines de la première Guerre Mondiale, 1871–1913* (Brussels, 1959); on anglophobia, E. Kehr, *Der Primat der Innenpolitik*, 2nd edn., ed. H.-U. Wehler (Berlin, 1970), pp. 149–75 ("Englandhass und Weltpolitik"); P. R. Anderson, *The Background of Anti-English Feeling in Germany, 1890–1902* (Washington, 1939). See W. Schenck, *Die Deutschenglische Rivalität vor dem Ersten Weltkrieg* (Aarau, 1967), on Weber, Ratzel, Lenz, Marcks, Meinecke, Hintze, Delbrück, Schäfer, Oncken, Schulze-Gävernitz. H. Pogge v. Strandmann, "Domestic Origins of Germany's Colonial Expansion under Bismarck", *Past and Present*, no. 42 (1969), pp. 140–59, very much overestimates the importance of the National Liberals for this policy. Some recent discussions of German colonial policy are based only on printed sources: W. O. Henderson, "German East Africa, 1884–1918", in V. Harlow *et al.*, eds., *History of East Africa*, ii (Oxford, 1965), pp. 123–62; M. Walker, *Germany and the Emigration, 1816–1885* (Cambridge, Mass., 1964), pp. 195–246; R. Cornevin, "The Germans in Africa before

1918", in L. H. Gann and P. Duigan, eds., *The History and Politics of Colonialism, op. cit.,* pp. 383–419. There are two new useful surveys offered by R. Tetzlaff, *Wirtschafts- und Sozialgeschichte Deutsch-Ostafrikas, 1885–1914* (Berlin, 1970); and K. Hausen, *Deutsche Kolonialherrschaft in Africa. Wirtschaftsinteressen und Kolonialaverwaltung in Kamerun vor 1914* (Zurich, 1970).

³⁸ K. v. d. Heydt to Hammacher, 30 June 1886, Hammacher Papers, vol. 57. DZA; cf. Wehler, *Bismarck und der Imperialismus,* pp. 483–5; A. Kruck, *Geschichte des Alldeutschen Verbandes, 1890–1939* (Wiesbaden, 1954); E. Hartwig, "Zur Politik und Entwicklung des Alldeutschen Verbandes, 1891–1914" (Jena, Phil. Diss., 1966, unpubl.); K. Schilling, "Beitrage zu einer Geschichte des radikalen Nationalismus in der Wilhelminischen Ara, 1890–1909" (Köln, Phil. Diss., 1968, unpubl.)

³⁹ Cf., with a similar interpretation, M. Weber, *Wirtschaft und Gesellschaft,* 4th edn. (Tübingen, 1965), ii, p. 527; R. Hilferding, *Das Finanzkapital* (Berlin, 1947), p. 506; O. Bauer, *Die Nationalitätenfrage und die Sozialdemokratie* 2nd edn. (Vienna, 1924), p. 494. This link was of course clearly seen by J. A. Hobson—cf. H. C. Schröder's introduction to the first German edition, *Der Imperialismus* (Köln, 1968), pp. 19–27, and by Lenin (cf. Meyer, *Leninism,* pp. 235–73); Wehler, *Bismarck und der Imperialismus,* pp. 116–20.

⁴⁰ Kehr, *Primat der Innenpolitik,* p. 164; Holstein, *op. cit.,* ii, p. 181.

⁴¹ *Grosse Politik der europäischen Kabinette,* iv, pp. 96 ff. (Bismarck to Münster, 25 Jan. 1885); H. v. Bismarck to Plessen, 14 Oct. 1886, RKA, vol. 603, pp. 21–9; K. v. Rantzau to Auswärtiges Amt, 29 Sept. 1886, Bismarck Papers, vol. 603; G. F. Parker, *Recollections of G. Cleveland* (New York, 1909), p. 195. For a comparison with American imperialist policy see above all William A. Williams, *The Roots of the Modern American Empire* (New York, 1969) and the literature cited there; H.-U. Wehler, "1889, Wendepunkt der amerikanischen Aussenpolitik. Anfänge des modernen Panamerikanismus—Die Samoakrise", *Hist. Zeitschr.,* lii (1965), pp. 67–109; id., "Sprungbrett nach Ostasien. Die amerikanische Hawaipolitik bis zur Annexion von 1895", *Jahrbuch für Amerikastudien,* x (1965), pp. 153–81; id., "Sendungsbewusstsein und Krise. Studien zur Ideologie des amerikanischen Imperialismus", *ibid.,* xiii (1968), pp. 98–133; id., "Der amerikanische Handelsimperialismus in China, 1884–1900", *ibid.,* xiv (1969), pp. 55–74; id., "Stützpunkte in der Karibischen See. Die Anfänge des amerikanischen Imperialismus auf Hispaniola", *Jahrbuch für Geschichte Lateinamerikas,* ii (1965), pp. 399–428; id., "Handelsimperium statt Kolonialherrschaft. Die Lateinamerikapolitik vor 1898", *ibid.,* iii (1966), pp. 184–318; id., "Cuba Libre und amerikanische Intervention", *ibid.,* v (1968), pp. 303–45.

⁴² Cf., B. Moore, *Social Origins of Dictatorship and Democracy,* 2nd edn. (Boston, 1967), pp. 433–52, 441; W. Sauer, "National Socialism: Totalitarianism or Fascism?", *Amer. Hist. Rev.,* lxxiii (1967), pp. 404–24; cf., K. Griewank, *Das Problem des christlichen Staatsmannes bei Bismarck* (Berlin, 1953). A theory of Bonapartism elastically applied would also provide possibilities for working out a theory of Fascism which would be worthy of discussion, cf., note 9.

⁴³ E. Rosenstock-Huessy, *Die Europäischen Revolutionen und der Charakter*

der Nationen (Stuttgart, 1962), p. 526; H. Arendt, "The Concept of History", in her *Between Past and Future* (New York, 1963), pp. 41–90; H. S. Hughes, *Consciousness and Society, 1890–1930*, 2nd edn. (New York, 1961); G. Masur, *Prophets of Yesterday* (New York, 1961); Rosenberg, *op. cit., passim;* Böhme, *op. cit.,* pp. 41, 419. On the consequences for foreign policy, specifically Bismarck's dilemma of being unable to react in another way, see Wehler, *Bismarck und der Imperialismus,* pp. 493–95.

[44] Miquel, 22 November 1897, according to Böhme, p. 316; cf., Kehr, *Primat der Innenpolitik, passim; id., Schlachtflottenbau und Parteipolitik* (Berlin, 1930); A. Gerschenkron, *Bread and Democracy in Germany,* 2nd edn. (New York, 1968) pp. 46 ff.; F. Meinecke, *Geschichte des deutsch-englischen Bündnisprobleme, 1890–1901* (Munich, 1927), pp. 6, 8; also Schmoller, *Charakterbilder,* p. 41; cf. Wehler, *Bismarck und der Imperialismus,* pp. 498 ff; Tirpitz, *Erinnerungen,* 2nd edn. (Leipzig, 1920), p. 52.

[45] J. Röhl, *Deutschland ohne Bismarck* (Tübingen, 1969), p. 229 (Bülow, 1897); Holstein to Kiderlen, 30 April 1897, Kiderlen Papers (supplied by H. Böhme).

[46] K. D. Bracher, *Deutschland zwischen Demokratie und Diktatur* (Munich, 1964), p. 155, cf. pp. 12, 151, 182 ff; *id.,* "Imperialismus", in Bracher and E. Fraenkel, eds., *Internationale Beziehungen* (Frankfurt, 1969), p. 123. On the problems of continuity see V. Berghahn, *Deutsche Rüstungspolitik, 1898–1908* (Mannheim, Unpubl. Phil. Habilschrift, 1970); *id.,* "Zu den Zielen des deutschen Flottenbaus unter Wilhelm II", *Hist. Zeitschr.,* ccx(i) (1970), pp. 34–100; H. Bley, *Kolonialherrschaft und Sozialstruktur in Deutsch-Südwestafrika, 1894–1914* (Hamburg, 1968); K. H. Jansen, *Macht und Verblendung, Kriegszielpolitik der deutschen Bundesstaaten, 1914–18* (Göttingen, 1963); F. Fischer, *Krieg der Illusionen, Die deutsche Politik von 1911 bis 1914* (Düsseldorf, 1969); *id., Griff nach der Weltmacht,* 3rd edn. (Düsseldorf, 1964); F. Stern, *Bethmann Hollweg und der Krieg: die Grenzen der Verantwortung* (Tübingen, 1968), pp. 22, 38, 45.

[47] H. Rothfels, "Probleme einer Bismarck-Biographie", *Deutsche Beiträge,* ii (Munich), 1948, p. 170; cf. however Rothfels's recent statement in his *Bismarck* (Stuttgart, 1970), pp. 8–12; Griewank,˙p. 55, comes to a similar conclusion. On continuity after the Kaiserreich: K. Hildebrand, *Vom Reich zum Weltreich. Hitler, NSDAP und koloniale Frage, 1919–1945* (Munich, 1969); and A. Hillgruber, *Kontinuität und Diskontinuität in der deutschen Aussenpolitik von Bismarck bis Hitler* (Düsseldorf, 1969).

8

**Domestic Factors in
German Foreign Policy
before 1914**

WOLFGANG J. MOMMSEN

Gordon Craig recently deplored the fact that political history, and particularly diplomatic history, no longer attracts the attention of historians or the public as much as has been the case up to now. In his opinion there is no proper reason why this should be so; foreign relations and diplomacy matter very much indeed, and deserve to be studied by historians on their own merits, at least up to a point.[1] However, there are valid reasons why diplomatic history nowadays is in a sort of crisis, and why more and more historians have come to believe that it is not enough to study the diplomatic files, however diligently this may be done, and to inquire about the deeds and motives of the fairly small groups that monopolize decision-making in foreign relations. Most historians nowadays are agreed upon the principle that foreign policy must be explained just as much by finding the social and economic factors conditioning it, as by analyzing the activities going on the level of official diplomacy.

With regard to German historiography it may be said that for more than a century the principle of the "primacy of foreign policy" was consid-

Revised and enlarged version of a paper read to the Conference of the Anglo-German Group of Historians at the Institute of Historical Studies in London on November 13, 1971. For helpful criticism as well as many suggestions I am indebted to Volker Berghahn, Paul Kennedy, Anthony Nicholls, Hartmut Pogge-v. Strandmann, and John Röhl.

ered as a fundamental truth, not only among professional historians, but also by the public. Ranke's famous statement that the
internal structure of any state is conditioned by its foreign relations remained for a long period almost undisputed; the example
of Bismarck seemed to have confirmed it absolutely.[2]

There has always been, however, a liberal tradition in German
historiography which was reluctant to underwrite the principle of
the "primacy of foreign policy" without reservation; in this context men like Droysen, Eyck, Ziekursch, Valentin may be mentioned. Even Meinecke, the historian of the ideology of the
"reason of state," adhered to it only partially. Yet the first historian who really challenged the validity of the principle, and who
depicted it as part and parcel of the conservative heritage, was
Eckart Kehr, first in his study on the social background of German naval policies in the late nineties, and a few years later
explicitly in an essay, "Englandhass und Weltpolitik," written in
1928. This essay was, in part, a critical corollary to Friedrich
Meinecke's *Geschichte des deutsch-englischen Bündnisprobleme*,
published only a year before. Kehr stated bluntly that the Ran-
kean principle of the primacy of foreign policy had become an
important element of "the official philosophy of power and the
political theory of the German Empire," because it was a useful
ideological instrument to induce the bourgeois classes to join
forces with the conservative ruling class in a common endeavor
to keep down the working classes.[3] Kehr went on to say that the
animosity of German public opinion towards Great Britain, and
also the deliberate abandonment of the alliance negotiations with
Great Britain in 1898 and 1901, must be explained on social and
economic grounds; in view of this he proclaimed—at least as
regards relations with Britain and Russia—the principle of the
"primacy of domestic politics," or to use the German phrase,
"Primat der Innenpolitik."[4]

In the late twenties Kehr's argument went almost unnoticed.
The rise of National Socialism then put an end to all serious
scholarship of this bent in contemporary history. Only in the
fifties was the discussion taken up again, one reason among others being that all attempts to deal with National Socialist foreign
policy along the traditional lines of diplomatic history seemed to

be futile. Yet for a variety of reasons which I cannot go into here, it was only in the sixties that Kehr was eventually rediscovered. It may be said that nowadays his opinion that foreign policies are primarily determined by social and economic structures, and in particular by the social and political interests of the ruling elites, is shared by a great majority of historians, though in different degrees, and with different emphasis.

This is the case in particular with regard to recent research in the politics of the Wilhelmine Empire. For this reason, in the first part of this paper some of the various approaches are discussed which have been undertaken on the assumption that foreign relations and in particular German imperialism must be dealt with in terms of domestic developments rather than by describing the complicated network of diplomatic actions and counteractions. In broad terms there can be distinguished five different types of approaches. A special position is held in this context by Marxism-Leninism. According to the Marxist-Leninist doctrine, politics is, at least in the last analysis, always conditioned by the economic system; or, to put it more precisely, it is but a particular aspect of the class struggle, at least under the conditions of bourgeois capitalism. Under the rule of imperialist capitalism the state is, directly or indirectly, the instrument of the bourgeois classes, and its policies are bound to serve two purposes, firstly the suppression of the working masses to the benefit of the capitalists, and secondly the defense and, possibly, the extension of the economic interest of its own groups of capitalists against their capitalist rivals beyond the borders, by means of force. Moreover, since Hilferding and Lenin it is an accepted principle of Marxism-Leninism that the more advanced, that is to say the more monopolistic, capitalist systems are, the more aggressive and violent they become.

It is important in this context to realize that this applies in the same way to domestic politics and to international relations. For this very reason the Marxist-Leninist approach does not recognize a strict separation of internal and foreign policies; there can be no "primacy" of foreign or of domestic policy. Suppression of the working classes in the interior and exploitation of subjected peoples abroad are but the two sides of the same coin. Militarism, for instance, is just as much a symptom of increasing exploitation and deprivation of the working classes as of a particularly aggressive foreign policy.

This explanatory pattern appears to be consistent and cogent indeed. The idea that monopolistic capitalism is of necessity associated with aggression, imperialist ventures, and warlike tendencies on the one hand, and intensified suppression of the working classes on the other, is a stock argument of Marxist-Leninist literature.[5] But it is not true no matter how often repeated. Obviously capitalist systems are not always inclined in the same degree to take recourse to suppression in the interior and expansion abroad by means of brute force; rather there seems to exist a great variety of possibilities. It may furthermore be pointed out that even orthodox Marxist-Leninists find it harder nowadays to attribute the aggressive tendencies of capitalist systems to the intrinsic necessities of capitalist production as such. Few will maintain today that the law of diminishing profits forces the capitalists to take recourse to imperialist policies in order to survive; this causal relationship must be formulated in a much more subtle way, in order to avoid flagrant contradictions with the more recent history of capitalist systems. In fact, Marxist-Leninists themselves have long since been forced to look for additional arguments, in the same eclectic manner which in their view is typical for present-day bourgeois history. Lenin had already pointed out that capitalism leads of necessity to imperialist wars not so much because of the greediness of the capitalists and their desire to constantly expand their business, but because of the uneven development of capitalist economies, which results of necessity in an enormous disproportion of economic and hence political strength of the various rival capitalist powers.[6] Yet similar arguments may be found today just as well with bourgeois economists, for instance, with Walt Whitman Rostow.[7] Apart from that, disproportionate economic growth is a constant source of trouble in the socialist part of the world also; it does not seem to be a specific quality of capitalist systems. And if more recent Marxist-Leninist authors emphasize that imperialist policies were a convenient strategy on behalf of the bourgeois classes to irritate, split, and partially bribe the working classes, this does not seem to be a very specific argument either. Once the principle is accepted that there is not just one capitalism, but a great variety of possible social systems which are more or less organized along the lines of a capitalist market economy, and in which the actual political influence of the capitalists as such may be great or limited, it becomes obvious that the analytical power of the Marxist-Leninist pattern of explanation is indeed limited, at least as long as its propositions are not going to be differentiated substantially.

Official Marxist-Leninist historiography so far is little inclined to modify its theoretical approach, as may be gathered from a recent study dealing with Wilhelmine Germany, *Deutschland im Ersten Weltkrieg*, published by a group of DDR historians under the chairmanship of Fritz Klein.[8] This is a most important and extremely valuable analysis, yet apart from various declaratory statements which we come across again and again and which are only loosely connected with the narrative as such, it is difficult to discover its Marxist quality. In fact, the authors do not succeed in bridging the gap between the general postulates of Marxism-Leninism and the actual description of the course of events. Admittedly they strongly emphasize the repressive and reactionary character of the political system of Wilhelmine Germany, as well as the aggressive character of German foreign policies. They also make the most of the monopolist structures of the German economy. Yet they fail to make a clear-cut case with regard to the government's being at the mercy of the capitalists, as one would expect. Instead they dwell at great length upon the role of the working classes, and in particular the left wing of the Social Democratic Party. They also pay much attention to the peace movement, thus redressing the balance a good deal, compared with traditional German historiography. Yet in their methodological approach, the authors do not differ markedly from Western positivistic accounts of the same era. The devotional references to the basic truths of Marxism-Leninism tend to obscure this, yet any analysis of the methodology and the theoretical framework of the book reveals that these references have little actual connection with the text. Those who expect a coherent and cogent analysis of Wilhelmine politics from the Marxist-Leninist viewpoint will be disappointed. This is, however, not the authors'

fault. Rather, we may conclude that the Marxist-Leninist pattern
is too general, as well as too inflexible, and not differentiated
enough, however valuable Marxist hypotheses may be in more
detailed research.

It is therefore worthwhile looking for other, perhaps less prominent, and at the same time less ambitious approaches in recent
research on Wilhelmine Germany by Western historians. It would
seem to me that the following four types can be distinguished,
among others:

1. The *socio-Marxist approach,* which emphasizes the influences of particular pressure groups that are interested in and
likely to benefit from imperialist policies; this approach is represented in particular by G. W. Hallgarten.[9]

2. The *moralistic approach,* or, as I have described it elsewhere, the "gesinnungsethische" approach, being primarily a
critical analysis of the prevailing ideological (that is to say,
antidemocratic) attitudes.[10]

3. The *"Kehrite" approach,* if I may be allowed to coin a new
phrase, which tends to explain developments in the political
sphere as the outcome of the defensive strategies of the ruling
classes against what may be called the process of democratization; at times this approach has rather strong Marxist
undertones.[11]

4. The *functional-structural approach,* which pays special attention to the functions and malfunctions of constitutional and
governmental systems under the impact of the various social
forces unleashed in particular by the advance of industrialization and mass culture, or to put it another way, under the
impact of modernization.[12] Here, the defense strategy of the
ruling classes is considered as just one factor among others,
the main argument being that disproportions between the social
and political systems tend to lead to an increasing degree of
open conflict, and to disturb the functioning of the governmental process, with the result that the recourse to war often is
little more than a "Flucht nach vorn."

It should be understood, however, that any classification of this kind will work only up to a point, for most historians tend to combine these approaches in one way or another, though with marked differences as to accentuation.

The position that can be dealt with most easily is perhaps the socio-Marxist. It is prominently represented in the works of George W. Hallgarten. Hallgarten was the first to try to describe German politics before the First World War in socioeconomic terms, and he also described the war itself as the logical outcome of imperialism. At first sight Hallgarten's concept of imperialism would seem to be very similar to the Marxist-Leninist one. However, a closer scrutiny reveals that he is narrowing imperialism down to a pattern of sinister political activities of particular business interests and pressure groups that seek to promote their own economic interests by inducing the men in power to pursue a policy of imperialist aggression. We find in Hallgarten's publications a personalistic version of the Marxist explanation of history; not the social structure of capitalist society as such, but rather the parasitical activities of particular individuals or groups are made responsible for imperialism. In view of this fact, it is not surprising to find that Hallgarten dissociates himself explicitly from Lenin's use of the term "imperialism," which, as he correctly points out, applies to practically every country with a modern capitalist economy, irrespective of "whether or not the individual nation-state concerned is expanding or not."[13]

Hallgarten likes to elaborate on cases in which it can be shown that business interests and administrative activities were mixed together. He pays particular attention to personalities who, holding key positions in the government, exerted influence on decision-making in the interest of specific economic groups with which they were affiliated either directly or indirectly, and often by kinship rather than through financial participation. The "real villains," however, would seem to be, according to Hallgarten, the "new International" of the armament industries which, he argues, were "ten times more powerful than the Second and the Third Internationals."[14]

In accordance with this pattern of explanation Hallgarten makes the most of the admittedly fairly intimate connection between William II and Krupp. He also emphasizes strongly the key role of heavy industry in supporting Tirpitz's naval policies. And with regard to Germany's diplomatic relations with the Ottoman Empire he again considers personal connections between the Young Turks and high personalities on the German side as being of decisive importance. It cannot be said, however, that this approach is particularly helpful with regard to German foreign policy before 1914. Hallgarten's contention, to mention just one point, that High Finance induced Kiderlen-Wächter to embark upon his rather risky Moroccan policy in 1911 is somewhat misleading; it actually worked the other way round, as Germany's business interests in Morocco were used merely as a pretext for a diplomatic move which was intended to force the French to cede the French Congo to Germany in exchange for a free hand in Morocco. Any attempt to explain German foreign policy in the last decade before 1914 exclusively as a product of the influence of particular interest groups does not get very far. It cannot be said, for instance, that particular economic pressure groups had any direct influence on the decisions taken by the German government on the eve of the First World War, or that special attention was given to particular economic problems by the men in power at that very moment. As far as we can trace any influence of men from business circles in June and July 1914, they were working against rather than in favor of going to war in 1914. High Finance definitely resented the course of events, and the mood of the industrialists, as far as it was articulated at the time, does not seem to have been particularly warlike. The *Rheinisch-Westphälische Zeitung*, at any rate, commonly considered a paper intimately affiliated with heavy industry, was one of the few papers which opposed the official line of support of Austria-Hungary against Serbia until late in July 1914.

The argumentation of Fritz Fischer appears to me to be much more important, and without doubt much more to the point. Whatever may be said about his opinions, he definitely deserves to be honored for having once more opened up the discussion of a vital issue which German historians had erroneously believed to be definitely settled. However, it remains to be seen whether his findings can also be considered the last word on German policy before 1914.

Fischer maintains that in the last analysis German foreign policy was the necessary outcome of an aggressive nationalism which pervaded almost all sections of German society and which, of course, was particularly strong among the ruling classes. In 1961 Fischer argued that Germany had been deliberately heading for a European war during the July crisis in 1914, in order to become a world power. Thereafter, step by step, he radicalized his position even more, eventually arriving at the thesis that Germany had decided upon going to war as early as 1911, or at any rate by December 8, 1912, in order to break out of the deadlock to which her previous attempts to acquire colonial territories and greater political influence overseas had led. He also maintained that the war aims Germany pursued after 1914 could be traced long before the war. He argued that this was particularly the case with regard to the acquisition of Longwy-Briey, but was also true with regard to the plan of establishing economic predominance on the European continent, possibly including the Balkans as well, by means of a German-led European Economic Association. In his most recent book, *Der Krieg der Illusionen*, Fischer assembled enormous source material, partially derived from Wernecke's study on German public opinion before 1914, in order to substantiate his thesis.[15]

It is not possible to present here a detailed critical analysis of Fischer's presentation of German politics between 1911 and 1915. Yet it seems obvious that he has been driven too far regarding his main thesis: Germany's "will to power." It may be said, for instance, that Fischer is not at all clear as to the question of which sections and groups of German society really advocated a policy of war in order to cut at one stroke the Gordian knot of German imperialism. Was it the government, the emperor, the military establishment, the Conservatives, the industrialists, or the nation at large, any one of them, or all of them? Actually Fischer's arguments constantly shift, charging at times one group, at times another with warlike tendencies; but they are never consistent in this respect. And he does not claim that the various groups and persons with which he is dealing were all, and at all times, committed to going to war. Although at many points we gain important new insights into what was going on, his overall thesis is far from clear.[16] To mention just one point, Fischer attributes the greatest importance to the informal war council which William II held on December 8, 1912, in a sudden outburst of war panic; Fischer contends that the German Empire was henceforth resolved to take up arms as soon as a convenient opportunity turned up, and that the German public was systematically prepared for war. This interpretation has been supported recently by J. C. G. Röhl in a somewhat qualified way; Röhl also is inclined to take literally Tirpitz's words in the so-called "War Council" of December 8, 1912, that the German Fleet would be ready for war by June 1914.[17] It is questionable, however, whether the decisions arrived at on this occasion were as crucial as Fischer, Röhl, and Geiss would have it. There is not the slightest evidence to support the argument that William II's excited order to prepare the country for war by means of an official press campaign was followed up by deeds. Neither can it be said that the German government henceforth was deliberately heading for war. The chancellor was informed of the conference of December 8 only eight days later, and even then only through semiofficial channels.[18] If the so-called "War Council" had indeed arrived at the decision that Germany should go to war within eighteen months, and that adequate support for this policy should be secured in the country by a systematic press campaign, it would have been very strange indeed to leave the responsible statesman as well as the *Wilhelmstrasse* completely in the dark about it for more than a week! Two things can be gathered from the discourse at the conference of December 8, namely, that the military establishment seriously considered solving the problems of German "world policy" by a preventive war, and that Moltke was in favor of going to war as soon as possible, on the grounds that the German military position was deteriorating rapidly. The conference also resulted in accelerating the preparation of the new armaments bill, which had already been under way. Otherwise, the direct effects of the conference were negligible. The plan to introduce another navy bill was effectively checked by Bethmann Hollweg. He also prevented the implementation of the emperor's order "ordentlich in die Presse zu gehen," to the extent to which it had been taken seriously at all, quietly and effectively.[19] There is little doubt that warlike tendencies were ascending both inside and outside official circles, but it is quite a different matter to say that the German government was bent on war from 1912 on.

It is also open to some doubt whether German imperialism had really come to a dead end by 1914, as is gloomily argued over and over again by Fischer. Germany's economic position in the Ottoman Empire had been consolidated, although this had necessitated some concessions both to French and British interests in this sphere. But it had *not* been diminished, even given the chronic problem of the relative scarcity of capital for "political" investments overseas.[20]

It would appear that the very nature of Fischer's approach makes it difficult for him to give proper consideration to the forces of moderation. He draws his conclusions rather from what people said than from what they actually did. Thus, the aggressive nationalist outbursts of the politicians concerned are often taken as the whole of the story. On the other hand, it must be admitted that Fischer makes a serious attempt to get beyond an interpretation dealing mainly with ideological aspects, at least in his "second" book, although not always with the same degree of success. Nonetheless, it seems warranted to conclude that he arrives at all too radical conclusions, mainly because he tends to isolate quotations of a nationalist or imperialist nature from the context, and bases his conclusions on those quotations rather than on a coherent analysis of the political and social structures.

There is still another point worth mentioning. The premise of Fischer's interpretation of Wilhelmine politics, that an aggressive nationalism lay at the bottom of all that happened, induces him to describe the actions of other powers as mere reactions prompted by German diplomacy itself. Yet neither French nationalism nor the growing militarist tendencies in Russia can be properly explained in such a way. A comparative study of European nationalism would reveal that the gradually growing participation of the masses of the population in the political process was everywhere accompanied by an intensified nationalism.

The "Kehrite" approach is in this respect much more rewarding, for it pays far more attention to universal factors such as industrialization—although it also tends to see things on a national level only. It is, furthermore, up to a point capable of explaining why imperialist tendencies of such magnitude developed particularly in Germany, in spite of the fact that a considerable proportion of the German people, in particular the working classes, would have none of it. German imperialism, according to this theory, was essentially a defensive strategy of the upper and middle classes against the Social Democrats and, in a wider sense, against the democratic tendencies of the age in general. There are, of course, differences in detail. Hans-Ulrich Wehler, for example, put forward the opinion that German imperialism resulted from a widespread feeling among the upper classes that the existing social order could be preserved only in a permanently expanding economy, and that therefore colonial and economic expansion had become a necessity, if not in objective economic terms, at any rate on sociopsychological grounds.[21] This model, however, developed with regard to what Wehler calls "Bismarck's Imperialism," is not particularly suited for explaining German imperialism from the nineties on, since the two decades after 1894 were a period of unprecedented and almost uninterrupted economic growth.[22] More to the point is Wehler's sociopolitical version of the same model, which seems to be derived from Kehr, namely, the argument that imperialism was a means of maintaining the ruling classes in their privileged position and holding down the Social Democrats. This interpretation has been accepted in particular by Dirk Stegmann, Volker Berghahn, and Helmut Böhme, among others. According to them, the "agrarian-industrial complex" was the most important social force in Wilhelmine Germany, and German foreign policy was, more or less, shaped under the influence of this group.

According to this theory the politics of imperialism and the construction of a huge battle fleet were primarily means to unite the conservative and bourgeois sections of German society against their common enemy, the Social Democrats. We find this thesis already with Kehr, who wrote in 1928: "In der Miquelschen Sammlungspolitik liegen die letzten Gründe der Aussenpolitik des deutschen Reiches, die in den Krieg steuerte."[23] Stegmann's book, *Bismarcks Erben*, is more or less an elaboration of this thesis, based on an enormous amount of material. In the manner of the Fischer school, Stegmann excels in applying the principle of continuity; the *Sammlungspolitik*, inaugurated by Bismarck in 1879 and put on a more formal basis by Miquel in 1893, continued, according to Stegmann, right up to 1932, and he considers it to be an important precondition for the rise to power of National Socialism. Böhme does not go that far in his recent essay on German imperialism, and he is also somewhat more reluctant to put all the blame on the industrialists; yet in principle he takes an essentially similar line.[24] Berghahn, in his recent studies of German naval policy, is perhaps a little more cautious; he points out that Tirpitz's naval policy was not only antiparliamentarian in tendency, but that it also had a distinctive social-imperialist function.[25]

How far do these models of explanation help us understand German foreign policy before 1914 better than before?

One point may be made right away. It would seem that both Stegmann and Böhme overrate the impact of the so-called *Sammlungspolitik* on German politics. Not fully convincing is Stegmann's elaborate attempt to show that, irrespective of the clash between the Conservatives and the business circles over the *Reichsfinanzreform* in 1909, there was from the early nineties an uninterrupted cooperation between the *Centralverband deutscher Industrieller* (CVdI, representing heavy industry) and the *Bund der Landwirte* (representing the agrarians). Yet even if one concedes for the moment that the coordinated activities of heavy industry and agrarians were indeed as far-reaching as Stegmann claims, why, then, did they achieve so little? Can the temporary halt in social legislation in 1914 really be considered as a first-rate victory? And can it really be said that the combined pressure of agrarians and industrialists was the only, or even the main factor which blocked progress in the constitutional field? It should be realized that the assumedly almighty CVdI manifestly failed even to gain substantial influence on the leadership of the National Liberal Party. Although the National Liberals became more inclined after 1912 to join forces with the Conservatives, they still objected to an outright reactionary policy, as advocated by the Conservatives and by the CVdI.

It follows from this that a more sophisticated explanation is needed than the "Kehrites" would have it in order to cope with the many-sided complex of German imperialism. In spite of Kehr's assertion to the contrary, there is no direct continuity from Miquel's *Sammlungspolitik* of the nineties to 1913.

There was, in fact, a substantial difference between Miquel's "Sammlung" of the "productive estates" in German society on an essentially reactionary platform, and the sort of *Sammlungspolitik* pursued by Bülow and Tirpitz, and in an even more straightforward manner by Bethmann Hollweg from 1909 on.[26] Miquel's concept was essentially antiparliamentarian, and was directed largely against the rising power of the Reichstag; he suggested not only an "adjustment" of the Electoral Law of the Reichstag on the Prussian pattern, but also an outright reactionary policy of suppression in regard to the Social Democrats. This political strategy was deliberately abandoned after about 1898 in favor of a much more elastic course that was able to put up with the existing constitutional framework, and to come to terms again with the Reichstag—or rather with the bourgeois parties in the Reichstag—while abstaining from any renewal of specific antisocialist laws. Yet, instead of making constitutional sacrifices to the Reichstag, Bülow and Tirpitz embarked upon a policy of popular imperialism, including the construction of a "bourgeois" battle fleet, which was designed to bring about a realignment of the middle parties with the government under the banner of a plebiscitarian *Kaisertum*.[27] This did not rule out a partial modernization of the political system, even at the risk of irritating the Conservatives to some degree. Bülow succeeded, by playing the nationalist, imperialist tune, in stabilizing the system of Imperial rule and checking the rising power of the Reichstag, at least for the time being. This explains why under Bülow *Weltpolitik* in the proper sense was actually pursued somewhat halfheartedly and without any realistic plan. In his opinion, it was primarily a means of alleviating political and social tensions at home by turning public attention to overseas problems. He was therefore more interested in prestigious results which increased the popularity of the government at home than in the actual acquisition of particular overseas territories. Imperialist expansion was not an aim in itself, but rather a means of bolstering the prestige of the emperor

and the political system, which had suffered a great deal in the
years since 1892. Consequently, it is hardly surprising that the
Bülow administration could never make up its mind as to where
German colonial activities should be concentrated. It also always
hesitated to go ahead with colonial policies if they might impair
the assumedly independent position of Germany between the
"British Lion" and the "Russian Bear." On the other hand, the
"sham" imperialism of Bülow matched the long-term goals of
Tirpitz's naval policies, for the latter required relative tranquillity
and peace until the battle fleet was strong enough to risk an
encounter with the British navy. After the abortive attempt to
undermine the Entente Cordiale in 1905, Bülow became increasingly concerned about the deterioration of Anglo-German relations; in 1908 he confronted Tirpitz with the question whether a
submarine fleet would not serve Germany's strategic interests
better than a battle fleet.[28]

In the first decade of the twentieth century, however, German
imperialism definitely became more than a skillful contrivance to
make a hitherto unpopular government popular again. Imperialism now became a serious concern of the middle classes, and not
only out of fear of the Social Democrats. Imperialism was now
associated with modernization and industrialization, and thus it
got a distinctly anticonservative tinge. While the imperialist ideology helped the integration of the middle classes into the existing
political framework, at the same time it greatly enhanced their
political influence, at the expense of the conservative nobility. It
is by no means surprising that the Reichstag elections of 1906,
which were fought explicitly on the issue of imperialism, resulted
in a Conservative-Liberal coalition which required sacrifices on
both sides. Yet this combination was not to last long. Domestic
issues once more became dominant, and the fragility of the
"Bülow Block" became apparent at once. Mainly because the
Conservatives were not prepared to pay their share of the bill,
they brought Bülow down in 1909, with the help of the Center
Party, on the issue of the *Reichsfinanzreform*.[29]

From 1909 onwards it becomes even more difficult fully to
account for the developments in German foreign policy by referring only to the now so fashionable catchword "social imperial-

ism.'' It cannot be said that it was the most reactionary sections of German society that were clamoring the loudest for territories overseas. The most outspoken supporters of an effective, if not aggressive German *Weltpolitik* were the upper middle classes, represented by the National Liberal Party, considerable sections of the intelligentsia (which were conspicuously numerous in the Pan-German League and the Navy League), and parts of the petty bourgeoisie. It was only in 1911 that the Conservatives came around to an unreserved support of an outright imperialist policy, although they continued to distrust industrialization, which appeared to be the twin brother of imperialism.[30] Their support of a nationalist imperialism resulted from opportunist calculations, for they hoped by doing this to regain their hold on the electorate. This hold was rapidly dwindling away, due to the increasing political mobilization of those groups of the population which hitherto had been largely apathetic and without much interest in political affairs. The rapid industrialization was about to break up even the last remnants of a tradition-bound society in which the word of the landlord was more or less willingly accepted as binding for everybody.

The repeated attempts of the Conservatives, as well as of the more reactionary groups of German industry (represented in particular by the *Centralverband deutscher Industrieller,* or rather its dominant right wing), to bring about a new ''Sammlung'' of the ''productive estates,'' that is to say, a realignment with the upper middle classes on a joint political platform, did not get very far. The National Liberals, for one, refused to join forces with them, for they regarded their taking part in a policy of repression in social as well as in constitutional matters as almost suicidal. They preferred to maintain their position as principal champions of what they called a reasonable and efficient German imperialism, combined with a policy of piecemeal modernization in domestic and constitutional affairs. The government of Bethmann Hollweg did not let itself be drawn in such a direction either, although it was ready to compromise with the Conservatives wherever this seemed possible. It is not surprising, therefore, that those sections of German society that stood for a policy of outright social imperialism became more and more ardent opponents of the government, on foreign issues as well as on domestic ones.

Precisely because Bethmann Hollweg (who in June 1909 had succeeded Bülow as chancellor) refused to embark on a policy of reckless imperialism associated with the straightforward suppression of the Social Democrats and other progressive forces at home, he was soon assailed by the Conservatives and parts of the upper bourgeoisie. This is borne out by the course of events from 1909 on. In the summer of 1909 manifest doubts as to whether the previous strategies of German diplomacy had been wise coincided with a severe internal crisis; for the first time in German history a chancellor had been forced to resign, if only indirectly, by a hostile coalition of parties. From the point of view of the ruling elite this was indeed a grave situation, because the Conservatives had thrown in their lot against the government and at the same time had antagonized at least a considerable section of the middle classes and the business community. Not a few people correctly assumed that the eventual outcome of the affair would be a gigantic victory of the Social Democrats at the polls, as most of the new taxes had been put on the shoulders of the masses of the population.

If, at the turn of the century, Bülow had succeeded in preventing an open conflict with the Reichstag by playing the imperialist tune, Bethmann Hollweg decided not to embark upon such a frivolous policy—with one notable exception with which we shall soon have to deal. He believed that the political situation after the crisis of 1909 was not a propitious moment for an adventurous foreign policy, and that time would be required to let things calm down again at home. Bethmann Hollweg's primary concern in the years from 1909 to 1911 was the stabilization of the position of the German Empire within the system of powers. Germany backed out of the somewhat odd position on Morocco which she had assumed at Algeciras, in spite of the noise the Mannesmann Brothers made on behalf of it. The government also tried to bring about a détente with Russia, an undertaking which initially appeared to have worked quite successfully. Otherwise, Bethmann Hollweg worked hard to improve relations with Great Britain, even after a not very sensible attempt to negotiate a neutrality agreement in return for a moderate limitation of naval construction had failed.[31]

The chancellor considered an understanding with Great Britain necessary above all to minimize the danger of a European war in which Germany might easily become involved growing out of a conflict between Austria-Hungary and Russia in the Balkans.[32] Still, a greater degree of security in Europe would also make it much easier to realize some of Germany's colonial objectives. The main goal of the government was the eventual creation of a coherent German Central Africa, through the acquisition of some of the Portuguese, Belgian, and French territories in this area. Apart from this, the government worked hard to strengthen, and whenever possible to expand, the German economic involvement in the Ottoman Empire.

Bethmann Hollweg assumed that for such a policy of moderate expansionism "without war" British support might come forward. He was fully aware, conversely, that a reconciliation with Great Britain was not an easy thing to bring about, if only in view of the rather Anglophobe attitude of German public opinion. He hoped that sooner or later the public would realize that there was no real alternative to such a political course. It is debatable how much chance there was for the realization of this political concept, in view of the fact that neither the emperor nor the middle classes was prepared to accede to a substantial reduction of the German naval armament program, a precondition for any rapprochement with Great Britain. Whatever chance there was, it was fatally reduced by the disastrous results of Kiderlen-Wächter's all too Machiavellian Moroccan policy of 1911.

In many respects, the Agadir crisis of 1911 must be considered the great divide in German politics before 1914. The shrewd calculations of Kiderlen-Wächter turned out to be absolutely wrong. Kiderlen-Wächter had optimistically assumed that a definite settlement of the Moroccan question would make a rapprochement with Great Britain easier.[33] In fact, the bold "forward move" of July 1, 1911, not only led to a serious deterioration of Anglo-German relations, but also brought about an outcry of German public opinion against Great Britain, alleging that she always stepped in whenever a chance turned up for Germany to score a success overseas.

The action against France on the Moroccan issue was not initiated by any economic interest groups; on the contrary, the Mannesmann Brothers, who really had a stake in southern Morocco, were deliberately left out of the game. A banking group in Hamburg was to supply, at the request of the Foreign Office, a convenient pretext for the German intervention, but in doing so they were left completely in the dark as to the real objectives of the government.[34] Much the same was true with regard to the press and even the Pan-German League, which were both officially encouraged to take a hard line on the Moroccan issue in order to scare the French into ceding the Congo as an appropriate compensation.[35]

The whole affair was undoubtedly undertaken, among other reasons, with an eye to the forthcoming Reichstag elections.[36] The cautious attempts of the chancellor to launch as an official election slogan the preservation of the present system of economic treaties had gotten but a meager reception, and a handsome success in foreign policy would have been welcome indeed. However, the modest results of Kiderlen-Wächter's diplomacy could not stand a comparison with the expectations of public opinion, which had been deliberately boosted by the government's own press policies. The domestic situation got completely out of control. The government was assailed from almost all quarters of German society for its allegedly "weak" policy. It was the Conservatives and the National Liberals who now embarked upon an avowedly imperialist course. At the culmination of the crisis, heavy industry also spoke up strongly in favor of what may be called a "forward" policy. The military establishment was also not satisfied with the course of events; Moltke maintained that Germany should have gone to war rather than sell out on what he believed to be dishonorable terms.[37] Tirpitz, on his part, quickly seized the opportunity to request a new naval bill.

Bethmann Hollweg was alarmed by the warlike spirit prevailing in important sections of German society, and he spoke out strongly against it.[38] But this was of little avail. Although there was no unanimity as to which objectives German policy should go after, the conservative and bourgeois classes tended to agree on one point: that Germany should act more vigorously whenever a new opportunity arose to acquire new territories abroad, perhaps even at the risk of a major war. Thus as early as 1912 there

developed a political constellation which foreshadowed the situation that existed in the first years of the war. On the one side we
find a government which, although in favor of an expansionist
policy, attempted to pursue an essentially moderate course. On
the other side there were strong groups within the upper classes,
supported by important sections of the parties, which advocated
a vigorous foreign policy, and which entertained the notion that if
Germany could not get her way otherwise she should not shrink
from taking up arms. In this struggle, the "civilian" government
did not succeed in getting its views accepted; rather, it was driven
step by step in the opposite direction.

This can be explained only by taking into account the peculiar
nature of the political system of Wilhelmine Germany in the pre-
war years. Since the turn of the century the internal situation had
undergone substantial changes, and it may be said that the governmental system was no longer in line with the social structures
emerging in the course of an accelerating process of industrialization. The social basis of traditional conservatism was dwindling
away. It was not only the shift from a primarily agricultural society toward urban industrialism which made life more and more
difficult for the Conservatives. It was rather the increasing speed
of social mobilization, associated with a growing diversification
of incomes, which cut into those sections of the population which
up to then had been oriented to traditionalist values and life-
expectations. From the socioeconomic point of view, the upper
middle class was about to become the dominant group in German
society. It was only the rapid growth of the working-class movement which afforded the conservatives another lease on political
predominance. But the speed of social change should not be over-
rated. The advance of industrialization was rapid enough to
frighten the traditional sections of German society very much
indeed; but its actual impact was not yet strong enough effectively to undermine their respective social positions altogether. In
1910 Germany was—in Rostow's terms—"a mature industrial
economy."[39] However, this does not mean that it was a fully
developed industrial *society*. Measured in socioeconomic terms,
the agrarian and, in particular the petit-bourgeois sections of German society were still in the majority, as is indicated by the

statistical figures concerning the average size of business enterprises before 1914, which was still surprisingly low. It is these
social groups which were all too ready to lend their support to
traditionalist and conservative politics, and upon whose sympathy the pseudoconstitutional governments of Bülow and Bethmann Hollweg could still count.

The traditionalist sections of German society were still remark-
ably strong, yet were no longer a sufficient basis for an outright
conservative policy. Neither did the opposite possibility exist.
The parties which could be called "progressive," namely the
Social Democrats, the Progressives, a part of the National Liberals, and to some degree the left wing of the Center Party, were on
the ascendant, but for the time being did not possess a majority.
In the middle range, their chances seemed to be very good indeed; but even as late as 1912 it did not pay to display too progressive an attitude. In spite of their great success in the
Reichstag elections of 1912, the Social Democrats and the Progressives were unable to exert any substantial influence on actual
legislation. The political influence of the Social Democrats stood
almost in inverse ratio to their numerical strength, for the government took care not to introduce any bill which could be passed
only with their support. Whenever the bourgeois parties were
about to join forces with the Social Democrats on a particular
issue, the government almost always succeeded in bringing them
to heel again by pointing out that such behavior was contrary to
the national interest. The National Liberals had to consider that a
great many of their voters were rather traditionalist. Consequently, they were particularly reluctant to join forces with the Left, as
this might have resulted in a breakup of the National Liberal
Party. The Social Democrats were not inclined to join a "coalition from Bassermann to Bebel" either, even if this had been
within their reach. Both the Social Democrats and the National
Liberals were tied down by traditional attitudes which made any
compromise extremely difficult. This situation was intensified by
the socioeconomic situation: after 1909 class conflicts had again
become more tense. The employers tried to check the rise of the
trade unions by the use of effective counterorganizations; and
they used all their means of influencing public opinion to bring a

stop to "Sozialpolitik." On the other hand, real wages, after a period of almost continuous rise, had again become almost stagnant, largely as a result of rising food prices. Active social reformers like Lujo Brentano and Max Weber were extremely worried whether the trade unions still had a fair chance against the employers; Weber complained late in 1912 that social reform was no longer fashionable, and tried in vain to create a propaganda organization to make it popular again.[40]

The almost complete deadlock in parliamentary politics which was caused in part by the antagonism between the Social Democrats and the liberal parties originated, in the last analysis, in the deep antagonisms within German society, which had been intensified by the momentous economic growth. None of the major political groups, the Conservatives, the bourgeois parties, or the Social Democrats, were at that time in a position to alter things substantially. The Conservatives, supported by the right wing of the Prussian National Liberals, controlled a strong defensive position thanks to their enormous strength in both houses of the Prussian Landtag. The Center Party and the National Liberals, although less and less inclined to join the conservative camp, were not strong enough to pursue a policy of moderate reform and at the same time to check effectively the further growth of the Social Democrats. The latter party was given almost no chance to exercise an effective influence on the course of politics, and the Social Democrats were rightly worried by symptoms which indicated that the potential reservoir of voters was approaching the point of exhaustion.

It was only this situation which enabled the semi-authoritarian government of Bethmann Hollweg to carry on in spite of its unpopularity in all political quarters. To put it another way, the stalemate of the party system was the main source of Bethmann Hollweg's relative strength. Apart from that Bethmann Hollweg was able to muster some support from those sections of the middle classes which still considered party politics "dirty business." Occasionally he appealed directly to these sections of the community to dissociate themselves from what he called the fruitless striving of the parties and to lend him their support.[41] It is fully in line with such a calculation that Bethmann Hollweg thought it best to keep clear of the parties as much as possible, and if possible to restrict the influence of the party leaders on the actual decision-making. However, maintaining a policy "above the parties" was bound to multiply the inherent evils of all authoritarian rule. Official policy and party politics were pursued side by side, with insufficient communication between them. This was the case in particular with foreign policy. Traditionally the Reichstag had no say at all in these matters, and so the chancellor did not care to inform the party leaders properly about the actual difficulties of German foreign policy; superficial consultations, followed up by appeals for support on national grounds, were still considered sufficient. Under these conditions the party leaders could afford to give themselves up to a rather irresponsible nationalist agitation, all the more so because they had to compete with extraparliamentary associations like the Pan-German League and the *Wehrverein*. As there was no proper exchange of political opinions between the government and the country at large, the gap between the ideologies of the day and the realities became wider and wider.

The stalemate between the various political groups was accompanied by sterile agitation and effectively blocked the way for any substantial change in the constitutional structure; but it did not necessarily strengthen the position of the government. On the contrary, as the government had to manage without any solid support by any of the Reichstag parties, it became increasingly dependent on the goodwill of the high bureaucracy, of the officer corps, and, in a wider sense, of the Prusso-German aristocracy. Without their support, the government had little chance of surviving the repeated onslaughts of the Reichstag, or of holding its own against the radical agitation of the Pan-German League and similar extraparliamentary political associations, and the less direct pressure of the *Centralverband deutscher Industrieller*.

Both the high bureaucracy and the officer corps, however, became more and more worried about the increasingly rapid advance of democratic ideas within German society. The officer corps was particularly sensitive to this trend; it therefore reacted disproportionately against any encroachment on its traditional rights by the Reichstag or public opinion. Bethmann Hollweg had a very difficult time clearing himself of the charges made against him in military quarters and court circles that he had not defended the rights of the army energetically enough during the debates in the Finance Committee of the Reichstag on the armament bill of 1913.[42] William II considered the *Kommandogewalt* the last vestige of supreme monarchial power. The chancellor therefore could not prevent an extension of the sphere to which the *Kommandogewalt* was held to apply, an extension which took place not so much in constitutional law as in actual practice, however strongly the Reichstag took objection.[43]

William II and the military establishment considered it the most important task of any chancellor to keep the Reichstag in check. Yet it became more and more evident that this was an impossible task, even under such favorable conditions as those of Wilhelmine Germany. The general trend toward more popular, if not democratic, forms of government made itself felt in German society as well as elsewhere, and resulted among other things in an enhanced self-consciousness of the Reichstag. It was no longer possible to discard the political requests of the Reichstag altogether. Conversely, the Conservatives and their fellow travellers were panic-stricken, and at least some of them felt that they were standing with their backs to the wall. In such a situation it was difficult to work out compromises, both on the social level and on the political level. The government was aware of this implication of the overall sociopolitical constellation, and therefore it decided to follow what it believed to be a neutral course. Bethmann Hollweg dared not seek political support on the Left; even if he had liked this idea—which, of course, he did not—it would have been difficult to pursue such a political line in view of the still intransigent attitude of the Social Democrats. On the other hand, he refused to join forces with the Right and embark upon a straightforward policy of repression of the Social Democrats and the democratic tendencies alike, although considerable sections within the ruling bureaucracy demanded this, and although the Conservative Party and important interest groups, in particular the CVdI, tried to push the government in this direction. The reason Bethmann Hollweg resisted such a policy, although he gave in at some points, is obvious: it would have resulted in further antagonizing the political parties and would have made it even more difficult to bring about a realignment of the bourgeois and Conservative parties, which he assumed would be the only way out of the present dilemma. In this sense Bethmann Hollweg's "policy of the diagonal," which did not please anybody, was a genuinely conservative policy.

The dissent within the ruling elite as to whether this kind of policy was right made itself felt, of course, in the sphere of foreign policy just as much as in internal affairs. In a way, Bethmann Hollweg deliberately discounted public opinion in matters of foreign policy, but he could afford to do so only if all sections of the government were willing to take a common stand on controversial issues vis-à-vis public opinion. The chancellor, however, became less and less capable of seeing that this principle was adhered to.

The chancellor believed that the only way out was to conduct foreign policy in almost absolute secrecy, holding back from the public at large, and even from the party leaders, all but the most elementary information. Bethmann Hollweg was fully aware that by doing this he exposed himself to vicious attacks from Conservatives and extreme nationalists alike, as his policy inevitably appeared to outsiders inconsistent and weak. In spite of this unfortunate fact, he refused to put forward any specific program. He did not act upon suggestions by Rathenau[44] to give the country a lead in matters of foreign policy, being convinced that publicity was bound to impair the chances of ultimate success. Riezler wrote at the time, not without some conceit, that only a foreign policy which did *not* care for the applause of the public, and which was *not* heading for quick results, was likely to achieve anything worthwhile.[45]

To put things another way: Bethmann Hollweg never tried and consequently never succeeded in selling his policy to the country at large, and for this reason he was largely at the mercy of the various groupings within the ruling elite. For the time being his political concept was accepted by the emperor and, though not without some misgivings, by the military establishment and the conservative bureaucracy. This was all the more true because Bethmann Hollweg had reluctantly given in to the requests of the navy as well as the General Staff by increasing both the army and the navy in 1912, and by putting through parliament another considerable increase of the army in 1913. A strong army was, up to a point, in line with his political concept, for he considered the strong, unassailable position of the German Empire on the European continent as the fundamental prerequisite for an expansive foreign policy elsewhere.[46] On the other hand, he sincerely believed that an improvement in Anglo-German relations would be the key to a solution of the difficult problems German diplomacy was facing. Better relations with Great Britain would serve two purposes. First, they would reduce the danger of a European conflagration, and this would enable Germany to steer somewhat more confidently through the troubled waters ahead, with a crisis-ridden Austria-Hungary as ally and a rapidly rising Russia as a possible enemy. Second, there was reasonable hope that Germany could secure some of her colonial objectives with British assistance, in particular in Central Africa, but also in the Near East and perhaps even in China.[47]

Bethmann Hollweg could reckon at least to some degree on the support of the National Liberal and Center parties, although the Anglophobia prevailing there was difficult to overcome. Furthermore, he was able to establish fairly intimate relations with some of the major banking houses; they could be induced, up to a point, to invest in the spheres of interest the government attempted to peg out in Africa and elsewhere in rather sophisticated diplomatic negotiations—even though the prospects for returns on such investments were gloomy indeed, apart from the fact that capital was scarce anyway.[48] Relations with big industry, however, were by no means good; and many of the industrialists were not at all interested in a German Central Africa. Their interests were more in the Near East, so far as they had any definite interests at all.[49] Some people, such as Rathenau, came around to the idea that it might be more useful to concentrate economic activities on the European continent, rather than pegging out claims for posterity overseas.[50] Bethmann Hollweg did his best to set the stage for a continuation of German economic penetration of the Ottoman Empire, though he took care to let the British have a share in this too. But it was only under the pressure of war that he joined a camp of the advocates of a European Economic Association dominated by Germany, as an alternative to old-fashioned territorial imperialism.[51]

There can be no doubt that the government of Bethmann Hollweg did not seriously contemplate attaining any of its objectives by war until May–June 1914—with the possible exception of a liquidation of the Ottoman Empire taking place without the Germans getting a proper share.[52] Bethmann Hollweg was confident that he could get along without a war, although by the end of 1913 he became increasingly worried about the deteriorating position of the German Empire within the European system of powers. He stuck to a peaceful policy, all the more so because he was convinced that the existing political order probably would not survive a war.[53] Fritz Fischer has argued again and again that Bethmann Hollweg's repeated attempts to negotiate a neutrality agreement with Great Britain were part and parcel of a policy of expansion by means of war. Britain should be made to stand aside in order to allow Germany safely to crush France and Russia—this, he maintains, was the core of German calculations.[54] This is, however, not borne out by the sources.[55] It will have to be admitted that a neutrality agreement—or something coming fairly close to it—played, so to speak, a token role in the internal struggle between Tirpitz and William II on one side, and Bethmann Hollweg and the Foreign Office on the other. This state of affairs existed behind the scenes during and after the visit of Lord Haldane to Berlin in February 1912. The group in favor of a hard line was not willing to make substantial sacrifices in naval construction unless the British would indicate that they were willing to change substantially their allegedly unfriendly attitude toward Germany. The inconsistent attitude of the German Foreign Office during February and March 1912 with regard to how much should be asked from the British government in return for a naval agreement cannot be explained except as a reflection of the ups and downs of the internal struggle going on in Berlin.

Bethmann Hollweg was unable at this time to carry out his policy. However, the failure of the Anglo-German negotiations in 1912 did not discourage him. He still thought that an improvement of relations with Britain, accompanied by colonial concessions, was within reach. Naturally, he came to be considered inside the ruling elite as an essentially pro-British statesman, and his political fortunes came to be tied up with the developments of Anglo-German relations. Early in December 1912 Sir Edward Grey conveyed to the German government an explicit warning that in case of a European war developing from the Balkan crisis, Great Britain would come to the assistance of France and Russia. In court circles this was considered positive proof that Bethmann Hollweg's expectations as regards Great Britain were unfounded (which, as a matter of fact, was not the case), and as mentioned already the emperor at once consulted Tirpitz and the military leaders, behind the back of the "civilians," as to how to prepare the country for the European war which in his opinion seemed imminent.[56] Bethmann Hollweg's prestige was at a low ebb. Although the chancellor soon regained ground, he henceforth was aware how unstable his position had become.

It must be realized, moreover, that since 1913 Bethmann Hollweg's moderate course had been challenged increasingly by a considerable section of the ruling elite, in particular by the General Staff. And, as has been shown above, the latter's influence had risen substantially. The military leaders were seriously worried about the reappearance of Russia as a first-rate military power, and—as we know now beyond doubt—they were harboring the idea of a preventive war against Russia and France, for within a few years the Schlieffen Plan would no longer work. Moltke, so far as we can see from the scattered sources, became increasingly annoyed with the diplomats, who kept saying that since relations with Great Britain were improving the dangerous period ahead could be overcome.[57] It is possible that the article of an *Oberleutnant* Ulrich published in March 1914 in the *Kölnische Zeitung*, which brought about a heated press controversy between German and Russian newspapers, had been initiated by somebody close to the German General Staff; although any proof for this is lacking, it seems possible, since this article expressed the fears and apprehensions in German military quarters rather precisely.[58]

It is at this point that pressure from the public at large also has to be given proper attention. The relations among the military establishment, the court, and the Conservatives were, of course, fairly intimate. In conservative quarters, as well as in the Pan-German League, the assumption was indeed widely held that a war was likely to have a healthy effect on German national character. Furthermore, a war appeared to be convenient in order to set the clock in the interior "right" again.

It goes without saying that this is only a part of the story. For the belief that the diplomatic situation had deteriorated alarmingly in the last years, and that a European war was imminent, had spread to a considerable proportion of the middle classes too. The warlike message of Friedrich Bernhardi's *Germany and the Next War*, which was couched in a language that may be called a peculiar mixture of the bourgeois cultural heritage and militant nationalism, did not fail to have some impact on the German intelligentsia. Yet the pressure exerted on the government by important sections of German society in favor of a tough line in matters of foreign policy does not suffice to explain the course of events which eventually led to the outbreak of the First World War. The popularity of imperialism accounts for much of what happened, but there is no evidence that specific influences of this kind played a major role in the deliberations of the German government on the eve of the war. It was, rather, the crisis of the governmental system as such which induced the men at the top to take refuge in an aggressive political strategy.

It has been pointed out already that the government of Bethmann Hollweg could not count on the support of any of the major political groupings in the Reichstag or in the country at large. For this very reason it was more dependent than any government since Bismarck on the goodwill of the conservative establishment, and in particular the entourage of William II, which was connected with the former through a great many social connections. Since 1913 the Conservatives had launched a series of vitriolic attacks against the chancellor, and had tried to convince the emperor that he was neither tough enough with the Social Democrats nor effective in holding the Reichstag parties in check. The Pan-German League hoped to exploit this situation. In October 1913 Class attempted to bring about the fall of the chancellor; with the assistance of the Crown Prince, a long memorandum in which General von Gebsattel assailed the supposedly weak foreign policy of the chancellor was brought to the attention of the emperor.[59] Although William II was not yet prepared to dismiss his chancellor, the position of Bethmann Hollweg was precarious indeed, and he had to fear the charge that his foreign policy was both weak and ineffective.

By far the most serious challenge to Bethmann Hollweg's foreign policy came, however, from the General Staff. The military leaders were extremely concerned about the prospect that the main premise of the Schlieffen Plan, namely, a slow Russian mobilization which would allow the German Army to crush France before the Russians became an effective military danger, was being undermined by the progress of Russian armaments, and in particular by the completion of the railways in western Russia. Their apprehensions were not reduced by the rather ambiguous official Russian reaction to press charges that Russia was preparing a war against Germany. In May or June 1914 Moltke therefore suggested that the government ought to bring about a war while Germany was still in a position to win it.[60] Obviously, the idea of a preventive war was gaining ground in governmental quarters. Even William II, who despite all his militaristic pathos was essentially in favor of peace, was in doubt as to whether it might not be wiser to take up arms before the Russian armament program was completed, as he confided to Warburg in June 1914.[61]

Outside the inner circle of the government other considerations also came into play. Quite a few people, such as Heydebrandt und der Lasa, maintained that a war would be a splendid opportunity to smash the Social Democrats.[62] Bethmann Hollweg was furious about such "nonsense,"[63] presumably because he was aware of the consequences for his political position if such views were taken up by the emperor. Bethmann Hollweg emphatically denied that a European war would strengthen the case of the conservatives. Rather, it was likely to benefit the Social Democrats; it might even result in the dethronement of some monarchs.[64] The somewhat scanty sources do not allow all too radical conclusions; yet it can be gathered from them that Bethmann Hollweg and Jagow apparently had a difficult time fending off such ideas. They were careful to make clear that they were not, in principle, against the idea of a preventive war—any other stand might have been interpreted as weakness—yet they nonetheless took exception to the suggestion of solving the problems of German diplomacy by a preventive war. Their main argument was that in view of the improving relations with Great Britain it would be folly to pursue such a policy.[65]

The strength of the position of the chancellor within the complicated governmental system of Wilhelmine Germany depended to a very large degree on his status as responsible leader of foreign policy. William II did not like the idea of changing the chancellor primarily because he feared the repercussions in diplomatic relations. In this respect, the fairly positive image which Bethmann Hollweg enjoyed in Great Britain was of great importance. Under such conditions the news about a forthcoming Anglo-Russian naval agreement—which had reached Berlin in May 1914 through a spy in the British Embassy in Saint Petersburg—had a disastrous effect on the domestic position of the chancellor. And just as in December 1912, the protagonists of a "forward policy" again got the upper hand. Bethmann Hollweg's main argument against a preventive war, namely, that the British government would help in preventing the Russians from going to war, had gone to pieces overnight. Even worse, the British seemed to be about to join forces once and for all with the Russians and the French; and this played into the hands of those who argued that since the military situation of the German Empire was getting worse and worse it would be better to fight the assumedly "inevitable" war as soon as possible. This situation is rather frankly alluded to in Bethmann Hollweg's message to Lichnowsky for Sir Edward Grey of June 16, 1914.[66]

Bethmann Hollweg was well known for his essentially pro-British orientation. Therefore, the sudden collapse of his hope that a rapprochement with Great Britain was within reach was grist to the mills of his domestic foes. For this reason Bethmann Hollweg was not very outspoken about his own estimate of the British attitude toward Germany in the event of a European war. It is worth noting that the chancellor did not reckon with British neutrality in a European war, although this was believed by many people at the time (and subsequently by many historians). In his opinion, more intimate relations between the German Empire and Great Britain would help to stabilize the German position on the continent, and reduce the danger of a European conflagration over a new Balkan crisis. Furthermore, it would ease German economic and political expansion overseas. Bethmann Hollweg was, however, well aware that the British would never allow Germany to crush France while standing aside themselves. The most the chancellor expected was that Great Britain might remain neutral in the initial phase of a European war, while trying to bring about a diplomatic solution. In 1914 he counted on British help in avoiding a European war, but not on British neutrality, all the more so because all available information pointed to the contrary.[67] The assumption that Great Britain might remain neutral did not play a key role in German calculations on the eve of the First World War. Rather, the opposite is true. It was the startling news that Great Britain was apparently about to join the opposite camp that set things in motion. It added additional strength to the argument of the domestic rivals of the chancellor that it might be wiser to forestall the formation of a more definite entente, which would encourage Russia to go ahead with warlike measures, by launching a preventive war as soon as a convenient opportunity was at hand.[68]

This is borne out by the course of events which culminated in the decision of Germany to let the Austrians and Hungarians have their punitive war against Serbia, whatever the eventual outcome might be, although the government was well aware that an Austro-Serbian conflict could easily escalate into a European war. Up to then German diplomacy had pursued a relatively pro-Serbian course; several times it had prevented the Austrians from interfering by force in the conflicts of the Balkan states. To the dismay of the Austrians, Berchtold had been told over and over again that it might after all be best to come to terms with Serbia in some way or other. In the first days after Francis Ferdinand's assassination the *Wilhelmstrasse* seems to have stuck to its previous line. This was indicated by the attitude of the Russophobe Tschirschky, to which early in July the emperor took violent exception. The decision to give Austria-Hungary a sort of "blank check" was a major shift in German policy, and it is reported that

Bethmann Hollweg agreed to it only after some hesitation.[69] In principle this decision was reached *before* Count Hoyos arrived in Berlin on July 5—presumably around the 2nd or 3rd.[70] This decision amounted to a sort of compromise between the position to which the chancellor and the Foreign Office had adhered hitherto and the General Staff's position that Germany should not work for peace if there was an opportunity to have right now the big showdown with Russia and France which they assumed would come anyway within the next few years. Bethmann Hollweg himself admitted (as he confessed later)[71] that, provided that the generals' estimatè of the situation of the Central Powers and the warlike tendencies of Tsarist Russia was correct, it might indeed be better to have the war at once rather than later. Consequently, Bethmann Hollweg embarked upon a "diagonal" course, that is, to let Austria act as an "agent provocateur," and make the Serbian war a test case regarding the question of whether Russia was bent on war anyway, or not.[72] In doing so he satisfied the request of the military establishment that Germany should *not* avoid a war, if it was in the offing, without fully endorsing their strategy, which was bent on a preventive war. He assumed that Russia was not ready for war, and that there was a genuine chance of breaking the ring of the Entente powers without a European war. Although all persons involved in this decision were fully aware of the fact that a Serbian action by Austria-Hungary could provoke a European war—in which case the chancellor expected Russia to begin the war within days[73]—he and the Foreign Office, at least, assumed that the Russians would back down, all the more so since neither France nor Great Britain was enthusiastic about going to war on behalf of Serbia.[74] It may be pointed out that a declaration of the British government to the effect that Great Britain would not remain neutral would not have altered the course of events a bit. On the contrary, it would have been grist to the mills of Moltke, and would have amounted to a further strengthening of his argument that in view of the steadily deteriorating position of the German Empire it was better to fight now, at a moment when in his opinion the war could still be won decisively within months, rather than later.

The political calculation of the German government amounted

to gambling with very high stakes indeed. Bethmann Hollweg himself called it "a leap in the dark" which was dictated by "most severe duty."[75] The chancellor's position was no longer strong enough to get any alternative accepted by the inner ring of the ruling elite. His plan was a fairly precise reflection of the deep division within the government itself. It was a compromise between two rival schemes. It did not directly work for war; rather, it favored a diplomatic solution of the crisis. Still, it satisfied the request of the military establishment insofar as it did nothing to avoid war. The attempt to maneuver Russia into a position in which *she* would have to decide about peace or war was not dictated only by the consideration that otherwise the Social Democrats might not rally behind the government. It was equally influenced by the calculation that only in this way could the forthcoming crisis be exploited diplomatically, and with the afterthought that, provided the Russians shrank back from extreme measures, the fears of the German General Staff could be positively disproved.

Hence, it was not so much lust for world power as weakness and confusion which induced Bethmann Hollweg to embark upon such a political strategy. The contradictions which can be discovered in the calculations of the German government in July 1914 are a rather precise reflection of the sharp antagonisms within the German ruling elite. It must be added, however, that this was possible only because those groups which were part of this elite (namely, the upper stratum of the governmental bureaucracy, the General Staff and behind it the officer corps, and the conservative entourage of the emperor) enjoyed a political influence which was out of proportion to their actual importance in German society as a whole. This was partly due to the fact that the stalemate on the level of parliamentary politics had enabled the government to carry on with its policies as if nothing had happened at all. It is noteworthy that the government could afford to disregard entirely the opinions of the party leaders in July 1914.[76] Indeed, there is no evidence that any of the party leaders was given the opportunity to have a say in the decisions of the government. The chancellor seems to have been confident that at least the bourgeois parties, with the possible exception of the Progressives, would support a bold course in preference to a policy which would pass over the opportunity of Sarajevo without any attempt to come to Austria-Hungary's assistance, and to exploit the crisis to the advantage of the Central Powers.[77]

It is doubtful whether Bethmann Hollweg, even if he had cared to consult the party leaders, would have found among the bourgeois parties wholehearted support against the champions of a preventive war. But surely the party leaders would not have agreed to a crisis strategy which was so designed as to please both the hawks and the doves, and which for this very reason was bound to fail. This is, of course, a rather speculative argument. Yet one point can safely be made, namely, that the desperate attempts of the government of Bethmann Hollweg to prevent any substantial constitutional change in the face of a more or less hostile Reichstag made it extremely dependent on the goodwill of those small groups within the German upper class which favored a policy of suppression in the interior just as much as a tough line in foreign politics.

In the last analysis, we may conclude, the causes of the First World War must be sought not in the blunders and miscalculations of the governments alone, but in the fact that Germany's governmental system, as well as Austria-Hungary's and Russia's, was no longer adequate in the face of rapid social change and the steady advance of mass politics.

NOTES

[1] Gordon A. Craig, "Political and Diplomatic History," in *Historical Studies Today*, ed. Felix Gilbert and Stephen R. Graubard (New York, 1972), pp. 356ff. (first published in *Daedalus* in 1971).

[2] For a more systematic treatment of this issue see Hans Rothfels, *Gesellschaftsform und auswärtige Politik* (Laupheim, 1956), and, more recently, the contributions to this problem in *Die anachronistische Souveränität. Zum Verhältnis von Innen- und Aussenpolitik*, ed. Ernst-Otto Czempiel (*Sonderheft* 1 of the *Politische Vierteljahrsschrift*, 1969). See also Karl Dietrich Bracher, "Kritische Betrachtungen über den Primat der Aussenpolitik," in *Faktoren der politischen Entscheidung. Festgabe für Ernst Fraenkel zum 65. Geburtstag* (Berlin, 1963), pp. 115ff.

[3] Eckart Kehr, *Der Primat der Innenpolitik*, ed. Hans-Ulrich Wehler (Berlin, 1965), p. 152.

[4] *Ibid.*, p. 155.

[5] A good example can be found in Willibald Gutsche and Annelies Laschitzka, "Forschungen zur deutschen Geschichte von der Jahrhundertwende bis 1917," *Historische Forschungen in der DDR (Zeitschrift für Geschichtswissenschaft, Sonderband*, 1970), p. 476.

[6] Cf. Lenin, *Selected Works* (Moscow, 1967), I, 770.

[7] *The Stages of Economic Growth* (Cambridge, 1968), pp. 106ff.

[8] *Deutschland im Ersten Weltkrieg, I: Vorbereitung, Entfesselung und Verlauf des Krieges bis Ende 1914*, by an *Autorenkollektiv* under the leadership of Fritz Klein (Berlin, 1968).

[9] George Wolfgang Hallgarten, *Imperialismus vor 1914* (2 vols.; 2nd ed. Munich, 1963). *Idem, Das Schicksal des Imperialismus im 20. Jahrhundert* (Frankfurt, 1969).

[10] This approach is particularly well represented by the earlier works of Fritz Fischer and some of his students, in particular Imanuel Geiss and Klaus Wernecke, Most important in this respect are: Fritz Fischer, *Griff nach der Weltmacht. Die Kriegszielpolitik des kaiserlichen Deutschland 1914–1918* (3rd ed., Düsseldorf, 1968). *Idem, Der Krieg der Illusionen. Die deutsche Politik von 1911 bis 1914* (Düsseldorf, 1969). *Idem, Weltmacht oder Niedergang. Deutschland im Ersten Weltkrieg* (Frankfurt, 1965). Imanuel Geiss, "The Outbreak of the First World War and German War Aims," *Journal of Contemporary History*, I (1966). *Idem, Julikrise und Kriegsausbruch 1914. Eine Dokumentensammlung* (2 vols., Hanover, 1963–64). Hartmut Pogge-v. Strandmann and Imanuel Geiss, *Die Erforderlichkeit des Unmöglichen. Deutschland am Vorabend des Ersten Weltkrieges* (Frankfurt, 1965). Klaus Wernecke, *Der Wille zur Weltgeltung. Aussenpolitik und Öffentlichkeit im Kaiserreich am Vorabend des Ersten Weltkrieges* (Düsseldorf, 1970). See also W. J. Mommsen, "The Debate on German War Aims," *Journal of Contemporary History*, I (1966), 47ff.

11 Right now this is a very influential methodological approach. It has been taken up by a fairly wide range of scholars, though not always with the same degree of stringency and radicality. See in particular the more recent writings of Hans-Ulrich Wehler, Dirk Stegmann, Helmut Böhme, and, with some limitations, Volker Berghahn: Hans-Ulrich Wehler, *Bismarck und der Imperialismus* (Cologne, 1969). *Idem, Krisenherde des Kaiserreichs 1871–1918* (Cologne, 1970). *Idem*, "Bismarcks Imperialismus und späte Russlandpolitik unter dem Primat der Innenpolitik," in *Das Kaiserliche Deutschland*, ed. Michael Stürmer (Düsseldorf, 1970). Dirk Stegmann, *Die Erben Bismarcks. Parteien und Verbände in der Spätphase des Wilhelminischen Deutschlands. Sammlungspolitik 1897–1918* (Cologne, 1970). Helmut Böhme, "Thesen zur Beurteilung der gesellschaftlichen, wirtschaftlichen und politischen Ursachen des deutschen Imperialismus," in *Der moderne Imperialismus*, ed. Wolfgang J. Mommsen (Stuttgart, 1971). Volker Berghahn, "Zu den Zielen des deutschen Flottenbaus unter Wilhelm II.," *Historische Zeitschrift*, CCX (1970). *Idem, Der Tirpitzplan. Genesis und Verfall einer innenpolitischen Krisenstrategie unter Wilhelm II.* (Düsseldorf, 1971). *Idem*, "Flottenrüstung und Machtgefüge," in *Das Kaiserliche Deutschland*, ed. Stürmer.

12 Such an approach, although as a rule not applied to foreign policies as such, may be found with scholars like Gerhard A. Ritter, Hans-Günther Zmarzlik, John C. G. Röhl, Gustav Schmidt, and Hans-Jürgen Puhle. Cf. Gerhard A. Ritter, Georg Kotowski, Werner Pöls, *Das Wilhelminische Deutschland* (Frankfurt, 1965). Hans-Günther Zmarzlik, *Bethmann Hollweg als Reichskanzler 1909–1914* (Bonn, 1957). J. C. G. Röhl, *Germany without Bismarck* (London, 1967). *Idem, Zwei deutsche Fürsten zur Kriegsschuldfrage, Lichnowsky, Eulenburg und der Ausbruch des Ersten Weltkrieges* (Düsseldorf, 1971). In his more recent publications Röhl, however, stands somewhat closer to the Fischer camp. Hans-Jürgen Puhle, "Parlament, Parteien und Interessenverbände 1890–1914," in *Das Kaiserliche Deutschland*, ed Stürmer. Gustav Schmidt, "Deutschland am Vorabend des Ersten Weltkrieges," *ibid.*

13 *Das Schicksal des Imperialismus im 20. Jahrhundert*, p. 140.

14 *Ibid.*, p. 34.

15 For Wernecke's book see n. 10.

16 For a more detailed assessment of Fritz Fischer's views, as well as of their development, see Mommsen, "The Debate on German War Aims," and *idem*, "Die Deutsche 'Weltpolitik' und der Erste Weltkrieg," *Neue Politische Literatur*, XVI (1971), 482ff.

17 Cf. Fritz Fischer, *Krieg der Illusionen*, pp. 231ff. The account given by John C. G. Röhl, "Admiral von Müller and the Approach to War 1911–1914," *Historical Journal*, XII (1966), demonstrates that Walter Görlitz, the editor of the diaries of Admiral von Müller (cf. *Der Kaiser, Aufzeichnungen des Chefs des Marinekabinetts Admiral Georg Alexander v. Müller über die Ära Wilhelms II.* [Göttingen, 1965], pp. 124ff.), on which almost all our knowledge about this conference depends, omitted vital passages from the text, in particular the second half of the following passage, beginning with the words "aber er." This passage clearly

shows Moltke in favor of a preventive war: "Der Chef des Grossen Generalstabs sagt: Krieg je eher, desto besser, aber er zieht nicht die Konsequenz daraus, welche wäre: Russland oder Frankreich oder beide vor ein Ultimatum zu stellen, das den Krieg mit dem Recht auf unserer Seite entfesselte. Nachmittags an den Reichskanzler wegen der Pressebeeinflussung geschrieben." It is difficult to escape the conclusion that the whole conference was dominated by the assumption that war might break out at any moment (as, indeed, it might have, for Europe was at the very height of a serious Balkan crisis), and that one vital issue was how to justify in the eyes of the German public a European war on behalf of Austria-Hungary's desire to create a semi-independent Albania. Hence the suggestion of William II: "Nun gehen Sie ordentlich in die Presse," according to Bethmann Hollweg's message for Kiderlen-Wächter of December 17, 1912. *Die grosse Politik der europäischen Kabinette* (Berlin, 1922–27), xxxix, No. 15553. Cited as *GP*.

[18] As follows from the last document cited in n. 17, the chancellor learned not before December 16 that there had been a sort of "War Council." Admiral von Müller apparently did not refer to the "conference" at all when he wrote on the afternoon of December 8 to the chancellor pointing out that something should be done to influence the press in order to bolster up public opinion in respect to the possibility of a European war on behalf of Austria-Hungary at that juncture. This would seem to indicate that von Müller was indeed of the opinion that the result of the conference had been "gleich null"! It is, by the way, not likely that von Müller would have led Bethmann Hollweg astray on purpose in this instance, as he usually acted as the chancellor's ally against Tirpitz.

[19] Bethmann Hollweg succeeded in calming the emperor down by explaining that Grey's message was, after all, not all that disastrous, at least as long as Germany avoided all provocative steps (cf. memorandum of Bethmann Hollweg of December 18, 1912, *GP*, xxxix, No. 15560, pp. 9f.). He had already suggested to Tirpitz and Heeringen that they not launch an official propaganda campaign for new armaments; cf. memorandum of December 14, 1912, *ibid.*, No. 15623. It makes rather amusing reading to see that on this occasion the chancellor pointed out to both men: "Ich müsse aber mit allem Nachdruck verlangen, dass sie sich hinter meinem Rücken auch seiner Majestät gegenüber nicht bänden, dass von Vorarbeiten, die sie innerhalb ihrer Ressorts etwa vornähmen, auch nicht das geringste in die Öffentlichkeit dringen dürfe, und dass ich irgendwelche Pressetreiberei zugunsten der Projekte unter keinen Umständen dulden könne" (*ibid.*, pp. 147f.). None of these gentlemen would seem to have dared taking recourse to the arguments put forward by William II a few days earlier at the so-called "War Council" of December 8, 1912!

[20] Fischer's interpretation rests upon the unspoken assumption that Germany had a position of predominant economic influence in the Ottoman Empire to start with, and that it was confronted with increasing competition by other industrial nations only in the last few years before 1914. In fact, all German enterprises in this area had been substantially dependent on assistance from the "Caisse de la Dette Publique," which was dominated by the French, and had been intimately associated with foreign, primarily French banking houses, in particular the

Banque Ottomane. The earlier sections of the Bagdad Railway could not have been built without the substantial support of these groups. Cf. Donald C. Blaisdell, *European Financial Control in the Ottoman Empire* (New York, 1966), pp. 124ff. It may be further pointed out that the Germans succeeded in increasing their proportion of shares in the "Dette Publique" from an initial share of 8% to about 30% by 1914, and consequently their influence was substantially enhanced, although the French continued to be the strongest group of shareholders. Cf. Raymond Poidevin, *Les Relations Economiques et Financieres entre la France et L'Allemagne de 1898 a 1914* (Paris, 1969), p. 697. The separation of the respective economic activities of the Western powers which took place in the Ottoman Empire after 1909 did not necessarily imply an infringement on the German position. The treaty between a German and a French group on February 15, 1914, regarding their respective spheres of interest and economic engagement in the Ottoman Empire, as well as the agreement reached in March 1914 between the d'Arcy Group and the *Deutsche Bank* on the joint exploitation of the Mesopotamian and Anatolian oil fields, could have been more favorable to the German side, but the *Deutsche Bank* was thoroughly pleased with it. See, for instance, *GP*, xxxvii/1, No. 14888, p. 435. Fischer's presentation in *Der Krieg der Illusionen*, pp. 424ff., is rather misleading.

[21] *Bismarck und der Imperialismus*, pp. 17ff., where Wehler presents his theory on a more general basis. Cf. my review of Wehler's book in *Central European History*, II (1969), 366ff. See also Wehler's introduction to *Imperialismus* ("Neue Wissenschaftliche Bibliothek," Cologne, 1970).

[22] This point is made also by Helmut Böhme, *op. cit.*, pp. 39ff.

[23] *Op. cit.*, p. 150.

[24] Böhme, *op. cit.*, pp. 48f. Böhme argues that German imperialism must be understood as "der Versuch der Staatsleitung und der sie tragenden Gruppen und Interessen . . . , im Gegensatz zum Entwurf 'des Sozialismus', die sozialen Veränderungen der sich durch die rasante Industrialisierung rasch wandelnden Gesellschaft nicht mit einer grundlegenden Reform, der Umwälzung der Eigentumsverhältnisse zu lösen, sondern mit Hilfe der Ablenking auf Grossmacht- und Weltmachtpläne zu paralysieren, um auf diese Weise den innenpolitischen Status quo ohne Reformen zu erhalten."

[25] Cf. Berghahn, "Zu den Zielen des deutschen Flottenbaus," pp. 34ff. *Idem, Der Tirpitzplan*, pp. 592ff. It may be mentioned that Berghahn maintains that Tirpitz's strategy had failed by 1909; from then on it would seem no longer to have been a major factor in German domestic politics, although Tirpitz continued to be very popular with the parliamentary politicians.

[26] This interpretation is to some extent in agreement with Berghahn, who also suggested in a recent article, "Das Kaiserreich in der Sackgasse," *Neue Politische Literatur*, xvi (1971), 497ff., that one ought to distinguish between a "kleine Sammlung," as suggested by the agrarians and by heavy industry, and a "grosse Sammlung," as pursued by Tirpitz and Bülow. It should be noted, however, that the difference is one not only of degree but of quality, in that the latter version sought to include the majority of the middle classes and the Center Party. Steg-

mann, of course, consistently confuses the two types of *Sammlungspolitik*, to the detriment of his argument.

[27] For Bülow's intention to revitalize the "personal rule" of William II see Röhl, *Deutschland ohne Bismarck. Die Regierungskrise im Zweiten Kaiserreich 1890–1900* (Tübingen, 1969—the German ed. of the book referred to in n. 12), pp. 123f., 147f., 251ff. As early as 1896, shortly before he became Secretary of State for Foreign Affairs, Bülow confessed that the solution of the constitutional problems could be found only in a "Royalismus sans phrase" (*ibid.*, p. 187). In 1897 he argued, "Ich lege den Hauptakzent auf die auswärtige Politik. Nur eine erfolgreiche Aussenpolitik kann helfen, versöhnen, beruhigen, sammeln, einigen" (*ibid.*, p. 229). The antiparliamentary tendencies of Tirpitz's naval policies are documented by Berghahn, "Zu den Zielen des deutschen Flottenbaus," pp. 36ff., and *Der Tirpitzplan*, pp. 14ff.

[28] Bülow to Tirpitz, December 25, 1908, in Otto Hammann, *Bilder aus der letzten Kaiserzeit* (Berlin, 1922), p. 148: "Ew. pp. enthalten sich aber einer Meinungsäusserung darüber, ob, angesichts der von Ihnen selbst hervorgehobenen derzeitigen grossen Überlegenheit der englischen Flotte über unsere Streitkräfte zur See—eine Überlegenheit, die überdies das englische Volk auch für die Zukunft unter allen Umständen aufrechtzuerhalten entschlossen scheint—es unseren Schlachtschiffen überhaupt möglich sein würde, entscheidend in Aktion zu treten. Ist aber die Befürchtung gerechtfertigt, dass unsere Flotte in ihrer gegenwärtigen Stärke von den übermächtigen englischen Seestreitkräften blockiert in unseren Hafen zurückgehalten werden würde, müssen wir mit der Wahrscheinlichkeit rechnen, in einem Seekrieg mit England vorläufig auf die Defensive angewiesen zu sein, so entsteht die Frage, ob sich nicht empfiehlt, der Verbesserung unserer Küstenbefestigungen, der Vergrösserung unseres Bestandes an Seeminen und der Schaffung einer starken Unterseebootflotte unsere Aufmerksamkeit zuzuwenden, anstatt uns ausschliesslich auf die Vermehrung von Schlachtschiffen zu konzentrieren. . . ."

[29] Cf. Peter Christian Witt, *Die Finanzpolitik des Deutschen Reiches von 1903 bis 1913. Eine Studie zur Innenpolitik des Wilhelminischen Deutschland* (Lübeck, 1970), pp. 303f.

[30] In fact, imperialist issues had played a rather secondary role in the Conservative ideology so far. The Conservative Party up until then had always taken the official line in imperialist issues, rather than putting pressure on the government. Although the *Bund der Landwirte* adhered to a rather aggressive version of nationalism, the Conservatives had no concrete ideas as to what kind of imperialist policy should be pursued; when their own economic interests were likely to be involved they opposed rather than supported imperialist ventures. See also Hans-Jürgen Puhle, *Agrarische Interessenpolitik und preussischer Konservativismus* (Hanover, 1966), pp. 96ff., 241f.

[31] A detailed, if uninspired, account of these negotiations is given by Alexander Kessler, *Das deutsch-englische Verhältnis vom Amtsantritt Bethmann Hollwegs bis zur Haldane Mission* (Erlangen, 1938). See also Hans Joachim Henning, *Deutschlands Verhältnis zu England in Bethmann Hollwegs Aussenpolitik 1909–1914* (published doctoral thesis, Cologne, 1962).

[32]See in particular Bethmann Hollweg's memorandum for Kiderlen-Wächter, April 5, 1911, *GP*, xxviii, No. 10347, p. 409.

[33]Cf. *GP*, xxix, pp. 107–108, note, and Kiderlen-Wächter's telegram for Schoen, June 30, 1911, where an allusion is made to his intention "das Marokko-problem endgültig als Reibungsfläche aus der internationalen Politik auszuschalten," *ibid.*, No. 10578, p. 155. See also Bethmann Hollweg's declaration in the Reichstag on November 9, 1911: "Marokko war eine dauernd schwärende Wunde in unserem Verhältnis nicht nur zu Frankreich, sondern auch zu England." "Die Erledigung der Marokkoangelegenheit [reinige] auch in unseren Beziehungen zu England den Tisch." *Verhandlungen des Deutschen Reichstages,* vol. 268, p. 7713 A, B.

[34] This is demonstrated beyond reasonable doubt by Alfred A. Vagts, "M. M. Warburg & Co. Ein Bankhaus in der deutschen Weltpolitik 1905–1935," *Vierteljahrsschrift für Sozial- und Wirtschaftsgeschichte*, xlv (1958), 253 ff. Cf. the diaries of Dr. Regendanz, who acted as an agent for the German government, F. W. Pick, *Searchlight on German Africa. The Diaries and Papers of Dr. Regendanz* (London, 1939). See also Joanne St. Mortimer, "Commercial Interests and German Diplomacy in the Agadir Crisis," *Historical Journal*, x (1967), who, however, substantially overrates the importance of the business groups behind Dr. Regendanz.

[35] The frivolous press policies of Kiderlen-Wächter were heavily criticized by the Reichstag as early as 1912. Cf. debates in the Budget Committee, as well as the Reichstag debates on February 17, 1912, *Verhandlungen des Reichstages*, vol. 283, pp. 96Aff. A full account of Kiderlen-Wächter's press politics now in Wernecke, *op. cit.*, pp. 26ff. Details as to Kiderlen-Wächter's negotiations with Class also in *Die Bürgerlichen Parteien in Deutschland*, ed. Dieter Fricke *et al.* (Leipzig, 1970), I, 11f.

[36] Cf. Kiderlen-Wächter's memorandum for William II, May 3, *GP*, xxix, No. 10549, p. 108: "Unsere öffentliche Meinung würde mit alleiniger Ausnahme der Sozialdemokratischen Partei das einfache Geschehenlassen der Dinge im Scherifenreich der Kaiserlichen Regierung zum Vorwurf machen, während andererseits mit Sicherheit angenommen werden darf, dass praktische Ergebnisse manchen unzufriedenen Wähler unstimmen und den Ausfall der bevorstehenden Reichstagswahlen vielleicht nicht unwesentlich beeinflussen würden."

[37] Helmuth von Moltke, *Erinnerungen, Briefe, Dokumente 1877–1916* (Darmstadt, 1922), p. 362.

[38] Cf. Bethmann Hollweg's speech in the Reichstag on November 9, 1911, in *Verhandlungen des Reichstages*, vol. 268, p. 756A, and also his letter to Eisendecher of November 16, 1911 in Nachlass Eisendecher, 1/1–7, Politisches Archiv des Auswärtigen Amtes, Bonn: "Krieg für die Gebrüder Mannesmann wäre ein Verbrechen gewesen. Aber das deutsche Volk hat diesen Sommer so leichtfertig mit dem Kriege gespielt. Das stimmt mich ernst; dem musste ich entgegentreten. Auch auf die Gefahr, den Unwillen des Volkes auf mich zu laden."

[39] *The Stages of Economic Growth*, p. 116.

[40] Cf. W. J. Mommsen, *Max Weber und die deutsche Politik 1890–1914* (Tübingen, 1959), pp. 133–35.

[41] He appealed, for instance, to men like Delbrück and Lamprecht to support the official scheme of a "Vermögensabgabe," in order to find the financial means for the armament bill of 1913 in a politically acceptable form.

[42] Cf. Bethmann Hollweg to Eisendecher, undated (July 1913), Nachlass Eisendecher, 1/1–7: "Der Kaiser ist wieder hochgradig nervös. Jeder törichte Beschluss, den die Reichstagskommission in der Wehrvorlage fasste, und es sind ihrer allerdings genug, reizt ihn aufs Äusserste und er möchte am liebsten jeden Tag auflösen oder doch mit der Auflösung drohen . . . ich kann mir nicht verhehlen, dass dem Kaiser meine Art, Politik zu treiben, von Tag zu Tag unerträglicher wird." See also Kurt Stenkewitz, *Gegen Bajonett und Dividende* (Berlin, 1960), pp. 117f., and Kuno Graf Westarp, *Konservative Politik im letzten Jahrzehnt des Kaiserreichs*, I (Berlin, 1935), 238.

[43] This trend of affairs is reflected in the Reichstag debates about various motions which suggested a more precise definition of the sphere to which the *Kommandogewalt* was supposed to apply, on January 23, 1914, and May 5 and 6, 1914; *Verhandlungen des Reichstages*, vol. 252, pp. 6730ff., and vol. 294, pp. 8480ff. On May 6, 1914, von Falkenhayn, the new minister of war, defined the royal privileges in such a way as fully to justify the semi-independent positions of the *Kaiserliches Militärkabinett* as well as of the War Ministry with regard to the Reichstag: "Die Befugnisse des Königs von Preussen gegenüber der bewaffneten Macht Preussens, sowie den ihr durch Konventionen angegliederten anderen Staaten sind in der Verfassung enthalten und durch die Reichsverfassung erweitert, aber in keinem Punkte eingeschränkt worden. Seine Majestät der König und Kaiser übt diese Befugnisse innerhalb der Gesetze völlig selbständig aus. Ein Mitwirkungsrecht des Reichstages besteht dabei in keiner Weise, obschon natürlich nicht bestritten werden soll, dass der Reichstag zuständig ist, bei seinen gesetzgeberischen Arbeiten seine Wünsche in Bezug auf das Militärwesen zur Sprache zu bringen." *Verhandlungen des Reichstages*, vol. 294, p. 8515B. See also Zmarzlik, *op. cit.*, pp. 135f.

[44] Cf. Walther Rathenau, *Tagebuch 1907–1922*, ed. Hartmut Pogge-v. Strandmann (Düsseldorf, 1967), p. 182.

[45] "J. J. Ruedorffer" [Kurt Riezler], *Grundzüge der Weltpolitik* (Berlin, 1913), p. 229.

[46] Cf. Bethmann Hollweg's speech in introducing the army bill on April 22, 1912, *Verhandlungen des Reichstages*, vol. 284, pp. 1300Bff.

[47] This strategy is perhaps revealed most clearly in a letter of Jagow's to Eisendecher of July 24, 1913, Nachlass Eisendecher.

[48] A satisfactory study of this aspect of German politics is lacking so far. Some useful information may be gathered from Vagts, *op. cit.* Up to now we have had to rely on Poidevin (above, n. 20) and a survey by Wolfgang Zorn, "Wirtschaft und Politik im deutschen Imperialismus," in *Wirtschaft, Geschichte und Wirtschaftsgeschichte, Festschrift zum 65. Geburtstag von Friedrich Lütge* (Stuttgart, 1966), pp. 340ff.

[49] Cf. Böhme, *op. cit.*, pp. 42f.

[50] Walther Rathenau, "Deutsche Gefahren und neue Ziele," in *Gesammelte*

Schriften. Zur Kritik der Zeit, Mahnung und Warnung (Berlin, 1925), pp. 272, 276. Cf. also *idem, Tagebuch,* pp. 168f., containing notes about a discussion on this topic with Bethmann Hollweg.

[51] Fischer argues that Bethmann Hollweg acceded to the idea of a Central European Economic Association under German leadership as early as 1912; it seems doubtful, however, that Rathenau's note "Bethmann allgemein einverstanden" indicates anything more than a vague sympathy with these ideas. There is, in fact, no indication that the decisions of the government were influenced at all by such ideas. Fritz Fischer suggested in his article, "Weltpolitik, Weltmachtstreben und deutsche Kriegsziele," *Historische Zeitschrift,* vol. 199 (1964), pp. 324ff., as well as in his *Der Krieg der Illusionen,* pp. 368ff., that the "Mitteleuropapläne" and the plans for a German Central Africa were but two sides of the same coin. It would seem to the present author that Egmont Zechlin's objections to this interpretation, in "Deutschland zwischen Kabinetts- und Wirtschaftskrieg," *Historische Zeitschrift,* vol. 199 (1964), pp. 398ff. are on the whole correct. Fischer's reply in *Der Krieg der Illusionen,* pp. 529f., is rather unconvincing. Even in September 1914 the *Reichsamt des Innern* thought that such plans were unrealistic, and suggested that the existing system of bilateral trade treaties should be continued.

[52] See, for instance, Jagow to Lichnowsky on January 23, 1913, *GP,* xxxiv/1, No. 12718.

[53] Cf. Bethmann Hollweg to Lerchenfeld, June 6, 1914 (author's translation): ". . . the emperor had not undertaken a preventive war, and neither was he going to do so. There were, however, circles in the empire who assume that a war might lead to a healthier state of affairs in Germany—in the conservative sense. He—the chancellor—thinks that on the contrary a world war with all its unpredictable consequences is likely to enhance the power of the Social Democrats—as they are preaching peace—tremendously, and might lead to the destruction of some thrones." *Bayrische Dokumente zum Kriegsausbruch und zum Versailler Schuldspruch,* ed. Pius Dirr (4th ed., Munich, 1928), No. 1, p. 113.

[54] *Griff nach der Weltmacht,* pp. 59ff.; *Der Krieg der Illusionen,* pp. 85ff., 182, and *passim.*

[55] Bethmann Hollweg's own position may be gathered from his memorandum for Kiderlen-Wächter of April 5, 1911; *GP,* xxviii, No. 10441, pp. 408f.

[56] Compare above, pp. 12–14, and nn. 17–19.

[57] Cf. Conrad von Hötzendorf, *Aus meiner Dienstzeit, 1906–18* (Vienna, 1921–23), iii, 670.

[58] A detailed account is given by Wernecke, *op. cit.,* pp. 244ff. There is, however, absolutely no evidence to support Wernecke's and Fischer's contention that this "press war" was staged deliberately in order to prepare the German public for war. Cf. *Der Krieg der Illusionen,* pp. 542ff.

[59] For the opposition of the Conservatives see Westarp, *Konservative Politik,* i, 182ff. The repeated attempts of the Conservatives in the Reichstag after 1913 to blame the government for its weak attitude toward the Social Democrats were mainly designed to undermine Bethmann Hollweg's prestige within the establish-

ment. For the Gebsattel affair see H. Pogge-v. Strandmann, *Erforderlichkeit des Unmöglichen*, pp. 16–31.

⁶⁰ Cf. Moltke's talk with Jagow in May or June 1914, published by Egmont Zechlin, "Motive und Taktik der Reichsleitung 1914," *Der Monat*, XVIII, No. 209 (February 1966), pp. 92–93.

⁶¹ Vagts, "M. M. Warburg" (above, n. 34), p. 353.

⁶² Cf. Riezler Diary, entry of July 25, 1914. Now published in Kurt Riezler, *Tagebücher, Aufsätze, Dokumente*, ed. Karl Dietrich Erdmann (Göttingen, 1972). Heydebrandt's statement, to which Bethmann Hollweg referred during July 1914, must have been made some time before that date, as Heydebrandt was not in Berlin then, and was politically inactive for the time being.

⁶³ *Ibid.*

⁶⁴ Statement to Lerchenfeld, quoted above, n. 53.

⁶⁵ This is indicated by a remark of Moltke's to Conrad, in which he tried to explain why the German government was reluctant to act upon the idea of a preventive war. Moltke complained that "we always expect a declaration of neutrality from Great Britain which she, however, will never give." Cf. Conrad von Hötzendorf, *op. cit.*, III, 670. In May or June 1914 Jagow took a similar line, insofar as he argued against Moltke's plea for a preventive war and that it would be wiser to sit back. Owing to the improving relations with Great Britain, a European war had become less likely, and, at any rate, would possibly be less serious. See n. 60.

⁶⁶ *GP*, XXXIX, No. 18883, pp. 628ff.

⁶⁷ Contrary to Albertini and Fischer, the German government did not base its political strategy on the assumption that Great Britain would remain neutral in the case of a major European war, although it naturally attempted to do its best to bring it about when the crisis came. In the secret debate in the Budget Committee of the Reichstag on April 24, 1913, Bethmann Hollweg pointed out clearly that Germany could not count on British neutrality in case of war. Cf. Dieter Groh, "Die geheimen Sitzungen der Reichshaushaltskommission am 24. und 25. April 1913," *Internationale Wissenschaftliche Korrespondenz zur Geschichte der deutschen Arbeiterbewegung*, No. 11/12 (April 1971). On June 5, 1914, Bethmann Hollweg said to Bassermann: ". . . wenn es Krieg mit Frankreich gibt, marschiert der letzte Engländer gegen uns." Cf. Bassermann's letter to Schiffer, June 5, 1914, Nachlass Schiffer 6, Hauptarchiv Berlin. This is also confirmed by Lerchenfeld's report of June 4, 1914: "Was England betrifft, so lauteten seine [i.e., Bethmann Hollweg's] Ausführungen ungefähr dahin: Zu allen Zeiten habe die britische Macht immer gegen die stärkste Macht auf dem Kontinent gestanden. Zuerst gegen Spanien, dann gegen Frankreich, später gegen Russland und jetzt gegen Deutschland. England wolle keinen Krieg. Er—der Reichskanzler—wisse bestimmt, dass die englische Regierung in Paris wiederholt erklärt habe, dass sie keine provokatorische Politik und keinen vom Zaun gebrochenen Krieg gegen Deutschland mitmache. Aber das hindere nicht, dass, wenn es zum Kriege käme, wir England nicht auf unserer Seite finden würden." Cf. *Bayrische Dokumente zum Kriegsausbruch*, No. 1, p. 112. As early as December 1912 the chancellor had

held a similar position, as can be gathered from a letter to Eisendecher, December 18, 1912, and Bethmann Hollweg's memorandum for William II, December 18, 1912, *GP*, xxxix, No. 15560.

[68] Hence, it is not the effect of the Anglo-Russian naval negotiations on foreign relations as such, as in particular Zechlin argues—cf. "Deutschland zwischen Kabinetts- und Wirtschaftskrieg" (above, n. 51), pp. 348ff.—that really matters, but rather its effect on the domestic situation.

[69] Report of Koester, July 20, 1914, *Deutsche Gesandtschaftsberichte zum Kriegsausbruch 1914. Berichte und Telegramme der badischen, sächsischen und württembergischen Gesandten aus dem Juli und August 1914*, ed. August Bach for the *Auswärtige Amt* (Berlin, 1937), No. 5.

[70] See also Fritz Fischer, *Der Krieg der Illusionen*, pp. 688–89.

[71] Cf. a report by Haussmann, February 24, 1918, quoted in Wolfgang Steglich, *Die Friedenspolitik der Mittelmächte 1917/18*, i (Wiesbaden, 1964), 418.

[72] It is impossible in this context to give a full account of the political calculations of the German government in July 1914. I hope to do this in a forthcoming study, *Die Politik des Reichskanzlers von Bethmann Hollweg als Problem der politischen Führung*. In the meantime, the reader may be referred to Wolfgang J. Mommsen, *Das Zeitalter des Imperialismus* (Frankfurt, 1968), pp. 272ff., and "Die latente Krise des Wilhelminischen Reiches 1909–1914," *Handbuch der deutschen Geschichte*, ed. Leo Just, Section IV, ii (Frankfurt, 1972). As regards the German intention to consider the Serbian issue a "Prüfstein" of Russia's warlike intentions, see Hoyos's notes about his interview with Victor Naumann, in *Österreich-Ungarns Aussenpolitik*, ed. L. Bittner (Vienna and Leipzig, 1930), viii, No. 9966, and Afred von Tirpitz, *Erinnerungen* (Leipzig, 1919), p. 227.

[73] Riezler Diary, entry of July 23, 1914.

[74] It has been argued time and again, in particular by Fritz Fischer and Imanuel Geiss, that the plan to isolate the Serbian war was not only a gross illusion, but was little else than a convenient pretext. It would seem, however, that the inner circle around Bethmann Hollweg did indeed believe in the possibility of getting along without a European "conflagration," as the chancellor used to put it. That this assumption was at any rate subjectively honest is borne out, for instance, by calculations in governmental quarters that provided the crisis passed without a European war, Germany might even conclude an alliance with Russia, at the expense of Austria-Hungary. Cf. Riezler Diary, entry of July 23, 1914, and the statement of Bethmann Hollweg to Theodor Wolff on February 5, 1915, which confirms Riezler's notes: "Ich habe Sasonow dann während der Krise—dies ganz unter uns—sagen lassen, er möge doch die Österreicher ihre Strafexpedition machen lassen, der Moment würde kommen, wo wir uns arrangieren würden. Natürlich nicht auf dem Rücken der Österreicher, aber gewissermassen auf ihren Schultern." Theodor Wolff, *Der Marsch durch zwei Jahrzehnte* (Berlin, 1936), p. 442.

[75] Riezler Diary, entry of July 14, 1914.

[76] In a way the Social Democrats must be excluded insofar as the government approached Haase, and a few days later the *Parteivorstand,* although only Süde-

kum was available. With regard to the negotiations of the government with the Social Democrats, there is a controversial literature which may be superseded by the forthcoming study of Dieter Groh, *Negative Integration und revolutionärer Attentismus. Die deutsche Sozialdemokratie am Vorabend des 1. Weltkrieges 1909-1914* (Berlin, 1973). In the meantime, see his "The Unpatriotic Socialists and the State," *Journal of Contemporary History*, I (1966), and "Negative Integration und revolutionärer Attentismus," *Internationale wissenschaftliche Korrespondenz zur Geschichte der deutschen Arbeiterbewegung*, No. 15 (1972). Little is known about contacts of the leading members of the bourgeois parties with the government. Westarp reports that he paid a few visits to the *Wilhelmstrasse* during the crisis, but apparently he was not told much (cf. *Konservative Politik*, I, 407). Heydebrandt, the leader of the Prussian Conservatives, was as late as August 3 still totally uninformed about what had been going on on the diplomatic stage (cf. letter of Heydebrandt to Westarp, August 3, 1914, Heydebrandt-Westarp correspondence; I am indebted for this information to *Freiherr* Hiller von Gärtringen, University of Tübingen).

[77] With regard to the attitude of the parties toward Bethmann Hollweg's policies in July 1914 we still have to rely largely on guesswork. Their overall attitude can nonetheless be rather clearly ascertained. The Conservatives were all in favor of a "forward policy"; it was, however, only fairly late that they actually began to press for war. It would seem that in the first weeks of July the *Post*, a leading conservative newspaper, was rather reluctant to join the chorus of pro-Austrian voices (cf. Jonathan French Scott, *Five Weeks. The Surge of Public Opinion at the Eve of the Great War* [New York, 1932], pp. 138, 191ff.). The National Liberals wished to have the energetic Tirpitz as chancellor rather than Bethmann Hollweg (cf. Bassermann to Schiffer, June 5, 1914, cited above, n. 67). They surely would have welcomed a policy which seemed to act upon the allegedly extremely successful strategy followed during the Bosnian crisis of 1908 once again. The Center Party, on the other hand, was since 1912 definitely in favor of any policy which was avowedly designed to assist Austria-Hungary. It is therefore not surprising to see that the Catholic press also took a similar line in the July crisis (cf. E. Malcolm Caroll, *Germany and the Great Powers, 1866-1914* [New York, 1938], pp. 747ff.).

Acknowledgments

The editor wishes to express his appreciation for permission to publish selections appearing in this volume: Karl Erich Born and Franz Steiner Verlag for "Structural Changes in German Social and Economic Development at the End of the Nineteenth Century"; Hans Rosenberg and the editors of the *Economic History Review* for "Political and Social Consequences of the Great Depression of 1873–1896 in Central Europe"; D. C. Heath and Company for "Conflict and Cohesion among German Elites in the Nineteenth Century"; Werner T. Angress and the Leo Baeck Institute for "Prussia's Army and the Jewish Reserve Officer Controversy before World War I"; John Röhl and Weidenfeld and Nicolson for "Higher Civil Servants in Germany, 1890–1900"; Otto Pflanze and the editors of *The Review of Politics* for "Bismarck's *Realpolitik*"; Hans-Ulrich Wehler and the editors of *Past and Present* for "Bismarck's Imperialism, 1862–1890"; and Wolfgang J. Mommsen and the editors of *Central European History* for "Domestic Factors in German Foreign Policy before 1914."

I am also grateful to Henry A. Turner, whose assistance in the preparation of this volume went well beyond the usual duties of a General Editor.

𝕭𝖎𝖇𝖑𝖎𝖔𝖌𝖗𝖆𝖕𝖍𝖞

The following is a very selective guide to the immense body of historical literature on Imperial Germany. I have tried to include those works that provide the most recent interpretations of historical problems and that offer the best guides to further reading. Under each of the various subject headings I have listed at least one work in English.

1. General Surveys and Guides to Research

The place to begin any systematic study of German history is one of the "Handbooks" that summarize recent research and give rather full bibliographical citations. The most accessible and easy to use of these is Bruno Gebhardt's *Handbuch der Deutschen Geschichte, vol. 3: Von der Französischen Revolution bis zum ersten Weltkrieg*, 9th ed., ed. K. E. Born, et al. (Stuttgart, 1970). For particular historical problems the series *Neue Wissenschaftliche Bibliothek*, ed. Hans-Ulrich Wehler (Kiepenheuer and Witsch) is of great value. Each volume in this series has a collection of articles on a historical theme ("Modern German Social History," "German Political Parties," etc.) and an extensive bibliography. Finally, there are two bibliographical articles on the post-Bismarckian empire: John Snell, "Imperial Germany's Tragic Era, 1888–1918," *Journal of Central European Affairs* 18, no. 4 (1959): 380–95 and 19, no. 1 (1959): 57–75 and James Sheehan, "Germany, 1890–1918: A Survey of Recent Research," *Central European History* 1, no. 4 (1968): 345–72.

Although there are a great many textbooks in English on German history, none of them can be recommended without reservation. The third volume of Hajo Holborn's *A History of Modern Germany* (New York, 1969) is the fullest account. Walter Simon's *A History of Modern Germany* (New York, 1966) is concise and largely political in focus. Perhaps the most stimulating, but at the same time the most uneven treatment of the Empire is in Koppel Pinson, *Modern Germany: Its History and Civilization*, 2d ed. (New York, 1966).

2. Bismarck and the *Reichsgründung*

The most complete guide to the voluminous literature on Bismarck is Karl Erich Born, *Bismarck-Bibliographie* (Cologne, 1966). The standard biography of the chancellor, now rather out of date but still worth reading, is Erich Eyck's *Bismarck*, 3 vols. (Erlenbach-Zürich, 1941–44); Eyck published a one-volume version of this work in English called *Bismarck and the German Empire*, which is available in a paperback edition (Norton Library). On Bismarck's early life and his political career down to 1871, the best work in English is Otto Pflanze, *Bismarck and the Development of Germany* (Princeton, 1963). Pflanze has promised a second volume covering the Imperial period. For the most recent German scholarship on the first chancellor see Lothar Gall, *Das Bismarck-Problem*, Neue Wissenschaftliche Bibliothek (Cologne and Berlin, 1971). There is a thoughtful summary of Bismarck's role in German history and historiography in Michael Stürmer, "Bismarck in Perspective," *Central European History* 4, no. 4 (1971): 291-331.

Pflanze's biography contains a lucid account of the formation of the Empire and a guide to the traditional literature on this subject. Since his book was published, historians have put increasing emphasis on the economic rather than the diplomatic aspects of national unification. The representative work in this process is Helmut Boehme, *Deutschlands Weg zur Grossmacht* (Cologne and Berlin, 1966). Boehme has summarized his own work and given a sampling of other interpretations in *Probleme der Reichsgründungszeit, 1848-1879*, Neue Wissenschaftliche Bibliothek (Cologne and Berlin, 1968). The most recent work in English on this period is Theodore Hamerow's *The Social Foundation of German Unification, 1858-1871*, 2 vols. (Princeton, 1969-1972).

3. Political Developments: General

E. R. Huber's *Deutsche Verfassungsgeschichte seit 1789*, 4 vols. of text and 3 of documents (Stuttgart, 1957-1969) is an extraordinarily rich source of information and bibliography on constitutional, legal, and political history. Huber is also a good example of the apologetic approach to the German past that once dominated the German historical profession. For some new and more critical judgments on Imperial political life, the reader can consult the articles edited by Michael Stürmer in *Das kaiserliche Deutschland* (Düsseldorf, 1970) and Hans-Ulrich Wehler's provocative synthesis, *Das Deutsche Kaiserreich* (Göttingen, 1973). Johannes Ziekursch's *Politische Geschichte der neuen Deutschen Kaiserreich*, 3 vols. (Frankfurt, 1925-1930) is somewhat outdated but still very much worth reading, especially the second volume on the Bismarckian Reich.

Wehler's *Bismarck und der Imperialismus* (Cologne and Berlin, 1969) analyzes the domestic basis of the chancellor's foreign policy and in the process generates some stimulating hypotheses about the Bismarckian political system. Wehler has been very much influenced by the work of Eckart Kehr, whose classic study *Schlachtflottenbau und Parteipolitik* (Berlin, 1930) remains one of best books on domestic political currents in the 1890s. Pauline Anderson's *Background of Anti-English Feeling in Germany* (Washington, 1939) was also influenced by Kehr and presents a good deal of material that is hard to find in English. The most recent analysis of Wilhelmian politics in this tradition is D. Stegmann's *Die Erben Bismarcks* (Cologne and Berlin, 1970). Finally, there are two good books in English that examine the impact of Bismarck's dismissal in 1890 on the German political system: J. Alden Nichols, *Germany after Bismarck: The Caprivi Era, 1890-1894* (Cambridge, 1958) and J. C. G. Röhl, *Germany without Bismarck: The Crisis of Government in the Second Reich, 1890-1900* (London, 1967).

4. Political Developments: Parties and Interest Groups

The best introduction to the data and literature on political organizations is D. Fricke's two-volume collection *Die bürgerlichen Parteien in Deutschland* (Leipzig, 1968–1970). Bernhard Vogel, et al., *Wahlen in Deutschland* (Berlin, 1971) is a guide through the complexities of the voting systems in the various German states. W. Mommsen's *Deutsche Parteiprogramme*, 2d ed. (Munich, 1964) has some of the most important documents on party programs. G. A. Ritter's volume *Die Deutsche Parteien vor 1918*, Neue Wissenschaftliche Bibliothek (Cologne, 1973) has some fine essays (see especially those by Nipperdey and Lepsius) and a splendid bibliography. The classic study of party organization remains Thomas Nipperdey's *Die Organisation der deutschen Parteien vor 1918* (Düsseldorf, 1961).

The following are some recent works on individual parties:

Conservatism

H. Booms, *Die deutschkonservative Partei* (Düsseldorf, 1954).

A. Dorpalen, "The German Conservatives and the Parliamentarization of Imperial Germany," *Journal of Central European Affairs* 11, no. 2 (1951): 184–99.

H.-J. Puhle, *Agrarische Interessenpolitik und Preussischer Konservatismus im Wilhelminischen Reich* (Hanover, 1967).

Liberalism

W. Gagel, *Die Wahlrechtsfrage in der Geschichte der deutschen liberalen Parteien, 1848–1918* (Düsseldorf, 1958).

H. Heffter, *Die Deutsche Selbstverwaltung im 19. Jahrhundert* (Stuttgart, 1950).

L. Krieger, *The German Idea of Freedom* (Boston, 1957).

Political Catholicism

R. Morsey, *Die Deutsche Zentrumspartei, 1917–1923* (Düsseldorf, 1966).

J. Zeender, "German Catholics and the Concept of an Interconfessional Party, 1900–1922," *Journal of Central European Affairs* 23, no. 4 (1964): 424–39.

Social Democracy

V. Lidtke, *The Outlawed Party: Social Democracy in Germany, 1878–1890* (Princeton, 1966).

G. A. Ritter, *Die Arbeiterbewegung im Wilhelminischen Reich*, 2d ed. (Berlin, 1963).

G. Roth, *The Social Democrats in Imperial Germany* (Totowa, N.J., 1963).

C. E. Schorske, *German Social Democracy: The Development of the Great Schism 1905–1917* (Cambridge, Mass., 1955).

In the past decade, historians of the Imperial era have become increasingly interested in the way in which interest groups interacted with political parties and influenced the direction of political developments. Some representative examples of this new scholarly concern for the relationship of economic organizations and politics are:

W. Fischer, "Staatsverwaltung und Interessenverbände im Deutschen Reich,

1871–1914," in *Interdependenzen von Politik und Wirtschaft: Festgabe fur Gert von Eynern*, ed., K. Böhret and D. Grosser (Berlin, 1967), 431–56.

H. Horn, *Der Kampf um den Bau des Mittellandkanals* (Cologne and Opladen, 1964).

H. Kaelble, *Industrielle Interessenpolitik in der Wilhelminischen Gesellschaft. Centralverband deutscher Industrieller, 1895–1914* (Berlin, 1967).

T. Nipperdey, "Interessenverbände und Parteien in Deutschland vor dem Ersten Weltkrieg," *Politische Vierteljahrsschrift* 2, no. 2 (1961): 262–80.

G. Schulz, "Über Entstehung und Formen des Interessengruppen in Deutschland seit Beginn der Industrialisierung," *Politische Vierteljahrsschrift* 2, no. 1 (1961): 124–54.

5. Military Institutions and Foreign Policy

There are several good works in English on military institutions. Gordon Craig's *The Politics of the Prussian Army, 1640–1945* (Oxford and New York, 1956) puts the political activity of the German officer corps into a broad historical perspective. Karl Demeter, *The German Officer Corps in Society and State, 1650–1945* (New York, 1965) emphasizes the sociological role of the army, as does Martin Kitchen, *The German Officer Corps, 1890–1914* (Oxford, 1968). Gerhard Ritter's massive but somewhat narrow study of what he calls "militarism" has been translated as *The Sword and the Scepter*, 4 vols. (Coral Gables, Fla., 1969–1973). On the navy, there is V. Berghahn's thoughtful study of *Der Tirpitz Plan* (Düsseldorf, 1971) and some good essays in H. Schottelius and W. Deist, eds., *Marine und Marinepolitik im kaiserlichen Deutschland, 1871–1914* (Düsseldorf, 1972).

The books by Eyck and Ziekursch cited above both have useful narratives of German foreign policy after 1871. Also worth reading are William Langer's two classic volumes, *European Alliances and Alignments, 1871–1890* and *The Diplomacy of Imperialism* (first published in 1931 and 1935, now available in Vintage Paperback editions). Wehler's study of *Bismarck und der Imperialismus* illuminates German policy in the 1880s, while his volume *Imperialismus* in the Neue Wissenschaftliche Bibliothek series (Cologne and Berlin, 1970) has some essays on the later period and a first-rate bibliography.

The liveliest topic in the history of German foreign policy has recently been (as it was a half century ago) Germany's role in the outbreak of the First World War. Much of the excitement surrounding this topic was generated by Fritz Fischer's *Deutschlands Griff nach der Weltmacht* (Düsseldorf, 1961, translated as *Germany's Aims in the First World War*, New York, 1967). Fischer's more recent study, *Krieg der Illusionen* (Düsseldorf, 1969), deals with the years immediately before 1914. A sample and guide to the debate which Fischer began can be found in Wolfgang Schieder, *Erster Weltkrieg: Ursachen, Entstehung, und Kriegsziele*, Neue Wissenschaftliche Bibliothek (Cologne and Berlin, 1969). In English, there is a very good summary of this literature in James Joll, "The 1914 Debate Continues: Fritz Fischer and his Critics," *Past and Present*, no. 34 (July, 1966), 100–13. Also worth reading are two contributions to this problem by American historians:

F. Stern, "Bethmann Hollweg and the War: The Limits of Responsibility," in *The Responsibility of Power: Historical Essays in Honor of Hajo Holborn*, eds., L. Krieger and F. Stern (New York, 1967), 252–85, and K. Jarausch, "The Illusion of Limited War: Chancellor Bethmann Hollweg's Calculated Risk, July 1914," *Central European History* 2, no. 1 (1969): 48–76.

6. Social and Economic History

When the second volume of H. Aubin and W. Zorn's *Handbuch der deutschen Wirtschafts- und Sozialgeschichte*, vol. 1 (Stuttgart, 1971) appears, it will be the best place to begin an examination of the large but uneven literature on German social and economic developments. For now, one can begin with Wilhelm Treue's contribution to Gebhardt's *Handbuch*, which is cited above. The two relevant volumes in the Neue Wissenschaftliche Bibliothek series are also very helpful: *Moderne deutsche Wirtschaftsgeschichte*, ed., Karl Erich Born (Cologne and Berlin, 1966) and *Moderne deutsche Sozialgeschichte*, ed., Hans-Ulrich Wehler (Cologne and Berlin, 1966). W. Hoffmann, *Das Wachstum der deutschen Wirtschaft* (Berlin, 1965) contains a great deal of useful data. Discussions of the historiography on industrial and agrarian developments can be found in O. Büsch, *Industrialisierung und Geschichtswissenschaft* (Berlin, 1969) and the essays by Hans Rosenberg published as *Probleme der deutschen Sozialgeschichte* (Frankfurt, 1969). The best recent discussion in English is Richard Tilly's article "*Soll und Haben:* Recent German Economic History and the Problem of Economic Development," *Journal of Economic History* 29, no. 2 (1969): 298–319. Additional literature can be found in James Sheehan, "Quantification in the Study of Modern German Social and Political History," in *The Dimensions of the Past*, eds., V. Lorwin and J. M. Price (New Haven and London, 1972), 301–31.

The following are some of the works available on individual social groups:

The Aristocracy

H. Rosenberg, "Die Pseudodemokratisierung der Rittergutsbesitzerklasse," in Wehler, *Moderne deutsche Sozialgeschichte* and Rosenberg, *Probleme der deutschen Sozialgeschichte*, both cited above.

L. Muncy, *The Junker in the Prussian Administration under William II, 1888–1914* (Providence, R.I., 1944).

The "Middle Classes"

W. Fischer, *Wirtschaft und Gesellschaft im Zeitalter der Industrialisierung* (Göttingen, 1972).

Hansjoachim Henning, *Das westdeutsche Bürgertum in der Epoche der Hochindustrialisierung, 1860–1914*, vol. 1 (Wiesbaden, 1972).

J. Kocka, *Unternehmerverwaltung und Angestelltenschaft* (Stuttgart, 1969).

A. Noll, "Wirtschaftliche und soziale Entwicklung des Handwerks in der zweiten Phase der Industrialisierung," in *Zur soziologischen Theorien und Analyse des 19. Jahrhunderts*, eds., W. Rüegg and O. Neuloh (Göttingen, 1971).

F. Zunkel, *Der Rheinisch-westfälische Unternehmer, 1834–1879* (Cologne and Opladen, 1962).

Manual Labor and the Urban Poor

R. Engelsing, *Zur Sozialgeschichte deutscher Mittel- und Unterschichten* (Göttingen, 1972).

W. Kollmann, "Politische und soziale Entwicklung der deutschen Arbeiterschaft, 1850–1914," *Vierteljahrschrift fur Sozial- und Wirtschaftsgeschichte* 50, no. 4 (1964): 480–504.

P. Stearns, "Adaption to Industrialization: German Workers as a Test Case," *Central European History* 3, no. 4 (1970): 303–31.

There is just beginning to be in Germany the kind of careful and systematic local studies which have so illuminated the social history of other European nations. A pioneering contribution to this enterprise is W. Köllmann's *Sozialgeschichte der Stadt Barmen* (Tübingen, 1960). The first product of what will be an outstanding local study can be found in David Crew's article "Definitions of Modernity: Social Mobility in a German Town, 1880–1901," *The Journal of Social History* 7, no. 1 (1973): 51–74.

Index